# The POPULAR MECHANICS

# ILLUSTRATED HOME HANDYMAN

# ENCYCLOPEDIA & GUIDE

EDITED BY THE STAFF OF POPULAR MECHANICS

J. J. Little & Ives Co., Inc., New York — 1961

# YOUTH BED

Inexpensive and easy to build, this Hollywood-type youth bed is just the thing for baby when he begins to outgrow his crib. Except for a headboard panel of ¼-in. plywood, the bed is made entirely of solid stock. Over-all dimensions of the bed and the length of the guard rails are not given in the detail as these are determined by the size of the mattress, the guard rails being approximately half the length of the bed. Note that the bed rails are fastened permanently to the headboard and the footboard by mitering the ends and gluing and nailing them into mortises in the tapered legs. After the bed is assembled, a rope spring (clothesline will do) is laced through notched strips of 1 x 1-in. stock screwed to the sides of the bed rails as well as to the headboard and the footboard. After all nails are set and puttied over, the bed is enameled, using either a two-tone effect or a color to harmonize with the bedroom.

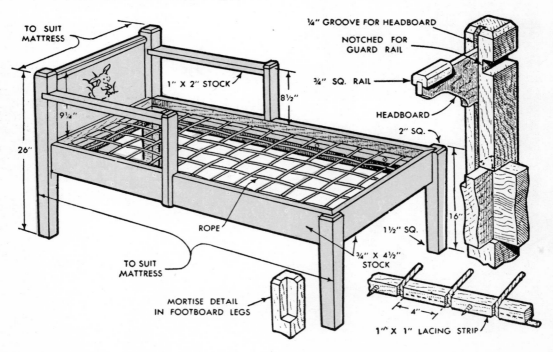

*Here is a bedroom suite whose beauty lies in modern lines matched by simplified construction appealing to any craftsman*

# MAKE YOUR OWN BEDROOM SUITE

PICTURE in your home this beautiful bedroom ensemble in honey maple, limed oak or rich walnut and then try to talk your way out of building it. Mom will want it by tomorrow, and if there is a teen-age daughter in your home she will say, "It's simply out of this world." Designed for flexibility, the pieces are functional and can be arranged, rearranged and interchanged to her heart's content.

All pieces are coordinated in size to fit together in sectional groups — chest, night stands and bed are all the same height. The group features a most practical bed which incorporates built-in storage space in the headboard. The front of it opens wide to reveal a spacious compartment for extra bedding and a roomy drawer pulls out at

each end of the headboard to provide storage for shoes. The chest-on-chest unit can be stacked to serve as a five-drawer highboy, or a pair of base units can be built and placed end-to-end under a large mirror to obtain the popular Mr. and Mrs. dresser. A novel three-piece vanity consists of two twin end units bridged with a separate top unit which opens to expose a cosmetic compartment and make-up mirror.

A product of a basement shop, the original furniture was built with the power tools shown. Only two tools, a saw and a jointer, actually are required as the construction involves just simple,

Right, edges of the plywood are mitered with the saw table tilted at a 45-deg. angle and planed accurately on the jointer to obtain a perfect fit

803

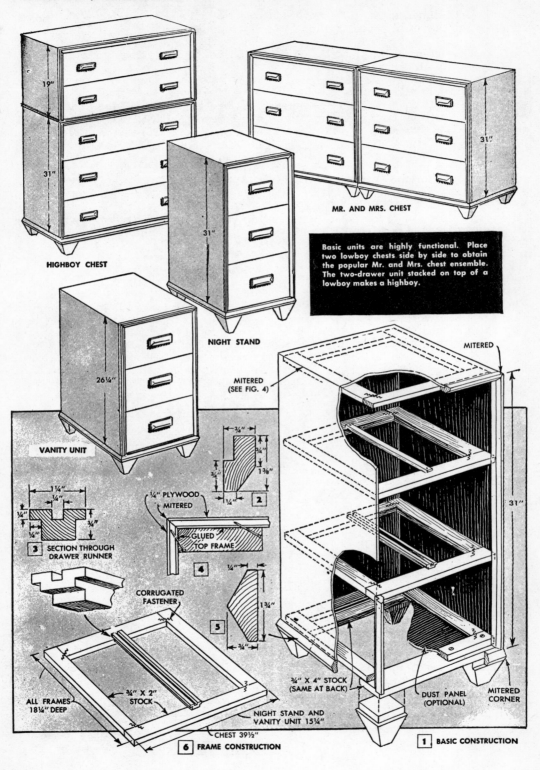

**HIGHBOY CHEST**

19"

31"

**MR. AND MRS. CHEST**

31"

**NIGHT STAND**

31"

Basic units are highly functional. Place two lowboy chests side by side to obtain the popular Mr. and Mrs. chest ensemble. The two-drawer unit stacked on top of a lowboy makes a highboy.

**VANITY UNIT**

26¼"

MITERED
(SEE FIG. 4)

MITERED

31"

¾"
¾"
¾"
1⅜"
¼"
**2**

1¼"
¼"
¼"
¼"
¾"

**3** SECTION THROUGH DRAWER RUNNER

¼" PLYWOOD MITERED

GLUED TOP FRAME

**4**

¼"
1¾"
¾"
**5**

CORRUGATED FASTENER

¾" X 2" STOCK

ALL FRAMES 18¼" DEEP

NIGHT STAND AND VANITY UNIT 15¼"

CHEST 39½"

**6** FRAME CONSTRUCTION

¾" X 4" STOCK (SAME AT BACK)

DUST PANEL (OPTIONAL)

MITERED CORNER

**1** BASIC CONSTRUCTION

straight cuts in dimensional stock and incorporates the use of plywood to simplify the work.

**Basic construction** of the night stands, chests and vanity units is exactly the same. It's merely a case of increasing the over-all height and width as given for each respective cabinet. Fig. 1 shows the extreme simplicity of construction. Each unit, with the exception of the two-drawer chest, requires three drawer frames and a top frame, four in all, which are made exactly alike as detailed in Fig. 6. Pine or other softwood will do for the frames, although the front rail of each frame can be of hardwood, if you wish. The top frame is of ½-in. stock while the others are ¾-in., and if the bottom frame is to be fitted with a dust panel, a groove is centered in the edge of the members to take a ¼-in. plywood panel. Otherwise, the frame pieces are merely butted, glued and joined together with corrugated fasteners.

The next step is to glue and screw the bottom frame to two ¾ x 4-in. base pieces. These pieces, which are placed across the front and back, are made the same length as the frame. Note that at the front the frame is placed 1⅛ in. in from the edge, while at the back the frame is glued flush with the edge of the base piece. Now, a 1¾-in. molding, Fig. 5, is mitered and glued to the edges of the base pieces so that it is flush with their top surfaces. The molding along the sides is cut ¼ in. longer than the depth of the base to allow for a ¼-in. plywood back. Glue blocks along the sides, plus screws driven at an angle through the edges of the base pieces from the inside, are used to anchor the molding.

**The edging** which conceals the laminated edges of the plywood at the front is ripped from ¾-in. stock according to Fig. 2. This is mitered and glued together as a separate assembly. The top piece of the edging is cut ½ in. longer than the width of the frame to allow for the side panels. Glue the pieces together on a flat surface and place a temporary brace across the bottom. Next, the top frame is glued to the edging. The frame is kept flush with the rabbeted edge and is fastened with long screws driven through the edge of the frame from the inside. Now, you are ready to attach the edging-and-frame assembly to the base, but first the back panel should be made ready as this is installed at the same time. The plywood back panel is made the same width as the frames and is cut ¼ in. less than the length of the edging. Nail the panel to the back edges of the top and bottom frames and then coat the ends of the edging strips with glue and clamp to the base with bar clamps. After the glue has dried, drill a pilot hole up into the end of each strip and drive a 1½-in. No. 9 flat-headed screw. The re-

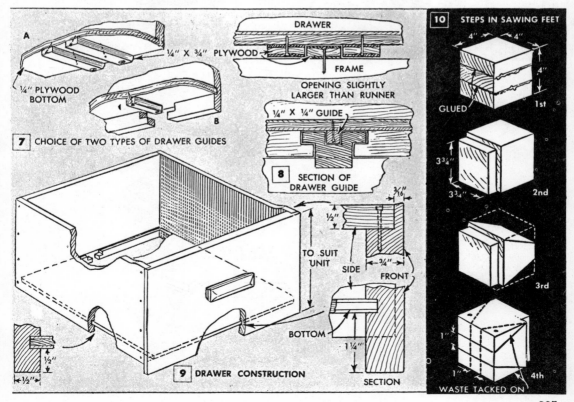

A

¼" PLYWOOD BOTTOM

B

**7** CHOICE OF TWO TYPES OF DRAWER GUIDES

DRAWER

¼" X ¾" PLYWOOD

FRAME

OPENING SLIGHTLY LARGER THAN RUNNER

¼" X ¼" GUIDE

**8** SECTION OF DRAWER GUIDE

TO SUIT UNIT

½"

¾"

SIDE

FRONT

¾6"

BOTTOM

1¼"

SECTION

½"

½"

**9** DRAWER CONSTRUCTION

**10** STEPS IN SAWING FEET

4"   4"

4"

GLUED   1st

3¾"

3¾"   2nd

3rd

1"

1"   4th

WASTE TACKED ON

maining two frames are spaced equally between the top and bottom ones. These are fastened to the inside of the edging strips with small screws. Pockets are formed for the screws by drilling and counterboring holes through the frame at an angle.

**Now, the framework** is ready to be covered with ¼-in. plywood. Fit and install the top piece first. In addition to obtaining a well-fitting mitered joint, it also is important to get a tight fit where the plywood abuts the rabbet of the front edging. Use bar clamps to draw this joint tightly and C-clamps to clamp the plywood firmly to the frame. Brads can be used here, as indicated in Fig. 4, although a good resin-type glue will hold sufficiently. Like the top piece, the sides fit flush with the outer face of the edging and the molding at the bottom. Clamps should be used to draw the mitered joint together. Brads can be used to reinforce the joint and to nail the plywood to the edge of the frames.

**Steps in sawing the feet** are given in Fig. 10. In most cases, the blocks for these will

have to be glued up using three or more pieces. The front feet require a ¼ x 1-in. rabbet on two adjacent edges, while the rear ones need a rabbet only along one side. The feet taper to 1 in. square at the bottom. After sawing two sides, the waste is replaced and held with either brads or cellulose tape so that a flat surface will be had to complete the sawing.

**Typical drawer construction** is detailed in Fig. 9. The method of fitting the bottom differs somewhat with the type of drawer runner used. Note that the lower edge of each drawer extends to cover the drawer frame. Drawer handles are detailed in Fig. 11. A choice of two types of drawer guides is given. One features a T-shaped runner, Fig. 3, over which the back of the drawer hooks to prevent the drawer from dropping down when all the way open. The runner is grooved for a ¼-in.-square guide, which is nailed to the underside of the drawer bottom as shown in Fig. 7, detail B. Note that the T-slot in the drawer, Fig. 8, is made slightly larger than the cross section of the runner. A more simple guide is pictured in Fig. 7, detail A. This is formed merely by nailing two strips of plywood to the drawer bottom to form a track for a plywood runner nailed to the frame. Fig. 1 shows both types of runners in place.

Construction of the highboy (two-drawer) chest unit, Fig. 12, differs from the other units in one respect; the bottom drawer frame is screwed to a mitered base frame which is beveled to match the edging.

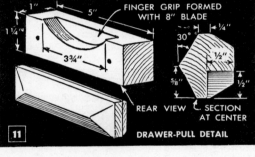

**11** — 1″ — 5″ — FINGER GRIP FORMED WITH 8″ BLADE — 1¼″ — ¼″ — 30° — 3¾″ — ½″ — ⅝″ — ½″ — REAR VIEW — SECTION AT CENTER — **DRAWER-PULL DETAIL**

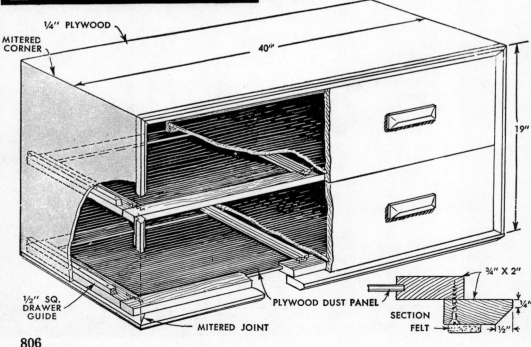

**12** CONSTRUCTION OF HIGHBOY-CHEST UNIT

¼″ PLYWOOD — MITERED CORNER — 40″ — 19″ — ½″ SQ. DRAWER GUIDE — MITERED JOINT — PLYWOOD DUST PANEL — ¾″ X 2″ — SECTION — FELT — ¼″ — ½″

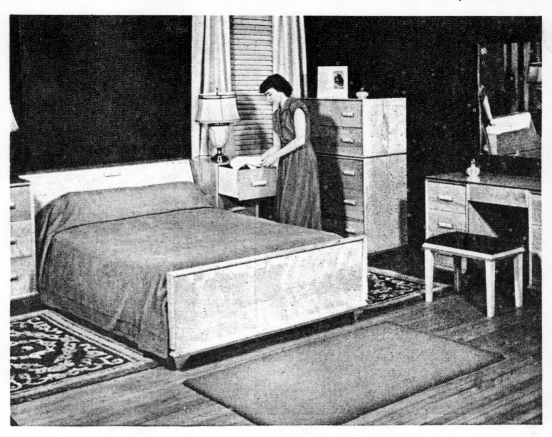

WITH THE night stands, chests and vanity units completed as described earlier, you can tackle the bed. In addition to its pleasing simplicity, it features a built-in storage compartment in the headboard for bedding and two roomy drawers for shoes. If twin beds are preferred to a full bed, the basic construction is the same. It would be merely a matter of making the bed narrower, installing only one drawer and eliminating the center partition in the storage compartment. Most of the bed is made of ¼-in. plywood. On the original bed, the lid of the storage compartment was a ¾-in.-plywood panel, but to save cost, this too can be of ¼-in. material by gluing it to a half-lapped frame as shown in Figs. 13 and 14.

The bed footboard consists of a ¼-in. plywood panel which is framed on three sides with a ¾ x 2-in. molding. The latter is chamfered and grooved

**Right, a jointer plus a bench saw are the only power tools needed. Here, base molding is being run on jointer after being ripped on saw**

A roomy drawer opens at each end of the bed headboard to provide storage space for seasonal footwear. Being concealed when the headboard is flanked with night stands, the drawers also provide a safe place for personal papers and jewelry

Another feature of this headboard is a convenient built-in storage compartment for bedding. If you wish, the compartment can be lined with aromatic, red cedar to protect woolen blankets from moths. Open, the lid rests on the bed

⅜ in. deep on its inside face to fit over the edge of the plywood. The panel is faced across the bottom with a ¾ x 1¾-in. molding which matches the molding on the night stands, chests and other pieces. This molding is glued to the plywood so that it overlaps the bottom edge ½ in., sectional detail Fig. 16, and then five rabbeted cleats, 6 in. long, are spaced along the inside and screwed to the molding. Note that the molding is mitered at the ends and returned at the corners for a distance of 4 in., Fig. 16. Note also that the lower ends of the grooved molding, which covers the edges of the plywood, are chamfered on two adjacent outside edges to fit flush with the bottom molding and the upper ends are mitered. The feet are made the same as detailed in Part I, except that here the shoulder must measure 1¼ in. long instead of 1 in. The feet are rabbeted on two adjacent sides and glued into the corners formed by the molding to bring them flush.

**The headboard** is built around a framework of scrap wood, Fig. 15. Start each end assembly with a ¾ x 4 x 11½-in. base piece and screw a ¾ x 2½ x 15-in. upright piece to it, ¼-in. in from the front edge. Note that the upper end of this piece is notched for a cross member. Another piece, ¾ x 1½ x 30¾ in., is attached vertically to the base piece, ¼ in. in from the rear edge. This piece is joined to the front piece with a cross member located 10 in. up from the top surface of the base, forming the drawer opening. Both end assemblies of the framework are joined together as shown, fitting a ¾ x 1-

13

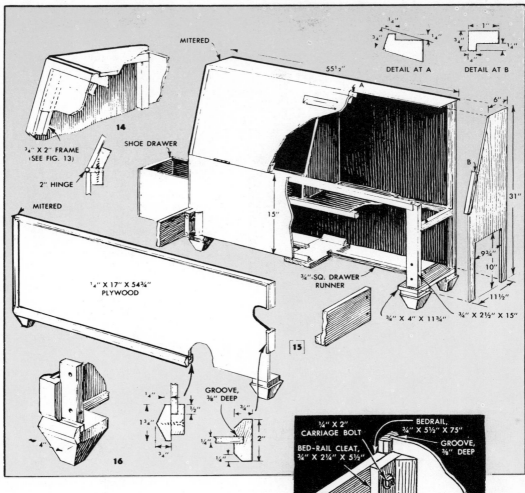

MITERED

55½"

DETAIL AT A

DETAIL AT B

14

¾" X 2" FRAME
(SEE FIG. 13)

2" HINGE

MITERED

SHOE DRAWER

A

B

6"

31"

15"

¼" X 17" X 54¾"
PLYWOOD

¾"-SQ. DRAWER
RUNNER

9¾"

10"

11½"

¾" X 4" X 11¾"

¾" X 2½" X 15"

15

GROOVE,
⅜" DEEP

¼"

½"

1¾"

¾"

¼"

¼"

2"

16

¼" X 2"
CARRIAGE BOLT

BED-RAIL CLEAT,
¾" X 2¼" X 5½"

BEDRAIL,
¾" X 5½" X 75"

GROOVE,
⅜" DEEP

¾"-SQ. BED-
SLAT CLEAT

¾" X 1½" X 6"
CLEAT (5 REQD.)

INSIDE CORNER AT FOOTBOARD    17

BED RAIL

½"

1¼"

4½"

GLUE
BLOCK

¼" X 4"
CARRIAGE BOLTS

18

INSIDE CORNER AT HEADBOARD

in. strip into the notched front uprights, another one below it at a point flush with the member at the top of the drawer opening and a third piece at the same height at the rear. These two latter strips form a ledge for the bottom of the compartment which is of plywood.

**Now, cover the back** of the framework. This requires a fir-plywood panel, ¼ x 30¾ x 55 in., which is nailed and glued so that the edges are flush with the framework. Next, fit the front panel, cutting it 15 x 55 in. The plywood pieces covering the ends of the headboard taper to 6 in. at the top from a point 15 in. up from the bottom. These are made right and left hand, selecting the best face of the plywood for the outside, and mitered at the top. After the ends are glued in place, the drawer-runner assembly is installed. The runners are simply ¾-in.-square strips, notched at each end to hook over the base pieces and a center piece fastened to the plywood with glue blocks.

Fit the panel forming the bottom of the bedding

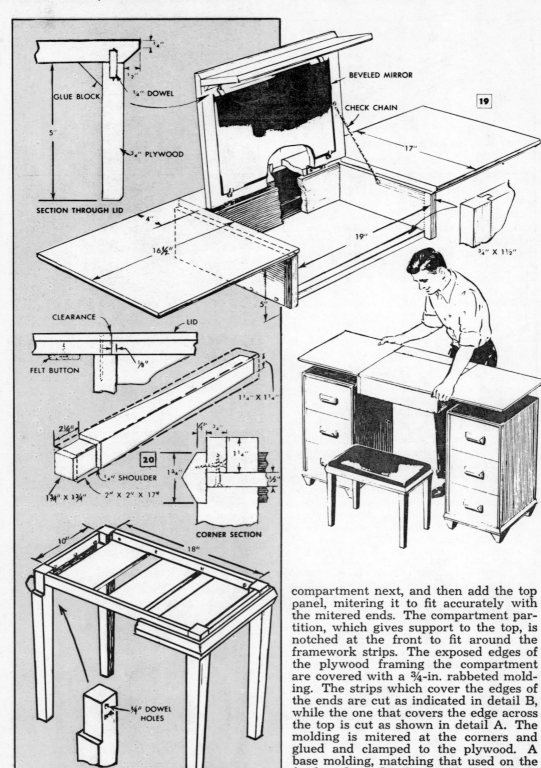

SECTION THROUGH LID

GLUE BLOCK

¼" DOWEL

¾" PLYWOOD

5"

¼"

½"

BEVELED MIRROR

CHECK CHAIN

19

17"

¾" X 1½"

4"

16½"

19"

5"

CLEARANCE

LID

FELT BUTTON

⅛"

1¼" X 1¼"

2¼"

¼" SHOULDER

1¾" X 1¾"

2" X 2" X 17"

20

¼" ¾"

1¼"

1¾"

½"

CORNER SECTION

10"

18"

¼" DOWEL HOLES

21 ASSEMBLY OF VANITY STOOL

compartment next, and then add the top panel, mitering it to fit accurately with the mitered ends. The compartment partition, which gives support to the top, is notched at the front to fit around the framework strips. The exposed edges of the plywood framing the compartment are covered with a ¾-in. rabbeted molding. The strips which cover the edges of the ends are cut as indicated in detail B, while the one that covers the edge across the top is cut as shown in detail A. The molding is mitered at the corners and glued and clamped to the plywood. A base molding, matching that used on the footboard, is fitted around the outside corners, gluing and clamping it to the edges of the base pieces of the framework.

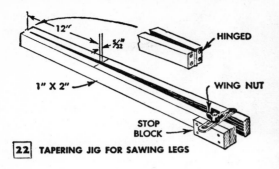

**22** TAPERING JIG FOR SAWING LEGS

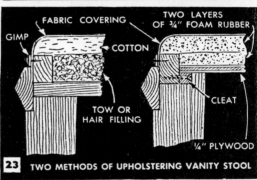

**23** TWO METHODS OF UPHOLSTERING VANITY STOOL

The compartment lid is hinged as shown in the sectional detail, Fig. 14, and drawers and handles are made as described earlier

Bedrails are attached to the head and footboard as detailed in Figs. 17 and 18.

**The separate top,** Fig. 19, which merely rests on two base units to form a vanity, is made of ¾-in. plywood and solid stock. The top requires a panel 17 x 52½ in. Three edges are chamfered on the underside and then the panel is cut into four pieces. The cosmetic compartment is made like a box. The sides and back are screwed to a plywood bottom and a fourth piece is installed to support the narrow fill-in piece to which the lid is hinged. Note how end grain of the side and bottom members of the compartment is concealed with edging strips, tongued and grooved. The outboard panels are nailed and glued to the top edges of the compartment ⅛ in. in from the inner faces to provide a shoulder for the lid. This is shown in the detail above Fig. 20. The front apron is attached to the lid with dowels and a triangular glue block is placed on the inside. The lid can be leaned against the wall when opened or a check chain can be used to hold it at the right angle.

Assembly of the vanity stool is detailed in Fig. 21. First make the legs by cutting a ¼ x 2¼-in. rabbet on two adjacent faces of each one. The legs taper from 2 in. square at the shoulder to 1¼ in. square at the bottom, Fig. 20. Before tapering the legs, bore holes in adjacent inner faces as shown for doweling ¾ x 1¼-in. rails flush with the face of the rabbets. A jig like the one shown in Fig. 22 may be used to rip the taper on each face, after which the cut is dressed smooth on a jointer. The corner-section detail at the right of Fig. 20 shows how a mitered face molding is attached to the rails with screws from the inside. A choice of two methods for upholstering the stool is given in Fig. 23. If tow or hair is used, the seat is supported by three ½-in. pieces spaced as in Fig. 21. If foam rubber is used, the bottom of the stool is covered with a piece of ¼-in. plywood held by cleats screwed to the rails.

When building new furniture or restoring old pieces, each step of the finishing process, from bleaching and filling to varnishing or lacquering, is of the utmost importance. Perfection, of course, comes only with practice, but the following information will get you off to a good start

AFTER COMPLETING the bedroom furniture described in the previous two pages it's time for the all-important job of finishing it, because right here you can either flatter or ruin the appearance of the furniture.

No doubt, you have built the furniture of a wood suitable to take the particular finish desired, whether it be harvest wheat or heather mahogany, ambered walnut or limed oak. Naturally, the kind of wood used is a determining factor as, for instance, one cannot expect to obtain a limed-oak finish on birch. The finishing schedules presented below give a condensed procedure to follow in producing a number of the popular, modern finishes, but, if the final results are to compare with finishes seen on store furniture, the finishing operation demands the same careful attention that you put into the cabinet work. Brushes and materials, as well as the room where the work is done, must be clean. Finishing should not be attempted in a cold room and the materials should not be cold. These precautions are important.

**Sanding:** Perhaps the most important

## FINISHING SCHEDULES

| FINISH | APPLICATION |
|---|---|
| Ambered walnut | Bleach. Stain with amber stain. Apply sealer coat of thin lacquer. Fill with natural filler. Finish with clear lacquer. |
| Old-World walnut | Bleach. Seal. Fill with natural filler lightly tinted with burnt umber. Seal. Shade with brown wiping stain. Finish with clear lacquer. |
| Honeytone maple or birch | Tone with blond toner, using 1 part white lacquer to 4 parts clear, flat lacquer. Finish with water-white lacquer. |
| Pickled pine | Bleach. Stain with gray stain for pine. Finish with water-white lacquer or clear varnish. |
| Limed oak | Bleach. Seal. Fill pores with white paste wood filler. Finish with water-white lacquer. |
| Harvest-wheat mahogany | Bleaching will give required wheat color. Fill with natural filler lightly tinted with raw-sienna color in oil. Finish with lacquer. |
| Tweed mahogany | Bleach. Seal. Fill pores with red paste wood filler. Finish with water-white lacquer or clear varnish. |
| Heather mahogany | Bleach. Seal. Fill pores with white paste wood filler. Finish with water-white lacquer or clear varnish. |

step in producing a beautiful, flawless finish is the sanding of the wood. Application of any number of finishing coats will not compensate for a careless job of sanding, but only tends to emphasize defects. Power sanders of the oscillating or belt types take the work out of sanding; however, if these are not available, you can do a satisfactory job of sanding by hand, wrapping the paper around a flat, felt-covered block and working with progressively finer grades of garnet paper from medium down to 5-0 grade.

**Bleaching:** Practically all of the so-called blond finishes are produced by first bleaching the wood to remove its natural color. This is done to obtain such popular mahogany finishes as harvest wheat, heather and tweed, and limed oak, and ambered walnut. Mahogany, when bleached and filled with white filler, is known as heather mahogany. When filled with red filler (natural filler with red oil

Above, a piano or draftsman's stool provides an excellent turntable when spraying lacquer on the smaller units. Below, a power sander makes play of sanding the broad, flat surfaces, but care must be used to avoid cutting through the top veneer

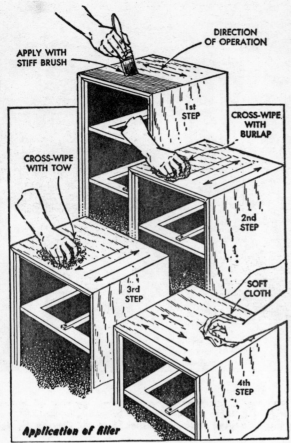

APPLY WITH STIFF BRUSH

DIRECTION OF OPERATION

1st STEP

CROSS-WIPE WITH BURLAP

CROSS-WIPE WITH TOW

2nd STEP

SOFT CLOTH

3rd STEP

4th STEP

*Application of filler*

the filler is applied liberally in the direction of the grain, preferably with a short-bristled brush. Do not cover more than 6 or 8 sq. ft. of surface at one time or you will get ahead of the wiping and cleaning-up operations that follow. As soon as the filler flattens, it is wiped off. This is done by wiping across the grain with a coarse cloth such as burlap, or excelsior, using a circular motion.

This is followed by cross-wiping with a fine material called tow, commonly used for upholstering purposes. This second wiping across the grain cuts the surplus filler flush with the surface of the wood.

A third cross-wiping with a soft cloth wrapped around a felt block is excellent practice. A second application of filler, somewhat thinner than the first, is sometimes required when filling mahogany or other wood having a very open grain. This is determined by noting whether the pores are completely filled.

Finally, the work is wiped lightly with the grain, using a soft cloth. This serves to remove any traces of filler missed in the towing-off operation. The filler should be allowed to dry 24 to 48 hrs. and then sanded very lightly with 5-0 waterproof garnet paper.

**Toning:** Toning is not successful on dark wood such as walnut, but very much so on naturally light-colored woods such as birch and maple. Toning, to some extent, takes the place of the bleaching process and is accomplished by spraying the bare wood with a semitransparent undercoat to further lighten the wood.

Toning is recommended for all extremely light finishes, as it does not obscure the grain, being almost as clear as water. Toner is made by adding white lacquer, 1 part, to clear flat lacquer, 4 or 5 parts. In the case of oak and mahogany, the toner should be made with tan-colored lacquer instead of white.

**Sealing:** Whether or not the bleached wood has been toned or stained, the surface must be sealed with a wash coat of shellac or lacquer before the work is filled. The wash sealer is made by cutting 1 part of clear shellac or lacquer with 6 parts of thinner. This coat is sanded lightly when dry, and then, after the grain is filled, a second sealer coat is applied. This likewise is sanded when dry, and followed with a coat of varnish or lacquer sealer. The latter coat, which fills any tiny open pores remaining, also is sanded. From here on, varnish or lacquer coats are applied, using a rubbed-effect or full-gloss type.

color added), it is called tweed, because of its pleasing pink tone. Bleached and filled with natural filler, it's called harvest-wheat mahogany. After bleaching, almost any color desired can be had by giving the wood a coat of diluted stain.

Bleaching is done with a commercial chemical solution consisting of two separate solutions which are mixed together and used immediately. As all bleaching solutions are highly corrosive, they should be handled carefully. You should wear **rubber** gloves. Use a sponge to swab the solution on the wood and see that you wet the entire surface evenly.

One application of bleach is usually sufficient although, in any case, it is good practice to make a test on a wood sample. Let the bleach stand and dry for at least 48 hrs.

**Filling:** Open-grained woods, such as oak, walnut, mahogany, etc., must be filled, that is, the pores of the surface and end grain must be packed level with a prepared paste filler. Fillers are available for either lacquer or varnish finishes and require cutting with benzine or turpentine to the consistency of thick cream before applying, so that they will sink into the pores.

Original vanity was framed in inexpensive woods and finished as you see it here with plastic veneer. Matching chairs and mirrors are made in duplicate

# DOUBLE VANITY DESK

## By John Bergen

FINE WOODS and conservative modern lines fit this double vanity desk into almost any arrangement of room furnishings. The simplest type of frame construction and drawer joinery make it easy to build, even with a small shop and limited equipment. At the start you have a choice of materials. You can use fine cabinet woods, such as cherry, birch, or primavera in solid stock or plywood faced with any of these three. The selection of wood depends on the color desired. Or you can use a less expensive wood, such as white pine or poplar, and face all exposed parts with a plastic veneer. The original vanity, pictured above, was made by the latter method.

Details of the cabinet-frame construction, also the top and drawers, are given in Figs. 1 and 2. Note first that the upper three drawers are of the flush type and are exposed, while those below in the cabinet, or pedestal, are housed behind doors. Build the lower part of the cabinet first. This unit consists of the base, bottom, side panels, back panel and drawer framing. These parts assemble into the unit pictured

in the photo in Fig. 1. All parts except the drawer framing are cut from plywood. Note that the base is inset on three sides the thickness of the plywood panels and doors. The top section, Fig. 2, consists of the top proper, a full-length back rail, end rails, and the drawer framing. Note especially in the perspective view in Fig. 2 how these parts are joined and that the top is flush at the back, ends and front. The top on the original piece was made from a ⅝-in.-plywood panel and covered with linoleum. The edges are finished with a strip of solid stock rabbeted and mitered as in a lower right-hand detail, Fig. 2. An alternate method of finishing the top, using a plastic laminate with edgings of the same material, also is shown. The sides of the drawers in the lower cabinet are grooved before assembly. Each drawer slides on a strip attached to the inner face of the end panel and on the center guide which is attached to the center stile. The slide grooves engage the guides as in the lower left-hand detail, Fig. 1. A clearance of ⅛ in. is provided between the drawers as in the lower right-hand detail, Fig. 1.

815

The drawers in the top section slide on flat rails and center guides which are a part of the top-section framing. The cutaway view, Fig. 2, shows how this framing is assembled into a unit and then attached to the lower cabinet, or pedestal. Assemble the top section completely before making and fitting the drawers.

The legs which support the overhang at

**Upper edge of all panels must be sanded or planed flush with the frame so top section will fit**

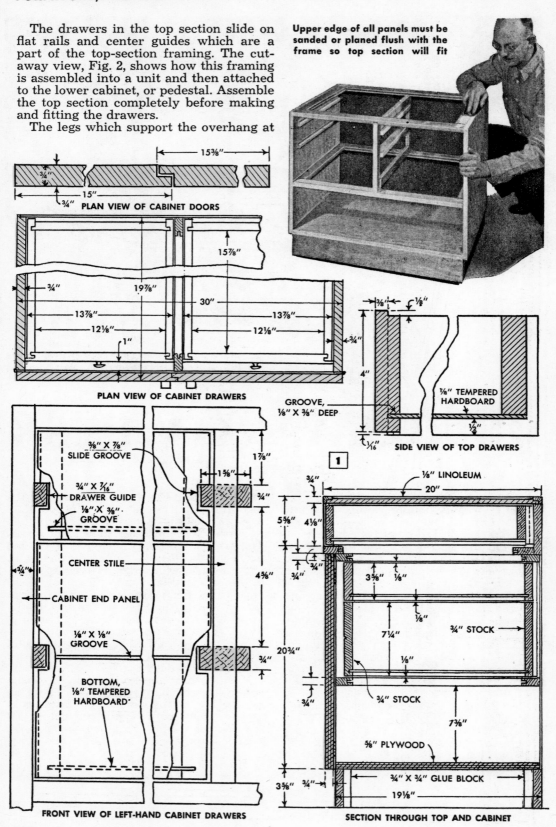

**PLAN VIEW OF CABINET DOORS**
15⅜"
¾"
15"
¾"

**PLAN VIEW OF CABINET DRAWERS**
15⅞"
¾"
19⅞"
30"
13⅞"
12⅛"
1"
13⅞"
12⅛"

**SIDE VIEW OF TOP DRAWERS**
⅜"
⅛"
¾"
4"
⅛" TEMPERED HARDBOARD
½"
GROOVE, ⅛" X ⅜" DEEP
1/16"

**FRONT VIEW OF LEFT-HAND CABINET DRAWERS**
⅜" X ⅞" SLIDE GROOVE
¾" X 7/16" DRAWER GUIDE
⅛" X ⅜" GROOVE
CENTER STILE
CABINET END PANEL
⅛" X ⅛" GROOVE
BOTTOM, ⅛" TEMPERED HARDBOARD
¾"
1⅞"
1⅝"
¾"
4⅜"
¾"
20¾"
3⅜"
¾"

**1**

**SECTION THROUGH TOP AND CABINET**
⅛" LINOLEUM
20"
¾"
5⅝"
4⅛"
¾"
¾"
3⅜"  ⅛"
7¼"
⅛"
¾" STOCK
⅛"
¾" STOCK
7⅜"
⅝" PLYWOOD
¾" X ¾" GLUE BLOCK
19⅛"
3⅜"  ¾"

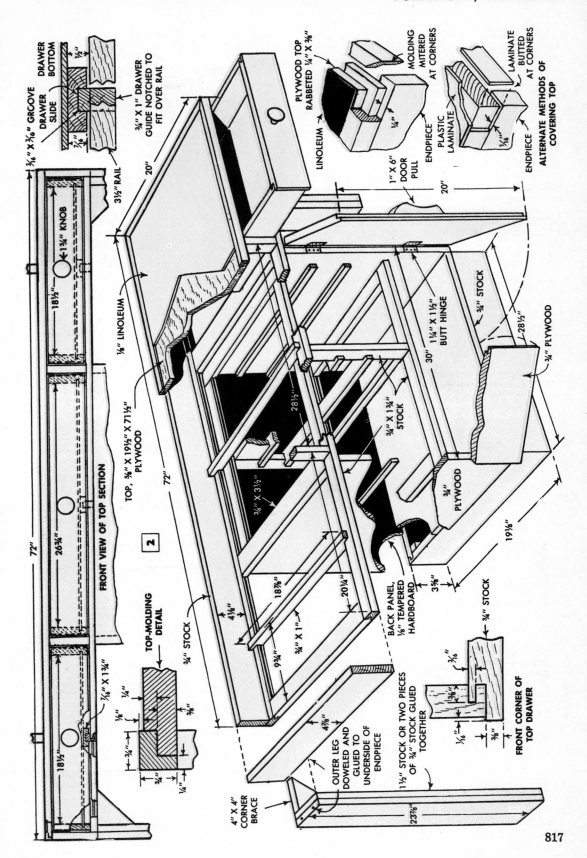

DRAWER BOTTOM

3/16" X 3/16" GROOVE

DRAWER SLIDE

3/4" X 1" DRAWER GUIDE NOTCHED TO FIT OVER RAIL

7/16"

1/2"

3 1/2" RAIL

20"

PLYWOOD TOP RABBETED 1/4" X 3/8"

MOLDING MITERED AT CORNERS

LINOLEUM

ENDPIECE

PLASTIC LAMINATE

1/4"

LAMINATE BUTTED AT CORNERS

ENDPIECE

3/16"

ALTERNATE METHODS OF COVERING TOP

1 3/4" KNOB

18 1/2"

1/8" LINOLEUM

TOP, 5/8" X 19 1/2" X 71 1/2" PLYWOOD

FRONT VIEW OF TOP SECTION

72"

26 3/4"

18 1/2"

7/16" X 1 3/4"

TOP-MOLDING DETAIL

2

3/4" STOCK

1/4"

1/8"

3/4"

3/8"

3/4"

1/4"

4" X 4" CORNER BRACE

OUTER LEG DOWELED AND GLUED TO UNDERSIDE OF ENDPIECE

1 1/2" STOCK OR TWO PIECES OF 3/4" STOCK GLUED TOGETHER

23 7/8"

1" X 6" DOOR PULL

20"

28 1/2"

3/4" STOCK

1 1/4" X 1 1/2" BUTT HINGE

30"

28 1/2"

3/4" PLYWOOD

3/4" X 1 3/4" STOCK

3/4" X 3 1/2"

3/4" X 1"

72"

4 1/8"

18 7/8"

9 3/4"

20 1/4"

BACK PANEL, 1/8" TEMPERED HARDBOARD

3/4" PLYWOOD

19 1/8"

3 5/8"

3/4" STOCK

3/16"

3/8"

3/16"

3/8"

FRONT CORNER OF TOP DRAWER

4 7/8"

each end of the top section are 5 in. wide and 1½ in. thick. If solid stock has been used in the construction of the cabinet then the legs should be cut from one piece of 1½-in. material. However, if the cabinet is to be finished with plastic veneer, then each leg can be built up to the required thickness by gluing two pieces of ¾-in. stock face to face as indicated.

Figs. 3 and 4 detail the twin mirrors and matching chairs. These units, of course, are optional. The mirrors may be attached to the wall as pictured on page 815, or pivoted on brackets attached to the back of the top cabinet section as in Fig. 3. In either case, the mirrors should be backed with ⅝-in. plywood. The chairs are of the swiveling type, the seat frame being mounted on a ball-bearing swivel, or fixture, as detailed in Fig. 4. The exposed legs and back braces are cut from wood that can be natural-finished to match the cabinet. All other parts of wood are covered by the upholstering materials. Upholstering consists of a simple padding and outer covering welted and tacked. ★ ★ ★

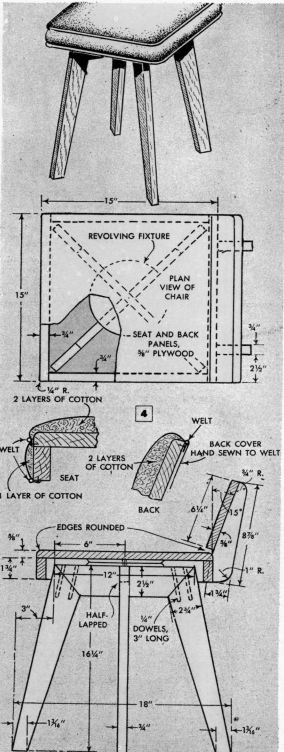

PLAN VIEW OF CHAIR

REVOLVING FIXTURE

SEAT AND BACK PANELS, ⅝" PLYWOOD

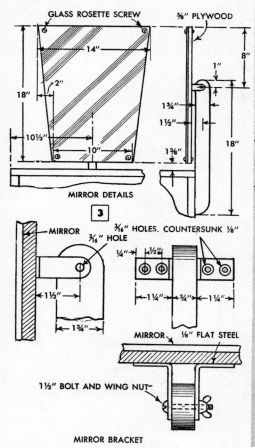

GLASS ROSETTE SCREW

⅝" PLYWOOD

MIRROR DETAILS

**3**

MIRROR

³⁄₁₆" HOLE

³⁄₁₆" HOLES. COUNTERSUNK ⅛"

MIRROR ¹⁄₈" FLAT STEEL

1½" BOLT AND WING NUT

MIRROR BRACKET

2 LAYERS OF COTTON

WELT

SEAT

1 LAYER OF COTTON

**4**

WELT

BACK COVER HAND SEWN TO WELT

2 LAYERS OF COTTON

BACK

EDGES ROUNDED

HALF-LAPPED

¼" DOWELS, 3" LONG

# CHILD'S CHIFFOROBE

DESIGNED to complete the furnishings of a child's room, this attractive chifforobe offers generous wardrobe space, a chest of drawers with a full-width storage drawer and a special compartment for toys or linens. It looks its best when made from a close-grained wood such as poplar or birch, and finished in ivory enamel with the interior drawer fronts finished in the natural color of the wood. As the first step in the construction, build up the top to the required width by edge-gluing four to six strips of selected stock. Allow ½ in. all around for trimming to finish size. Although the detail on page 820 shows the edge of the top molded, this can be omitted if no shaper is available. While the glued-up top is drying, cut selected stock for the drawer fronts, corner posts and the scrolled front and back aprons. Bandsaw the edges of the drawer fronts and the aprons, laying out the curves full size from the patterns given below. Round the bandsawed edges and sand smooth. Groove and rabbet the front and back posts. Frame the ends by fitting top and bottom rails and then glue and clamp the parts together. Note that the front posts are cut off square at the lower ends, flush with the scrolled edge of the apron, and are fitted with turned feet. Drill a hole in the lower end of each front post to take a ½ x 1¼-in. tenon. After turning out the feet, glue the parts together.

Note the assembly of parts in sections A-A and B-B, then build up the top and bottom frames, using grooved stretchers

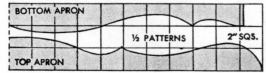

BOTTOM APRON

½ PATTERNS    2" SQS.

TOP APRON

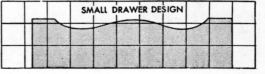

SMALL DRAWER DESIGN

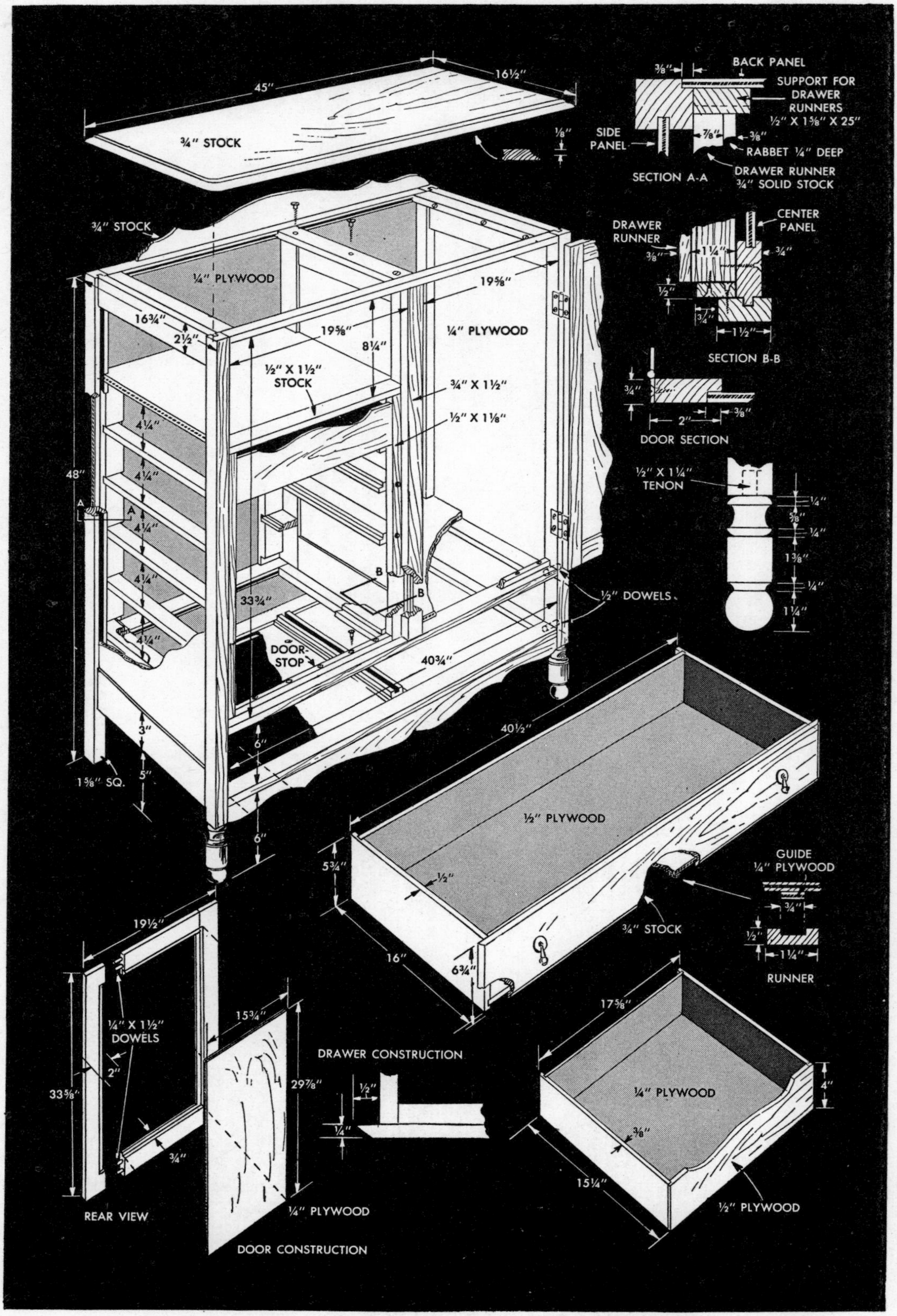
45"
16½"
¾" STOCK
⅛"
BACK PANEL
⅜"
SUPPORT FOR DRAWER RUNNERS ½" X 1⅝" X 25"
SIDE PANEL
⅞"
⅜"
RABBET ¼" DEEP
SECTION A-A
DRAWER RUNNER ¾" SOLID STOCK
¾" STOCK
DRAWER RUNNER
CENTER PANEL
1¼"
¾"
⅜"
½"
¾"
1½"
SECTION B-B
¼" PLYWOOD
19⅝"
16¾"
2½"
19⅝"
8¼"
¼" PLYWOOD
½" X 1½" STOCK
¾" X 1½"
½" X 1⅛"
¾"
2"
⅜"
DOOR SECTION
½" X 1¼" TENON
¼"
⅝"
¼"
1⅜"
¼"
1¼"
48"
4¼"
4¼"
4¼"
4¼"
4¼"
33¾"
½" DOWELS
DOOR-STOP
40¾"
3"
6"
5"
1⅝" SQ.
6"
40½"
½" PLYWOOD
5¾"
½"
GUIDE ¼" PLYWOOD
¾"
½"
1¼"
RUNNER
¾" STOCK
16"
6¾"
19½"
¼" X 1½" DOWELS
2"
33⅝"
¾"
REAR VIEW
15¾"
29⅞"
¼" PLYWOOD
DOOR CONSTRUCTION
DRAWER CONSTRUCTION
½"
¼"
17⅝"
¼" PLYWOOD
4"
⅜"
15¼"
½" PLYWOOD

above are formed by a paneled partition supported on the intermediate frame. Make up this paneled partition first and join to the top and intermediate frames with screws and glue. Now, groove the back drawer-runner supports and screw them in place. The front-runner supports are ripped to the same width but are not grooved, the front ends of the runners being attached with screws as in the detail and section B-B. Rabbet the runners and glue and screw them in place. Attach the top, then fit plywood bottoms in the storage and wardrobe compartments. Now all that remains is the making and fitting of the drawers and doors. Construction of the drawers is clearly shown in the details, but note that the large drawer is fitted with a ½-in.-plywood bottom for added rigidity and also is fitted with a center guide. Doors can be paneled in the manner shown or the panels can be housed in grooves cut in the stiles and rails. The doors are hinged to close flush, but the lower drawer front is rabbeted all around and the outer edges are beveled to give a raised-panel effect. After the cabinet has been completely assembled, sand all exposed surfaces and apply a coat of sanding sealer. When this is dry, sand lightly and finish with two coats of ivory enamel. Apply a sanding sealer to the inside drawer fronts, sand lightly when dry, and finish in the natural color with two coats of varnish or one coat of water-white lacquer. The exposed center upright and the front drawer-runner supports also can be finished in the natural color if desired. Attach two pulls to the lower drawer.

and the tenoned rails. Note that the bottom frame is paneled to provide dustproof construction, and that the back stretchers are rabbeted to take the back panel. Build up the intermediate frame, then drill blind holes for ½ or ¼-in. dowels which join the frames to the posts. After making a trial assembly of the parts to check the fit, apply glue to the doweled joints and clamp the parts together. Check the assembly for square corners before the glue dries, and cut and fit the back panel while the assembly is in the clamps. Attach the panel with screws, but do not use glue in the joints. Now, note that the back ends of the inside drawer runners are housed in grooves cut in uprights fitted into the corners of the drawer compartment, and that this compartment and the special storage space

# Simple Bed Tray You Can Make in One Evening

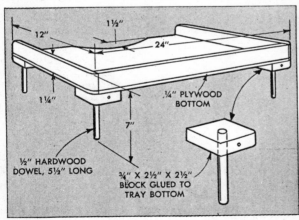

12"

1½"

24"

1¼"

¼" PLYWOOD BOTTOM

7"

½" HARDWOOD DOWEL, 5½" LONG

¾" X 2½" X 2½" BLOCK GLUED TO TRAY BOTTOM

This simple and attractive lap tray will help mother in a dozen ways around the house to save time and eliminate extra cleaning, especially in the sickroom. Complete meals can be placed on the tray and carried to a bedridden child or adult, then placed on the bed over the patient's lap. Between meals, the cleared tray can be used as a play surface for a youngster or as a card or writing table for an adult.

The suggested dimensions for the tray can be varied to suit the individual needs, but care should be taken to see that it is not so large as to be awkward to handle the tray nor so small that it is impractical. The cutout at the back of the table top, which allows the tray to fit closer to the person using it, was cut with 1½-in. radius on the original. This size is all right for a child, but might have to be increased for an adult. For purposes of storage, the dowel legs of the tray could be removable.

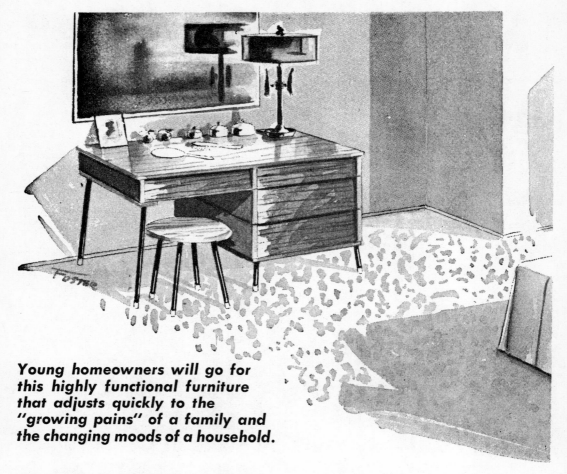

**Young homeowners will go for this highly functional furniture that adjusts quickly to the "growing pains" of a family and the changing moods of a household.**

# Stacked-Drawer

### By Tom Riley

HERE IS build-it-yourself furniture that is ideal for the young couple who have little cash, but own a circular saw and have the desire for fine furnishings. The furniture is easy to make and yet has all the eye appeal and quality look of expensive purchased furniture. You assemble the pieces by stacking two or more individual drawer units, attaching ready-made legs and adding a simple top. This assembly method makes the furniture completely functional. When you tire of one grouping, you can unstack the drawer units and rearrange them to make completely new-appearing pieces. And when more storage space is needed, you simply add another

# BEDROOM FURNITURE

drawer to the stack, or make a double chest from a single one by adding a stack alongside. To provide both shallow and deep drawers, the units are built in two heights, 5 in. and 8 in. These two dimensions also allow you to assemble vanity bases and other pieces that will work out to the proper height when using ready-made legs of standard lengths. Fig. 9 shows how legs of various lengths are used on different pieces of furniture and, also, how the drawer units can be assembled to produce a variety of furniture.

### Drawer Units

Building the drawers and their outer frames can be a production job. In other words, you can cut all similar pieces at the same time with the same setting of

your circular saw, simplifying the job and assuring greater accuracy. Only the drawer front and the two sides of the drawer frame need to be hardwood. And these can be either solid stock, or hardwood-faced ¾-in. plywood. When plywood is used, cover the end grain with plywood-veneer tape. Figs. 2, 3 and 4 give construction details of both the 5-in. and the 8-in. drawers. Note in the right-hand detail in Fig. 2 that the top of the drawer is offset ¾ in. To maintain this offset on both the 5 and 8-in. drawers, different angles must be cut on the drawer sides. On the 5-in. drawers, the sides are cut at an 8-deg. angle; on the 8-in. drawers the sides are cut at 5 deg.

In Fig. 3 a ³⁄₁₆ x ³⁄₁₆-in. rabbet is indicated along the bottom edges, as well as the front and back of the frame sides. This

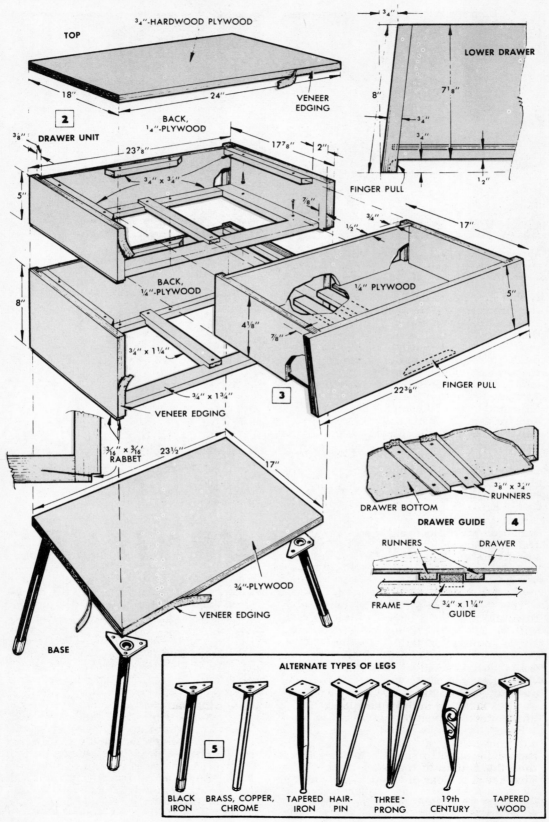

¾"-HARDWOOD PLYWOOD

TOP

18"

24"

VENEER EDGING

**2**

¾"

LOWER DRAWER

8"

7⅛"

¾"

¾"

FINGER PULL

½"

BACK, ¼"-PLYWOOD

⅜"

DRAWER UNIT

23⅞"

17⅞"

2"

5"

¾" x ¾"

⅞"

¾"

17"

½"

8"

BACK, ¼"-PLYWOOD

¼" PLYWOOD

5"

4⅛"

⅞"

¾" x 1¼"

**3**

22⅜"

FINGER PULL

VENEER EDGING

¾" x 1¾"

3/16" x 3/16" RABBET

23½"

17"

DRAWER BOTTOM

⅜" x ¾" RUNNERS

DRAWER GUIDE **4**

RUNNERS     DRAWER

FRAME

¾" x 1¼" GUIDE

¾"-PLYWOOD

VENEER EDGING

BASE

**ALTERNATE TYPES OF LEGS**

**5**

BLACK IRON

BRASS, COPPER, CHROME

TAPERED IRON

HAIR-PIN

THREE-PRONG

19th CENTURY

TAPERED WOOD

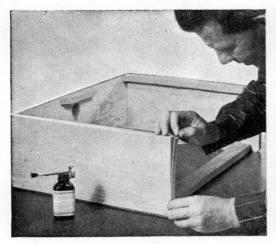

Above, veneer tape is applied to the edges of all plywood. Above right, rabbet is cut along bottom edges, front and back of drawer-frame assemblies

rabbet becomes a decorative groove when the drawers are stacked, and hides any small variation in the width or lengths of the drawers. Handles can be installed on the drawers or they can have hidden finger pulls cut on the inner edge of the bottom of the drawer fronts, as indicated in Figs. 2 and 3. There need be no exposed nails or screws showing on the drawers or frames. Glue and clamp all components of drawers and frames. Use nails on the drawer back only. To attach the inner pieces of the drawer frames, glue and nail or screw from the inside. Where it might seem imperative to nail the front framing into the side pieces, small finishing nails can be hidden by being driven through the rabbet, as indicated in the left-hand detail, Fig. 3. Notch the center drawer guide into the framing so it projects only ½ in. above the frame. Then turn the assembled drawer-and-frame unit upside down and position the two runners on the drawer bottom.

## Tops and Bases

The simple tops for the stacked-drawer furniture are sheets of ¾-in. plywood, and will be 24, 48 or 72 in. long to cover a single, double or triple side-by-side assembly. Use hardwood-faced plywood and tape the exposed edges. With all tops 18 in. wide, the dimensions will provide a slight overhang all around to cover any variation in the sizes of individual units. Fig. 1 illustrates the effect of this overhang.

Bases for single or multiple units are cut from sheets of ¾-in. fir plywood, and should be slightly smaller in dimensions than the bottom of the piece of furniture. This keeps it clear of the drawers and the

**One above the other, or side-by-side, drawer units are held together by screws driven through frames**

TWIN-BED HEADBOARD

½" OR ¾". HARDWOOD PLYWOOD

40"

36"

¾"

2½"

¾"

1¼"

¾"

3"

1"

¼" HOLES FOR BEDFRAME BOLTS

HEADBOARD TRIM

6

1¼" WOOD SCREWS

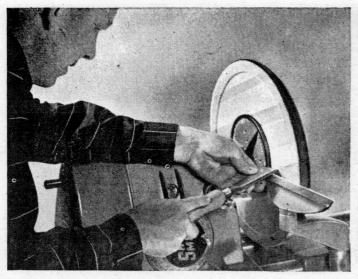

Upper right-hand photo, "chopping block" vanity stool is made by gluing together strips of hardwood of contrasting grain and color. Left-hand photo shows how bevel is turned on bottom of seat for leg angle

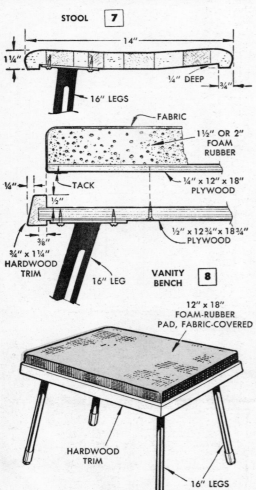

**STOOL** `7`

14"

1¼"

¼" DEEP    ¾"

16" LEGS

FABRIC

1½" OR 2" FOAM RUBBER

¼" x 12" x 18" PLYWOOD

¼"    TACK

½"

½" x 12¾" x 18¾" PLYWOOD

⅜"

¾" x 1¼" HARDWOOD TRIM

16" LEG

**VANITY BENCH** `8`

12" x 18" FOAM-RUBBER PAD, FABRIC-COVERED

HARDWOOD TRIM

16" LEGS

rabbet on the lower edges of the drawer frame. The edges of the base can be taped, or strips of ¾ x 1-in. hardwood can be used. The latter extend ¼ in. below the base to cover the edges of the leg plates.

Matching headboards, Fig. 6, are easy to make. Simply cut a ¾-in. groove in lengths of trim stock to fit on three sides of a sheet of ¾-in. hardwood-faced plywood. Miter the two corners of the trim. For a single bed the headboard is 40 in. wide, for a double bed it is 65 in. wide.

## Vanity Stools and Benches

The latest idea in vanity seats is a light-weight three-legged stool. The top can be turned from a single piece of hardwood and ready-made legs attached. Less expensive is the "chopping block" stool, Fig. 7. Scrap lengths of hardwood are glued and clamped together to form the seat which is turned on a lathe. The bottom side of the seat is beveled as indicated, both to hide the leg plates and to give the legs a greater angle. The legs of a three-legged stool must be angled as much as possible to provide stability when sitting near the edge. Detailed in Fig. 8 is a vanity bench, which is preferred for a large vanity. The seat consists of a piece of ½-in. plywood to which four legs are screwed. A piece of foam rubber 12 x 18 in. then is cemented to a piece of ¼-in. plywood and it is covered with fabric that is folded under and tacked to the plywood. This assembly is dropped onto the bench and attached with screws.

Although all furniture described in this article is for a bedroom, stacked-drawer construction also could be used for dining-room and living-room furniture.    ★ ★ ★

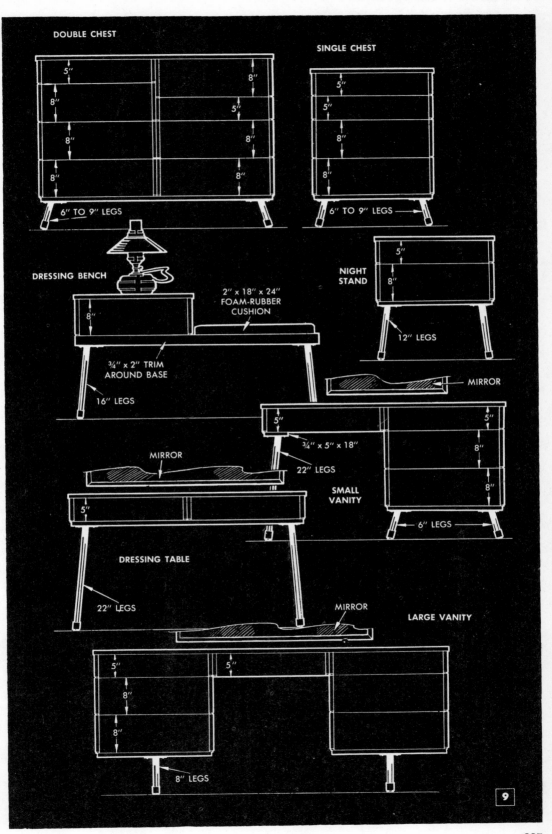

DOUBLE CHEST

5"
8"
8"
8"
8"
5"
8"
8"
6" TO 9" LEGS

SINGLE CHEST

5"
5"
8"
8"
6" TO 9" LEGS

DRESSING BENCH

2" x 18" x 24" FOAM-RUBBER CUSHION

8"

¾" x 2" TRIM AROUND BASE

16" LEGS

NIGHT STAND

5"
8"
12" LEGS

MIRROR

5"
¾" x 5" x 18"
22" LEGS

5"
8"
8"

SMALL VANITY

MIRROR

5"

DRESSING TABLE

22" LEGS

6" LEGS

MIRROR

LARGE VANITY

5"
5"
8"
8"
8" LEGS

9

827

# Desk-Chair

WITH ONE SIMPLE MOTION, this novel youth-size chair can be converted into a neat little desk that is just right for play or school homework. When used as a chair, the back locks firmly in place. By sitting astraddle the chair backwards and pushing the back up and outward, the chair is changed into a desk. A small metal clip locks the desk top securely in place. Releasing this clip permits the desk top to be returned to its original position as a chair back. A small drawer that opens at one side is handy for pencils, crayons and paper.

### Any Wood Will Do

The drawings show how the parts are made and fitted together. Dowels, screws and glue are used in assembling the parts. Hardwood is best for this project but any clear, straight-grained wood can be used. All screwheads are deeply sunk and the holes plugged wherever they show.

A spring clip on the underside holds the desk top in place. It is placed so that it locks over the upper dowel rung at the top of the legs. The recess at this point is to allow space for the clip to operate freely. The clip is released by pressing upward on it if you want to change from desk to chair.

### Drawer Under the Seat

Standard drawer construction is used in making the drawer. It is mounted on guide strips fastened to the inside face of the seat rails and the drawer sides are grooved to fit the guides. Glue and nails are used in assembling the drawer, and a small knob is attached to the front.

Each back leg is cut from a piece 4 x 25 in. Follow the side-view drawing in laying them out. Where possible it is best to bandsaw or jigsaw them as a pair to assure identical shape and also sand and bore the holes for the dowel rungs while the two

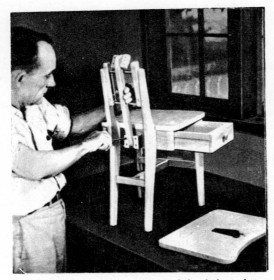

Pivot blocks for the lower end of the desk-top brace are attached securely with screws to side of chair seat rail. Brace must work freely to fold properly

back-leg pieces are still tacked together.

Dowel pins and screws are used in assembling the chair frame. Glue is applied to all joints at the time of final assembly. Three rails are all that are used in the chair, one side being left open for the drawer. Screws for attaching the seat board are placed in counterbored holes in the rails. Corners of both the seat board and back board are rounded as shown. The arm should be made of ¾-in. plywood for strength and to prevent splitting at the ends.

The desk action of the chair back is easy to see in the side view. The holes for the countersunk screws are plugged with plugs made of ⅜-in. dowel. These are glued and sanded down smooth. Holes and moving parts may have to be filed or sanded a little to make the parts work freely. The completed project can be finished with wood stain and varnished or painted. ★★★

The combination desk-top-and-chair-back is attached with screws to slotted cleats that ride on dowel rungs. Notice how notched ends of cleats hook over lower rung to lock desk top in chair-back position

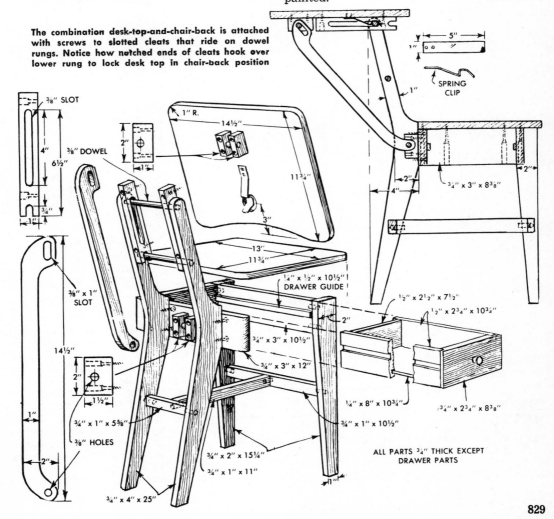

ALL PARTS ¾" THICK EXCEPT DRAWER PARTS

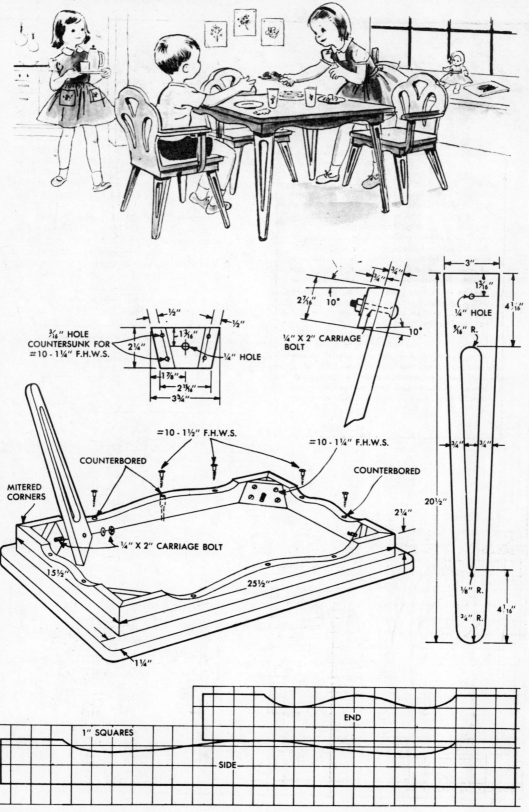

¾₁₆" HOLE
COUNTERSUNK FOR
#10 - 1¼" F.H.W.S.

½"
½"
1³₁₆"
2¼"
¼" HOLE
1⅞"
2¹³₁₆"
3¾"

¾"
¾"
2⁷₁₆"
10°
10°
¼" X 2" CARRIAGE BOLT

3"
1³₁₆"
¼" HOLE
⁵₁₆" R.
4¹⁄₁₆"
¾"
¾"
20½"
⅛" R.
¾" R.
4¹⁄₁₆"

#10 - 1½" F.H.W.S.
COUNTERBORED
#10 - 1¼" F.H.W.S.
COUNTERBORED

MITERED
CORNERS
¼" X 2" CARRIAGE BOLT
2¼"

15½"
25½"
1¼"

END

1" SQUARES

SIDE

# Children's Dinette Set

Always appealing to little girls and boys, a pint-sized dinette set means tea parties in style as well as a fine place for drawing and playing games. The table top may be a 20 x 28-in. piece of ¾-in. plywood or the sink-cutout blank from a plastic-laminated counter top. Rails and legs are made of ¾-in. lumber and assembled as in the details. It ordinary ¾-in. plywood is used for the table top, it may be covered easily with plastic laminate. Make as many chairs as you like, using the patterns shown below. The back and seat are of ¾-in. plywood, with legs, rails and arms of ¾-in. lumber. When assembling both chairs and table, apply glue to all joints before fastening them together with wood screws. Then simply bolt the legs to the corner blocks. The exposed surfaces of the wood can be enameled or stained and varnished

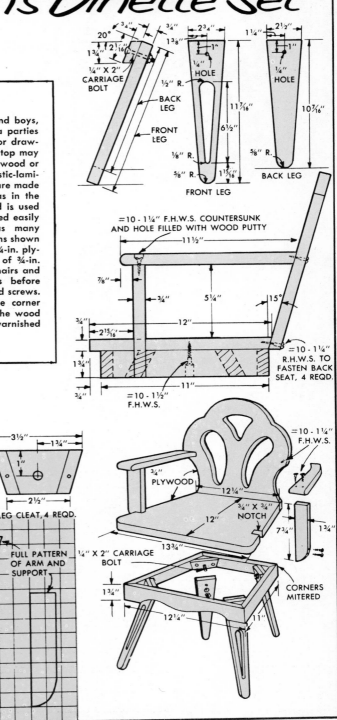

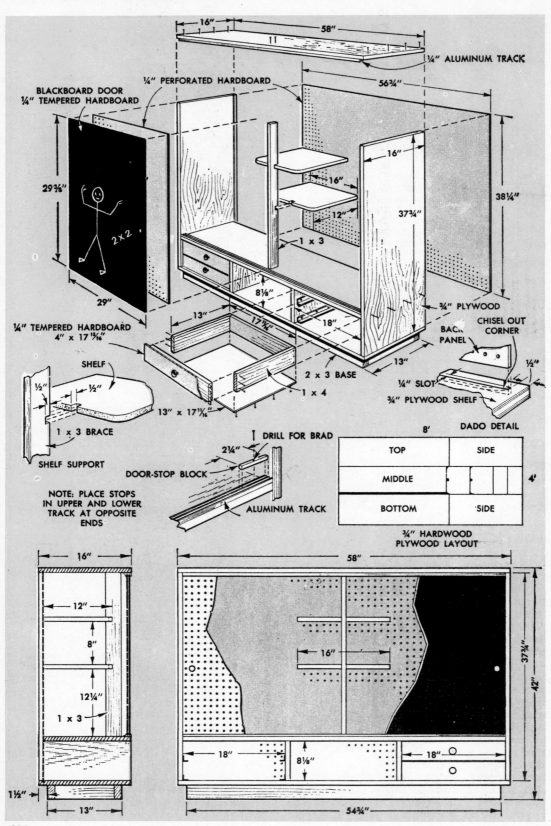

16"
58"
11
¼" ALUMINUM TRACK

BLACKBOARD DOOR
¼" TEMPERED HARDBOARD

¼" PERFORATED HARDBOARD

56¾"

29⅜"

2 x 2

16"

16"

38¼"

12"

37¾"

1 x 3

¼" TEMPERED HARDBOARD
4" x 17¹³⁄₁₆"

29"

¾" PLYWOOD

SHELF

8⅛"

½"    ½"

13"

17¼"

18"

BACK
PANEL

CHISEL OUT
CORNER

½"

1 x 3 BRACE

13" x 17¼"

2 x 3 BASE

13"

¼" SLOT

SHELF SUPPORT

1 x 4

¾" PLYWOOD SHELF

NOTE: PLACE STOPS
IN UPPER AND LOWER
TRACK AT OPPOSITE
ENDS

DRILL FOR BRAD

2¼"

DOOR-STOP BLOCK

ALUMINUM TRACK

DADO DETAIL

8'

| TOP | | SIDE |
|-----|---|------|
| MIDDLE | | | | |
| BOTTOM | | SIDE |

4'

¾" HARDWOOD
PLYWOOD LAYOUT

16"

58"

12"

8"

16"

37¾"

12¼"

42"

1 x 3

18"

8⅛"

18"

1½"

13"

54¾"

REAR VIEW

*By Dave Swartwout*

# CHILD'S WARDROBE
## Is Island of Storage and Play

GROWING FAMILIES having a shortage of wardrobe space can relieve some of the "bulging-at-the-seams" by building one or more wardrobes like this one. Designed as a child's wardrobe, it may be backed against a wall, or located as above so as to project into the room like a divider.

The upper three-fourths of the wardrobe-divider has two shelves and two clothes hanging compartments, while the lower part has four good-sized drawers and a shoe compartment. Two sliding doors enclose the front, one of which is perforated hardboard. The other is tempered hardboard that may be painted flat black or green to serve as a blackboard. The back of the unit is covered with a panel of ¼-in. perforated hardboard, providing a pin-up surface for play, inset above, or for hanging things on utility hooks such as are available for this purpose. Sides, top, middle and bottom shelves, plus drawer partitions and center

shelves of the wardrobe are cut from a 4 x 8-ft. panel of ¾-in. solid-core hardwood plywood as indicated in the layout detail. Drawer sides, backs and fronts are made of 1 x 4-in. lumber. Bottoms and drawer-front facings are ¼-in. tempered hardboard. The drawers slide on ⅛ x ¾ x ¾-in. aluminum angles screwed to the wardrobe as shown in the drawings.

After cutting out all wardrobe parts, begin assembly with the base, which consists of 2 x 3s nailed on edge to the ¾-in. plywood bottom. Then install the drawer slides and dado the wardrobe sides, top and bottom to take the hardboard panel at the back, which is glued and nailed in place. Drawer partitions, drawers and shelf assembly are installed next, followed by the sliding doors, which are fitted in a double aluminum track as shown in the track detail. Installation of pull-out-type clothes hanger or brackets and a coat or two of paint, completes the wardrobe. ★ ★ ★

# YOUNGSTER'S

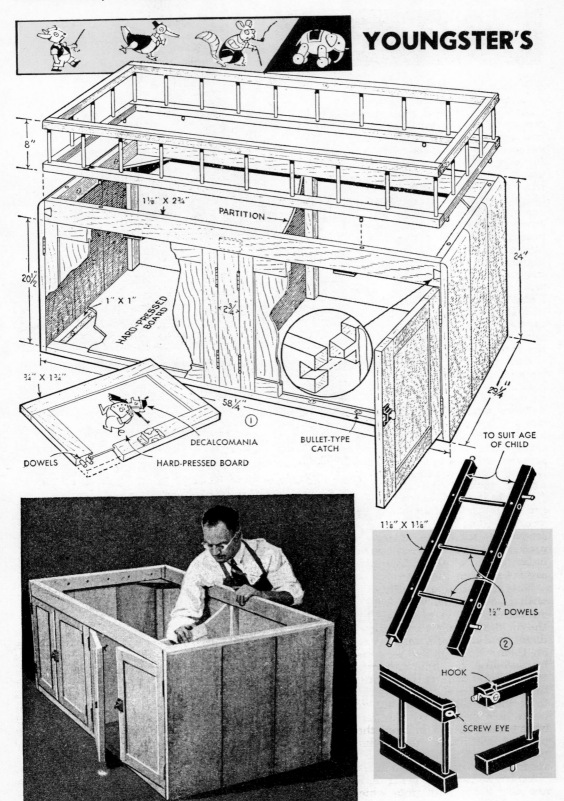

8"

1⅛" X 2¾"

PARTITION

20½"

1" X 1"

HARD-PRESSED BOARD

2¾"

24"

29¼"

¾" X 1¾"

58¼"

①

DECALCOMANIA

HARD-PRESSED BOARD

DOWELS

BULLET-TYPE CATCH

TO SUIT AGE OF CHILD

1⅛" X 1⅛"

½" DOWELS

②

HOOK

SCREW EYE

# CHEST-BED

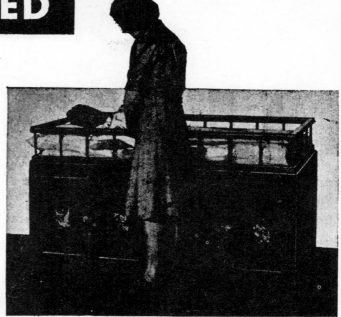

IN SMALL homes and apartments where it is impossible to furnish a room for the child, this combination bed and chest will be of real value, as it serves as a comfortable bed at night and provides storage space for extra blankets, toys and other household items. In daytime, removing the railings and covering the chest with an appropriate drapery converts it into a useful couch. If made higher than shown in Fig. 1, the railings can be removed and set up separately to form a child's play pen. When used in this way, however, a floor for the pen must be assembled and drilled for pegs to keep the railings in place.

Before assembling the frame, have the springs at hand so they can be measured, as the exact size of the chest depends upon these dimensions. Corners of the frame are dovetailed and glued, with triangular blocks glued and screwed to the underside of the top members at each corner to support the springs. Note that the ends of the chest are built up of tongue-and-groove stock, glued and screwed to the frame. To improve the appearance, the outer edges of these boards are rounded at the top.

Note that the chest is fitted with a partition which is curved at the top to prevent

the springs hitting it when they are pressed down by weight of a person sitting or lying on them. Railings are assembled quickly by clamping the upper and lower members together and drilling them both at the same time. The holes should be just large enough to provide a sliding fit for the dowels, these being held in place by glue and small finishing nails driven in from the sides. To prevent shifting of the railings, tapered pegs are fitted in the lower members to correspond with holes drilled at the top of the chest frame as shown in Fig. 2. End railings are also fitted with pegs which slip into holes drilled in the side railings. Hooks and screw eyes lock the railings together.

Doors are hung with hinges having removable pins for convenience in detaching them, in case the edges need planing to make them fit accurately. A stop block at the top and bullet-type catches in the bottom rail hold the doors shut. Or, you can fit them with elbow catches and cabinet latches, if desired. Although the bed is somewhat higher than cribs in general, this gives the advantages of adding to the storage space, Fig. 3, and facilitating making the bed with a minimum of stooping for the housewife. Low railings are also a convenience where the bed is made without removing them. Decalcomania transfers are applied in the center of each door.

# YOUNGSTER'S 4-IN-1

HERE'S A DESK youngsters won't out-grow. Preschoolers will have fun with it as a play center, and then continue to find it useful as a homework desk all through the grades and even high school. It makes good use of the small space it takes, for it not only provides storage galore for books and toys, but incorporates a king-size blackboard on the underside of the desk. Best of all, the desk part swings up out of the way so the unit takes even less space when closed.

### Most of It Is Hardboard

The complete unit consists of two sep-arate cabinets (a base and a top) both of which are assembled from simple wooden frames faced with tempered and perforated hardboard. The latter is used for facing of ends on the inside and, in turn, to hold the hangers that are used to support the shelves. With the exception of the frame for the writing desk, which is made of 1 x 4s, all frames are cut from 1 x 2s. Glue and corrugated fasteners are used to join the frame members.

Both upper and lower units are simple boxlike assemblies. The end frames can be faced with perforated hardboard at this time, but the outside, as well as the entire assembly, is not covered with hardboard until after the frames are glued and nailed together. You'll notice in the case of the base unit, Fig. 4, that the top frame differs from the bottom one in that wider end members are used, and that the bottom frame fits inside the ends, whereas the top frame laps the latter. In the case of the top unit, Fig. 3, identical pairs of frames are made and, in turn, lapped and nailed to the ends of the end frames. Only the bottom and ends are covered both sides.

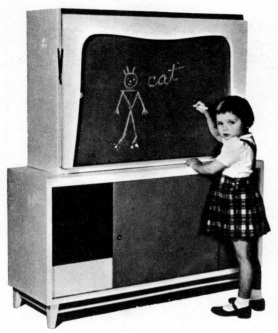

It's a blackboard, desk, bookcase and toy box all in one. Makes compact play center for preschool tot and future home-study desk for teen

# PLAY DESK

### "Veneering" the Outside

In gluing the hardboard panels to the framework, a better job will result if you have a few C-clamps on hand to clamp the work. Start by adding the back panels first. These are kept flush all around and will add rigidity to the units. Both units are covered in much the same manner, the main difference being that both sides of the bottom frame of the upper unit are covered with hardboard, whereas just one side of the bottom frame of the base unit is covered. The panels covering the tops of both units lap the panels covering the ends, and all panels lap the edges of the back panels. When facing the sides of the writing-desk frame, apply both panels at one time to avoid unequal stress and possible warping. The three shelf frames, one for the toy chest and two for the bookcase, can be faced on just one side, although if

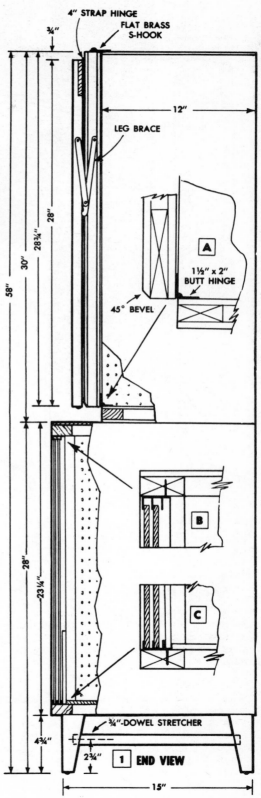

4" STRAP HINGE
FLAT BRASS S-HOOK

LEG BRACE

12"

A

1½" x 2" BUTT HINGE

45° BEVEL

¾"

58"
30"
28¾"
28"

28"
23¼"
4¾"
2¾"

15"

B

C

¾"-DOWEL STRETCHER

**1 END VIEW**

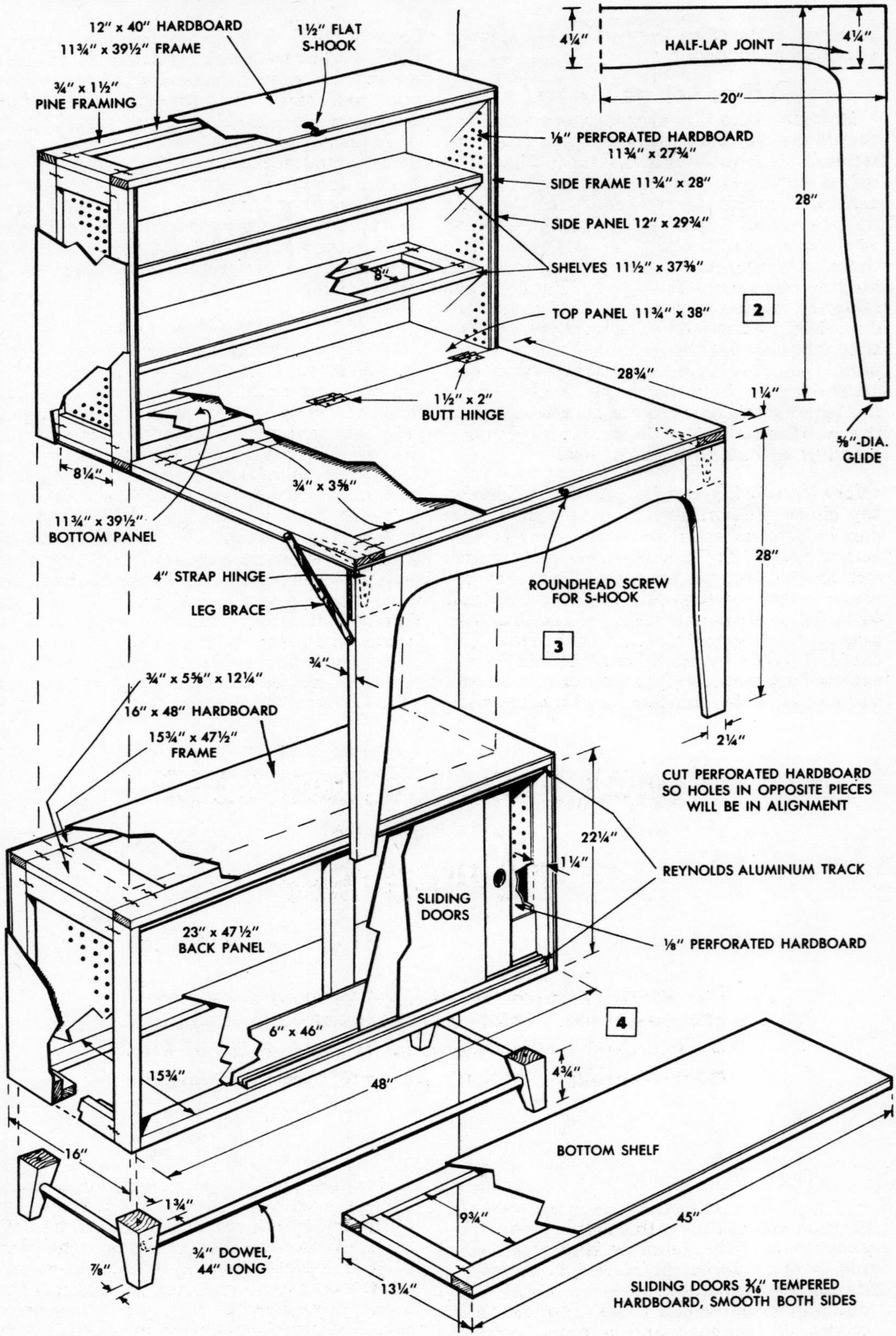

12" x 40" HARDBOARD
11¾" x 39½" FRAME

1½" FLAT
S-HOOK

¾" x 1½"
PINE FRAMING

HALF-LAP JOINT

4¼"

4¼"

20"

⅛" PERFORATED HARDBOARD
11¾" x 27¾"

SIDE FRAME 11¾" x 28"

SIDE PANEL 12" x 29¾"

28"

SHELVES 11½" x 37⅜"

TOP PANEL 11¾" x 38"

2

8"

28¾"

1¼"

1½" x 2"
BUTT HINGE

⅝"-DIA.
GLIDE

8¼"

¾" x 3⅝"

28"

11¾" x 39½"
BOTTOM PANEL

4" STRAP HINGE

ROUNDHEAD SCREW
FOR S-HOOK

LEG BRACE

¾"

3

2¼"

¾" x 5⅝" x 12¼"

CUT PERFORATED HARDBOARD
SO HOLES IN OPPOSITE PIECES
WILL BE IN ALIGNMENT

16" x 48" HARDBOARD

15¾" x 47½"
FRAME

22¼"

1¼"

REYNOLDS ALUMINUM TRACK

SLIDING
DOORS

⅛" PERFORATED HARDBOARD

23" x 47½"
BACK PANEL

4

6" x 46"

15¾"

48"

4¾"

16"

BOTTOM SHELF

1¾"

45"

7⅞"

¾" DOWEL,
44" LONG

9¾"

13¼"

SLIDING DOORS ³⁄₁₆" TEMPERED
HARDBOARD, SMOOTH BOTH SIDES

faced on both sides they will hold a lot of books without bowing.

### Adding Legs and Doors

Holes for the dowel stretchers that join the legs are bored before the legs are tapered. If you should find it difficult to buy a dowel 44 in. long, thin-wall conduit can be used for the stretchers. In tapering the legs from 1¾ in. square at the top to ⅞ in. square at the bottom, note that only the inside adjacent faces are tapered, the outside faces are left straight. The legs are fastened to the corners of the base with 2-in. No. 10 flathead screws driven down through the hardboard and frame members. Use glue in addition to screws and set the legs ⅞ in. in from the corners. Both the legs for the base and those that support the writing desk should be made of hardwood to withstand years of use.

The bypassing hardboard doors for the toy chest slide in aluminum tracks which can be purchased at hardware stores. Details B and C, Fig. 1, show where the tracks are located, top and bottom. They are set about ⅛ in. in from the front edges and fastened with small nails. A 1 x 2 center post gives support to the base unit, and this is installed next, gluing and nailing it top and bottom, and positioning it at the very edge of the bottom hardboard panel.

Finally, a 6 x 46-in. hardboard strip is fitted across the front, gluing it to the post and to the edges of the hardboard bottom and perforated side panels. The sliding doors measure 20⅞ in. high and 23¾ in. wide and are fitted with regular brass finger grips pressed into ¾-in. holes bored 1¼ in. from the outer edges. It should be mentioned that when installing the tracks, the track with the wide flange is placed at the top, otherwise the doors will not engage the upper track and will appear to be too short.

### Cutting Desk Legs

Fig. 2 gives a half pattern for the scroll-cut desk legs. This is a one piece unit which is assembled from three members that are half-lapped at the corners and later bandsawed, after gluing. Strap hinges are used to attach the legs to the writing desk and three butt hinges are used to pivot the writing desk to the upper cabinet. In both cases, the hinges are surface mounted. Card-table leg braces hold the legs in the open position, and a round-headed screw and a flat brass S-hook are used to hold the desk when swung up. Green blackboard paint is applied to the hardboard; the rest is painted to suit.

Any nails exposed in the hardboard surfaces should be set below the surface and puttied over before painting.  ★ ★ ★

# MAKE THIS COMPLETE

# DINING SET

**This smart-looking seven-piece dining-room group—one of a special series of fine furniture for the entire house— is our answer to the tremendous response received for more home-built furniture of good, practical design**

Designed expressly for the craftsman working with small home-workshop tools, this complete dining ensemble, which is sufficient to furnish a full-size dining room, consists of seven pieces, including an extension table for eight, four chairs, a credenza and a china cabinet. However, if you haven't room for the entire group, you can eliminate the china cabinet or, in the case of an exceptionally small dinette or dining alcove, the base section of the two-piece china cabinet can be built and used alone as a server to take the place of the large credenza. The table is designed to take an extra leaf which permits serving as many as eight persons, and the seats of the upholstered chairs are spring-filled for real added comfort, a feature not found in all commercial suites.

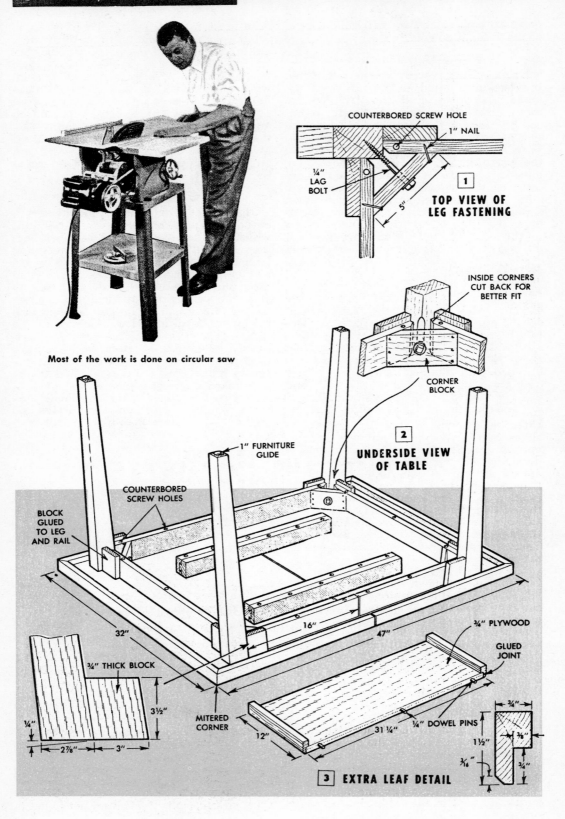

Most of the work is done on circular saw

**COUNTERBORED SCREW HOLE**

**1" NAIL**

¼" LAG BOLT

5"

**1**

### TOP VIEW OF LEG FASTENING

INSIDE CORNERS CUT BACK FOR BETTER FIT

**CORNER BLOCK**

**2**

### UNDERSIDE VIEW OF TABLE

1" FURNITURE GLIDE

COUNTERBORED SCREW HOLES

BLOCK GLUED TO LEG AND RAIL

32"

16"

47"

¾" PLYWOOD

GLUED JOINT

¾" THICK BLOCK

3½"

¼"

2⅞"

3"

MITERED CORNER

12"

31¼"

¼" DOWEL PINS

¾"

1½"

³⁄₁₆"

¾"

⅜"

**3** **EXTRA LEAF DETAIL**

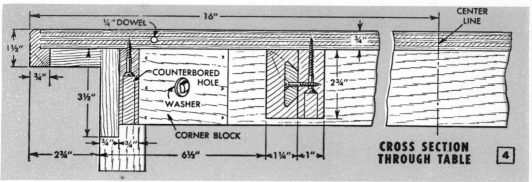

**CROSS SECTION THROUGH TABLE** 4

¼"DOWEL 16" CENTER LINE 1½" ¾" ¾" COUNTERBORED HOLE 2¾" WASHER 3½" CORNER BLOCK 2¾" ¾" ¾" 6½" 1¼" 1"

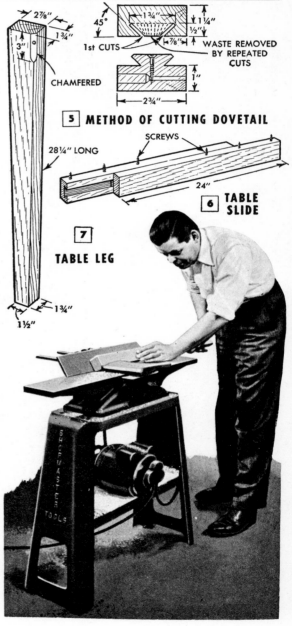

2⅞" 1¾" 3" CHAMFERED

28¼" LONG

TABLE LEG 7

1¾" 1½"

45° 1¾" 1¼" ½" 1st CUTS ⅞" WASTE REMOVED BY REPEATED CUTS 1" 2¾"

**METHOD OF CUTTING DOVETAIL** 5

SCREWS 24" **TABLE SLIDE** 6

**Construction of the table** is detailed in Figs. 1 to 7 inclusive. Like the living-room suite, which incorporated the use of both plywood and solid stock, the table top and extra leaf are cut from ¾-in. plywood to save the work of gluing up solid stock. All the rest of the table is made of solid material. A ¾ x 1½-in. facing or edging strip, mitered at the corners and rabbeted on the back, is glued and nailed to the edge of the plywood to conceal the laminations. The top, of course, consists of two separate sections having the conventional aligning pins and holes in the edges at the joint. The sectional view in Fig. 4 indicates the position of the legs and the slides and also shows how the 3-in. aprons, or rails, are screwed to the underside of the top. The ends of the end aprons are cut off squarely, while the two-piece side ones, which butt together at the joint, are cut at an angle to match the slant of the tapered legs. Locate the side aprons 3½ in. in from the edge of the top and the end ones 6 in. inward. Then glue and screw them securely to the plywood.

The tapered legs, Fig. 7, are cut from 1¾-in. stock. Note in the detail at the left of Fig. 3, that the tops of the legs are cut at a ¼-in. angle. Each leg is placed in the corner formed by the aprons and drawn up rigidly with lag screws. Corner blocks are drilled for the screws and then glued and nailed to the aprons as shown in Fig. 1. The lag screws are the only fastenings the legs require and, if the legs loosen with use, it is easy to make them rigid simply by drawing the lag screws tighter. Additional rigidity is had by the eight overlay blocks which are applied to the face of the aprons at the corners. Note that the blocks at the sides of the table are fitted flush with the face of the legs.

Figs. 4, 5 and 6 show how the dovetail joint is formed in the table slide. The

tenon on the male member of the slide consists of a separate strip shaped as shown and screwed to the face of the piece. This strip engages a matching groove in the female member. The groove can be cut on the circular saw by first making the two 45-deg. outside cuts and then removing the waste portion with repeated cuts, varying the angle of the blade slightly each time. The male members of the slide are glued and screwed to one half of the table and the female members to the other, using three screws in counterbored holes. A coating of wax will make the slides work smoothly.

**Chair-frame construction** is detailed in Figs. 9 to 12 inclusive. Whether four or more chairs are built, at least one should be made a guest, or host, chair by adding arms as shown in Fig. 8 and increasing the width of the front and back, Fig. 11. The over-all height and depth remain the same. Identical parts can be mass-produced to save time by using stops and jigs on the saw. As the legs are the only part of the

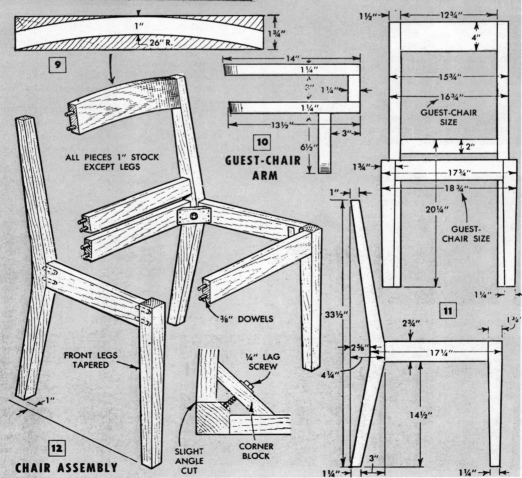

**9**

**10 GUEST-CHAIR ARM**

ALL PIECES 1" STOCK EXCEPT LEGS

GUEST-CHAIR SIZE

GUEST-CHAIR SIZE

3⁄8" DOWELS

FRONT LEGS TAPERED

**11**

**12 CHAIR ASSEMBLY**

¼" LAG SCREW

SLIGHT ANGLE CUT

CORNER BLOCK

frame exposed, the rest of the assembly can be rough. Note in Fig. 12 that all members are doweled and each corner of the seat is braced with lag screws the same as the table. The curved back rail is bandsawed from a piece 1¾ x 4 in., Fig. 9, while the front legs are tapered on all four faces from a point 2¾ in. from the top. The exposed part of the legs should be finished before upholstering.

**Upholstering the chairs:** The first step is to tack furniture webbing to the seat bottom, Fig. 13. Six strips are interlaced and stretched tautly in the manner indicated in the detail to the right of Fig. 16. The ends of the webbing are left about 1 in. long for folding back and double-tacking. Five No. 1 plain-end coil springs are used in the seat. These are placed in position, tack-sewed to the webbing, and then tied and crosstied to the bottom of the seat rails as shown in Fig. 14. The dots in the drawing indicate knots. The springs are compressed so that the center one is about 1½ in. above the top of the seat. The spring twine is brought down through holes punched in the webbing and tacked securely to the underside of the rails. Next, the springs are covered with burlap, Fig. 15. The edges are tacked, folded over and retacked, and then a welt edging is tacked around the outer edge on three sides, Fig. 16. The welt used here is the same as used later on the back, Fig. 25, except that being hidden it can be made up of scrap material wrapped around a length of ¼-in. rope. Hair, tow or moss filling is added next, Fig. 17. This is held in place by tack-sewing it to the burlap. A layer of cotton is applied over the filling so it covers the sides of the seat rails, Fig. 18. After this, the whole job is covered with the finished fabric, and the completed seat should look like Fig. 19. Patterns for the seat covering as well as the rest of the chair are given in Fig. 24. When completed, the underside of the seat is covered with black cambric, the edges being folded under.

Two strips of webbing are tacked to the back, Fig. 20, and then it is covered with burlap, moss and finally cotton. The cotton is brought around the sides and over the top

**13** WEBBING ENDS DOUBLE-TACKED

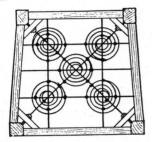

**14** SPRINGS CROSSTIED LIKE THIS

**15** BURLAP IS TACKED OVER SPRINGS

**16** THEN WELT IS TACKED TO EDGE

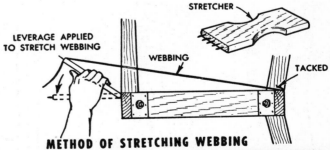

STRETCHER

LEVERAGE APPLIED TO STRETCH WEBBING

WEBBING

TACKED

**METHOD OF STRETCHING WEBBING**

**17** MOSS FILLING COMES NEXT

**18** THEN IS COVERED WITH COTTON

**19** AND HERE'S THE COMPLETED SEAT

**20** FIRST, WEBBING IS APPLIED TO THE BACK

**21** THEN WEBBING IS COVERED WITH BURLAP

**22** LAYER OF MOSS IS TACK-SEWED TO BURLAP

**23** COTTON IS ADDED NEXT, THEN THE FABRIC

and the lower edge is folded up under the moss. Note in applying the covering to the front of the back that the fabric is first pulled through and tacked to the face of the rear seat rail, Fig. 25. Before the back covering is applied, a welt made of the finished fabric is tacked to three sides. Then a strip of cardboard, ½-in. wide, is cut to fit across the top between the welt at the sides. The fabric is tacked at the top first, driving the tacks through the cardboard strip as in Fig. 25. With the top tacked, the fabric is brought down over the back, the edges folded under and hand-stitched to the welt. Blued gimp nails are used in tacking the covering where it passes over the exposed surface of the legs. This method is called blind tacking. In addition to concealing the tacks, the cardboard strip provides a firm edge which avoids irregular pleats when the cloth is pulled taut.

(Note—Traditional methods of upholstering are shown here. For instructions on foam rubber upholstering, see page 788.)

**24** ## PATTERNS

These fabric patterns were taken from the actual covering on one of the chairs and are somewhat approximate in size. While over-all measurements are ample, the various cuts and folds indicated should be made while fitting to avoid an error

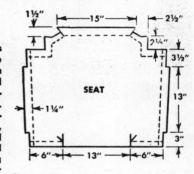

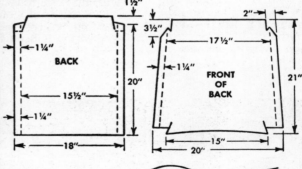

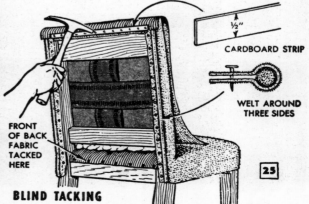

FRONT OF BACK FABRIC TACKED HERE

CARDBOARD STRIP

WELT AROUND THREE SIDES

**25**

## BLIND TACKING

WITH THE table and chairs completed as detailed **earlier**, you should be ready to tackle the more pretentious pieces of the dining-room group — the credenza and the china cabinet. Construction of the credenza is fairly simple as revealed in the cutaway drawing in Fig. 28. Over-all dimensions for this piece are given in Fig. 26, and a view of the interior, Fig. 27, shows how the doors are hinged, where friction catches are installed and how finger pockets in the rails are provided to facilitate

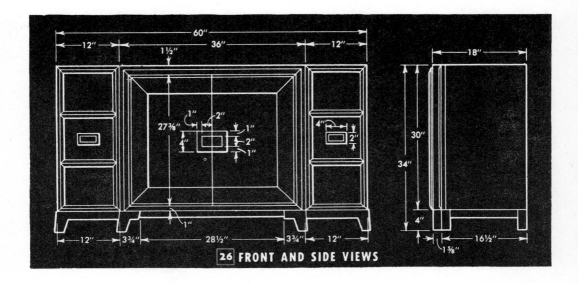

**26 FRONT AND SIDE VIEWS**

removal of the two silverware drawers.

**Start the credenza** by making the base framework. Each end is made up exactly the same, right and left hand, and then joined together with front and rear members. Section A-A in Fig. 28 gives the sizes of these members and shows how they are screwed together. Note that the ¾ x 1½-in. strip placed on edge runs the full length of the base and is glued and doweled to the two rear legs. All legs are the same size and shape, six being required, three of which are made for the right side and three for the left. All are doweled to the rails. Note that the outside faces of the end rails are beveled to match the flare of the legs. Section D-D shows how intermediate rails are rabbeted along one edge to receive ¼-in. plywood bottoms. Cleats are fitted on the three other rails to support the plywood. Center legs of the credenza are doweled to the face of the front rails 12 in. in from the corner. Then, the 1 x 1⅛-in. strip is screwed to the projecting ends of the rails and small overlay blocks are used to conceal the screwheads. Section A-A shows how the back rail is built up of two additional pieces, both being the same length and set between the intermediate rails.

**Next, the side members** of the end compartments are installed. These are cut to size from ¾-in. plywood. The upper ends of the outside panels are mitered 45 deg. while the lower ends are trimmed off squarely and bored for three ¼-in. dowels, which are located in the base to bring the outer panels flush with the rail. The rear edges of the two outer panels are rabbeted for a ¼-in. plywood back. The inner panels of each compartment are made ¾

in. shorter than the outer ones and narrower to permit covering the plies of the wood with a ¾ x 1⅝-in. strip of solid stock as detailed in section B-B. This strip is edge-glued and may be doweled for additional strength. The two panels of each unit are held together at the top with a frame of ¾ x 1½-in. stock. Front and rear pieces of the frame are grooved on the inside edges for tenons on the sidepieces. The frame is screwed in place through the edge so it is even with the bottom of the miter and flush with the top of the inner

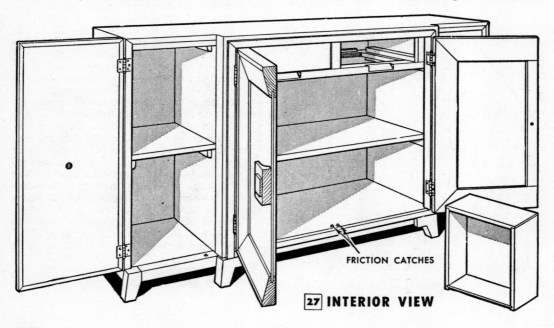

FRICTION CATCHES

**27** INTERIOR VIEW

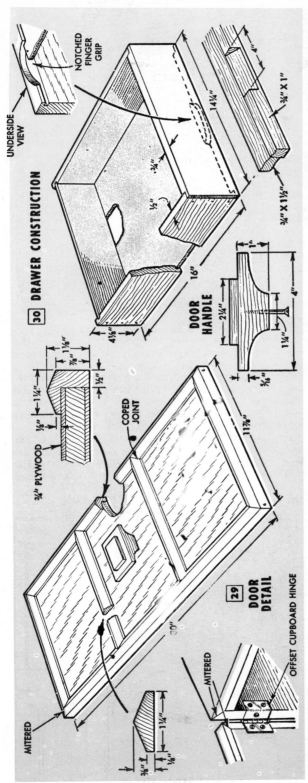

**NOTCHED FINGER GRIP**

**UNDERSIDE VIEW**

14¼"

¾" X 1"

¾" X 1½"

½"

¾"

16"

4⅝"

**30** **DRAWER CONSTRUCTION**

2¼"

1¼"

4"

**DOOR HANDLE**

⁵⁄₁₆"

1⅛"

⅞"

½"

1¼"

⅛"

**¾" PLYWOOD**

**COPED JOINT**

11⅞"

30"

**OFFSET CUPBOARD HINGE**

**MITERED**

1¼"

¾"

⅛"

**MITERED**

**29** **DOOR DETAIL**

panel. The plywood back is added next to strengthen the assembly. This is nailed into the rabbets of the outer panels, to the edge of the inner panels and to the framing at the top and bottom.

**Next comes the top.** This is cut 15¾ in. wide and is mitered at each end to make a perfectly fitting joint with the end panels. As in the case of the inner panels, a ¾ x 1⅝-in. strip of solid stock is edge-glued to the top to build it out flush with the sides. With this done, the center door molding is applied. Sections A-A and B-B give the size of the molding. The side and top members are rabbeted on the outer edge to fit over the edge of the top and inner panels, while the bottom member is rabbeted to take a ¼-in. plywood bottom panel. Facing edges of the molding are beveled according to the sectional views and mitered to fit perfectly at the corners. Note, however, that the center shelf and the drawer frame should be installed before the molding is applied.

**The drawer frame** is made similarly to the frames at the top of the end units. Drawer runners are installed in the center and at each side after the frame is in place. Note that the front edge of the frame is faced with a hardwood strip which is notched at a 45-deg. angle to provide a finger pocket for each drawer. While the dimension for this is missing in Fig. 28, it is included in Fig. 30. The center doors are built up according to section C-C. They can be made in one piece by framing ¼-in. plywood with a heavy molding grooved to fit over the edge and then sawing in half. A ⅜ x 1½-in. strip is used to reinforce the plywood along each side of the saw cut. Construction of the doors for the end units is detailed in Fig. 29. Plywood is framed with a rabbeted molding to conceal the laminations, and overlay strips, coped at the ends, are surface-glued to the plywood to divide the doors into three equal panels. Regular offset cupboard hinges are used on the end doors, while 3-in., loose-pin hinges are used on the center doors.

**The china cabinet** consists of two separate units which are held together at the back with a cleat. If space is so limited that you can accommodate neither the large credenza nor the complete china cabinet, just the base of the latter can be built and used as a small server. Fig. 31 shows the general construction of both units of the cabinet. Top, sides, back and dust panels of the lower unit are ¼-in. plywood. Top and bottom frames are joined at the back with ¾ x 1¾-in. posts which are notched for the shelves and two drawer frames. Fig. 32

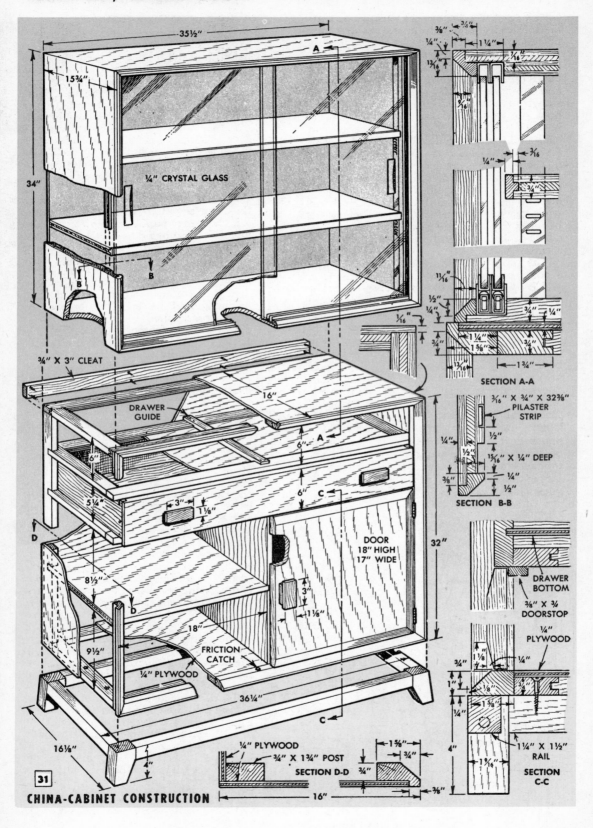

35½"

15¾"

A

¼" CRYSTAL GLASS

34"

B

B

B

¾" X 3" CLEAT

DRAWER GUIDE

16"

A

6"

6"

5¼"

3"

1⅛"

6" C

D

DOOR
18" HIGH
17" WIDE

32"

8½"

D

3"

1⅛"

18"

FRICTION CATCH

9½"

¼" PLYWOOD

C

36¼"

16⅛"

4"

¼" PLYWOOD
¾" X 1¾" POST
SECTION D-D

1⅝"
¾"

16"

⅜"

⅜"  ¾"
¼"
1¾"
1⅜"
¼"
1/16"
5/16"

11/16"
½"
¼"

1¼"
1⅝"

1⅜"

¾"
¼"

¾"  ¼"
¾"

1¾"

**SECTION A-A**

3/16" X ¾" X 32⅜"
PILASTER STRIP

¼"
½"
½"

15/16" X ¼" DEEP

⅜"
¼"
½"

**SECTION B-B**

DRAWER BOTTOM
⅜" X ¾
DOORSTOP

¼"
PLYWOOD

¾"
1⅛"
¼"

1"
⅜"

¼"
1⅝"

4"

1⅝"

1¼" X 1½"
RAIL

**SECTION C-C**

**CHINA-CABINET CONSTRUCTION**

shows how the drawer frames are assembled. The top and bottom frames are supported at the front by a rabbeted molding which is mitered and assembled as a picture frame and then glued to the front edges of the frames at top and bottom. Side and top panels fit the rabbeted molding as shown in section D-D. Section C-C shows how the bottom frame is screwed to the base. Note that the top panel is rabbeted at each end to overlap the side panels. Drawers are assembled as in Fig. 30 and made to fit the openings. A grooved runner which rides on the guide is nailed to the underside of each drawer. Fig. 34 shows the simple wooden drawer pull. If desired, a silverware drawer can be included, Fig. 33. A bevel is run around the outer edges of the doors ¼ in. deep and 1⅛ in. wide to give a raised panel effect.

**The top unit** of the cabinet is made like a box from ¾-in. plywood. Sections A-A and B-B show how the pieces are rabbeted at the front edge to receive a molding which covers the laminations. Note that the rabbets at the top and bottom are made wide enough to house a standard showcase door track (see section A-A) and that rabbets also are made along the sidepieces to provide end grooves for the sliding glass doors. Note in section B-B that a groove is run at the front and back edges of the sidepieces for a standard adjustable shelf pilaster. In ordering glass panels for the doors, notice in section A-A that they must be short enough to permit inserting in the top track and then down into the lower one. Use crystal glass as it is less expensive. Any glass shop can grind the finger grips.

The china cabinet makes the seven-piece group complete. Featuring sliding glass doors, it's designed as two separate units to simplify moving and to permit base alone to be built and used as dinette server

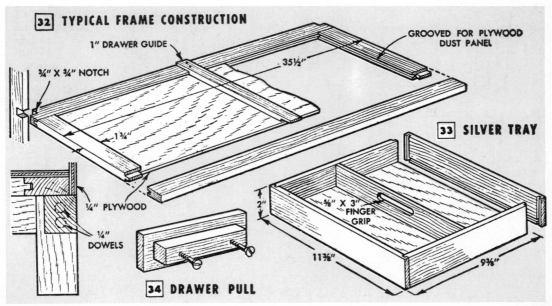

**32 TYPICAL FRAME CONSTRUCTION**

GROOVED FOR PLYWOOD DUST PANEL

1" DRAWER GUIDE

¾" X ¾" NOTCH

35½"

1¾"

¼" PLYWOOD

¼" DOWELS

**34 DRAWER PULL**

**33 SILVER TRAY**

2"

⅝" X 3" FINGER GRIP

11⅜"

9⅜"

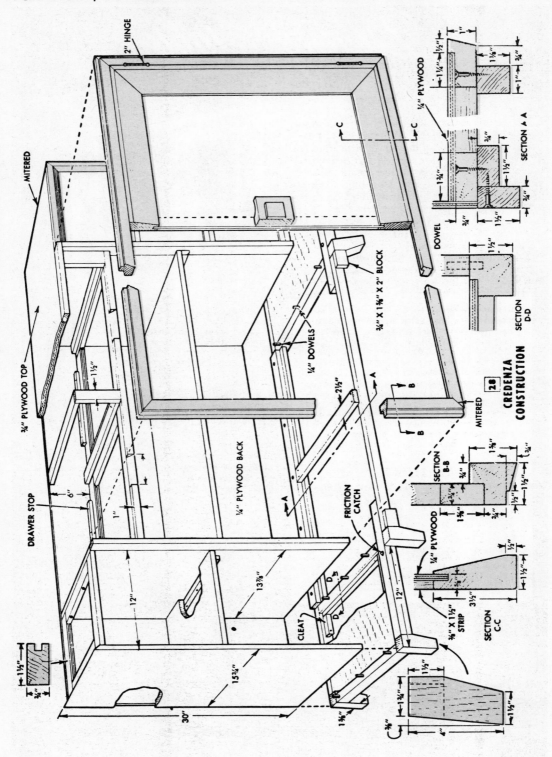

2" HINGE

MITERED

¾" PLYWOOD TOP

DRAWER STOP

1½

6"

1"

1½"

12"

13⅞"

CLEAT

15¾"

30"

¾"

1½"

¾" X 1¾" X 2" BLOCK

¼" DOWELS

DOWELS

¼" PLYWOOD BACK

2½"

A

A

B

B

C

C

FRICTION CATCH

D

D

12"

1⅝"

½" PLYWOOD

1"

1¼"

1½"

1⅛"

¾"

1"

1"

SECTION A-A

DOWEL

1¾"

¾"

1½"

1½"

¾"

¾"

1½"

SECTION D-D

**CREDENZA CONSTRUCTION** 28

MITERED

SECTION B-B

1⅝"

¾"

1½"

¾"

1⅝"

¾"

½"

¼" PLYWOOD

½"

1½"

3½"

⅝"

¾"

SECTION C-C

¾" X 1½" STRIP

1½"

1¾"

1½"

4"

¾"

# Dining Table

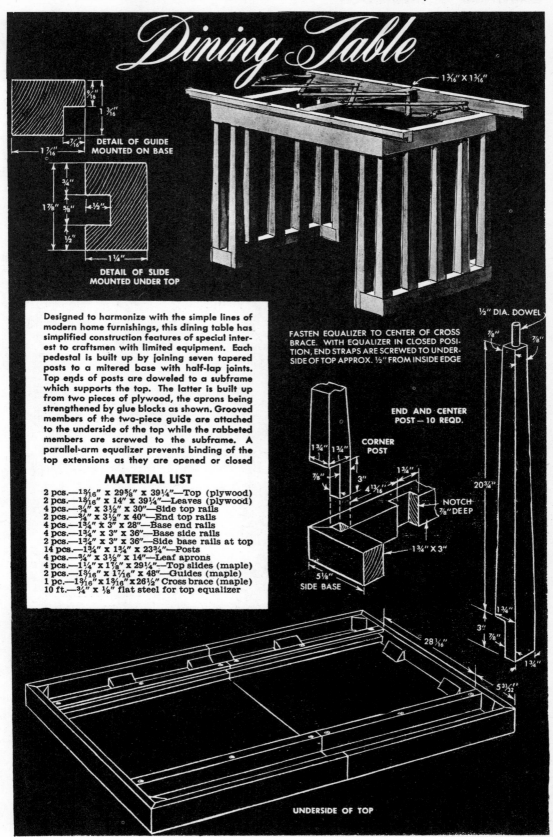

DETAIL OF GUIDE MOUNTED ON BASE

DETAIL OF SLIDE MOUNTED UNDER TOP

1¾₆" X 1¾₆"

Designed to harmonize with the simple lines of modern home furnishings, this dining table has simplified construction features of special interest to craftsmen with limited equipment. Each pedestal is built up by joining seven tapered posts to a mitered base with half-lap joints. Top ends of posts are doweled to a subframe which supports the top. The latter is built up from two pieces of plywood, the aprons being strengthened by glue blocks as shown. Grooved members of the two-piece guide are attached to the underside of the top while the rabbeted members are screwed to the subframe. A parallel-arm equalizer prevents binding of the top extensions as they are opened or closed

## MATERIAL LIST

2 pcs.—1⅜₆" x 29⅝" x 39¼"—Top (plywood)
2 pcs.—1⅜₆" x 14" x 39¼"—Leaves (plywood)
4 pcs.—¾" x 3½" x 30"—Side top rails
2 pcs.—¾" x 3½" x 40"—End top rails
4 pcs.—1¾" x 3" x 28"—Base end rails
4 pcs.—1¾" x 3" x 36"—Base side rails
2 pcs.—1¾" x 3" x 36"—Side base rails at top
14 pcs.—1¾" x 1¾" x 23¾"—Posts
4 pcs.—¾" x 3½" x 14"—Leaf aprons
4 pcs.—1¼" x 1⅞" x 29¼"—Top slides (maple)
2 pcs.—1⅜₆" x 1⅞₆" x 48"—Guides (maple)
1 pc.—1⅜₆" x 1⅝₆" x 26½" Cross brace (maple)
10 ft.—¾" x ⅛" flat steel for top equalizer

FASTEN EQUALIZER TO CENTER OF CROSS BRACE. WITH EQUALIZER IN CLOSED POSITION, END STRAPS ARE SCREWED TO UNDERSIDE OF TOP APPROX. ½" FROM INSIDE EDGE

½" DIA. DOWEL

END AND CENTER POST — 10 REQD.

CORNER POST

NOTCH ⅞" DEEP

1¾" X 3"

SIDE BASE

UNDERSIDE OF TOP

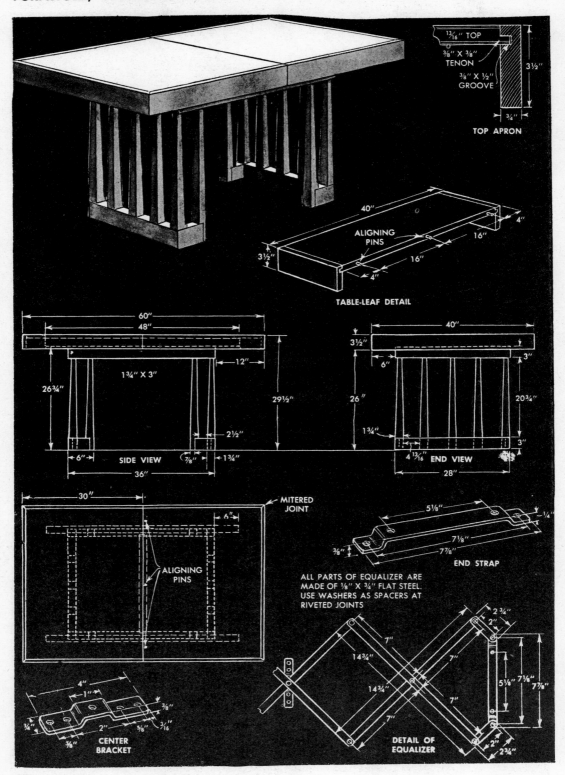

TOP APRON

13/16" TOP
3/8" X 3/8" TENON
3/8" X 1/2" GROOVE
3 1/2"
3/4"

TABLE-LEAF DETAIL

40"
ALIGNING PINS
4"
16"
16"
4"
3 1/2"

SIDE VIEW

60"
48"
12"
1 3/4" X 3"
26 3/4"
29 1/2"
2 1/2"
6"
7/8"
1 3/4"
36"

END VIEW

40"
3 1/2"
6"
3"
26
20 3/4"
1 3/4"
4 13/16"
3"
28"

MITERED JOINT
30"
6"
ALIGNING PINS

END STRAP

5 1/8"
1/4"
7 1/8"
7 7/8"
3/8"

ALL PARTS OF EQUALIZER ARE MADE OF 1/8" X 3/4" FLAT STEEL. USE WASHERS AS SPACERS AT RIVETED JOINTS

CENTER BRACKET

4"
1"
3/8"
3/4"
2"
5/8"
3/16"
3/8"

DETAIL OF EQUALIZER

2 3/4"
2"
7"
14 3/4"
7"
14 3/4"
7"
7"
5 1/8"
7 1/8"
7 7/8"
2"
2 3/4"

# Dining Table Commode

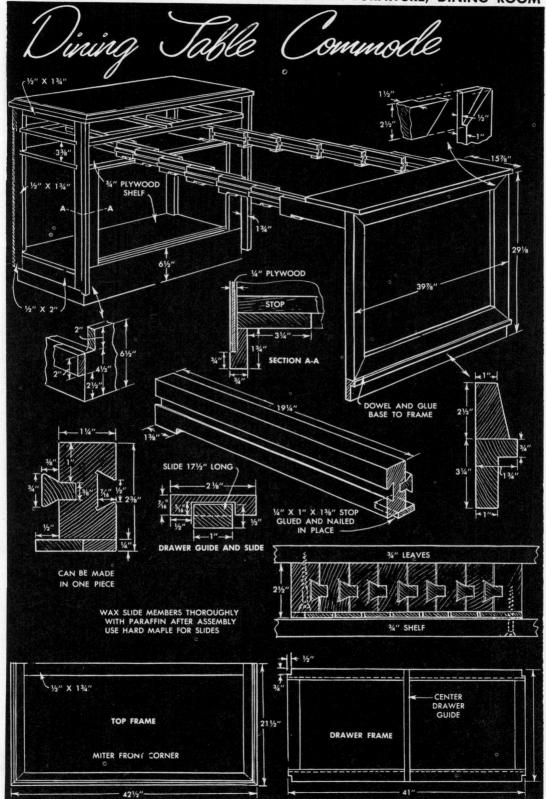

½" X 1¾"

3⅜"

½" X 1¾"

¾" PLYWOOD SHELF

A

A

6½"

½" X 2"

2"
6½"
2"
4½"
2½"

1½"
2½"
½"
1"

15⅞"

29⅛"

39⅞"

DOWEL AND GLUE BASE TO FRAME

1"
2½"
¾"
3¼"
1¾"
1"

¼" PLYWOOD
STOP
3¼"
1¾"
¾"
¾"
SECTION A-A

19¼"
1⅜"

¼" X 1" X 1⅜" STOP GLUED AND NAILED IN PLACE

1¼"
1"
3⅜"
¾"
½"
7/16"
½"
2⅜"
¼"

CAN BE MADE IN ONE PIECE

SLIDE 17½" LONG
2⅛"
7/16"
5/16"
½"
1"
½"

DRAWER GUIDE AND SLIDE

¾" LEAVES
2½"
¾" SHELF

WAX SLIDE MEMBERS THOROUGHLY WITH PARAFFIN AFTER ASSEMBLY USE HARD MAPLE FOR SLIDES

½" X 1¾"

TOP FRAME

MITER FRONT CORNER

21½"

42½"

½"
¾"

DRAWER FRAME

CENTER DRAWER GUIDE

41"

853

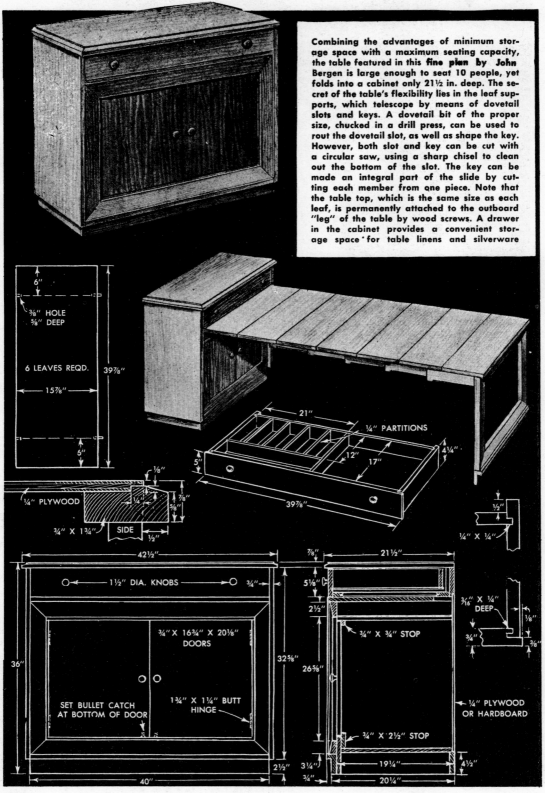

Combining the advantages of minimum storage space with a maximum seating capacity, the table featured in this **fine plan by John Bergen** is large enough to seat 10 people, yet folds into a cabinet only 21½ in. deep. The secret of the table's flexibility lies in the leaf supports, which telescope by means of dovetail slots and keys. A dovetail bit of the proper size, chucked in a drill press, can be used to rout the dovetail slot, as well as shape the key. However, both slot and key can be cut with a circular saw, using a sharp chisel to clean out the bottom of the slot. The key can be made an integral part of the slide by cutting each member from one piece. Note that the table top, which is the same size as each leaf, is permanently attached to the outboard "leg" of the table by wood screws. A drawer in the cabinet provides a convenient storage space for table linens and silverware

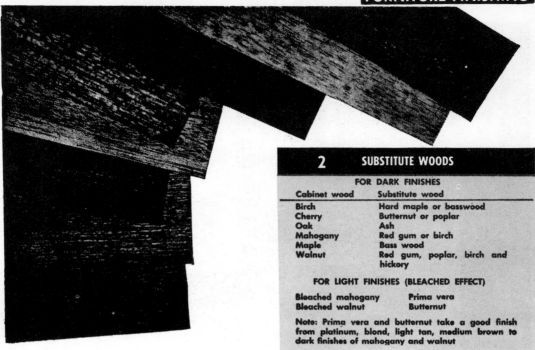

| 2 | SUBSTITUTE WOODS | |
|---|---|---|
| **FOR DARK FINISHES** | | |
| Cabinet wood | Substitute wood | |
| Birch | Hard maple or basswood | |
| Cherry | Butternut or poplar | |
| Oak | Ash | |
| Mahogany | Red gum or birch | |
| Maple | Bass wood | |
| Walnut | Red gum, poplar, birch and hickory | |
| **FOR LIGHT FINISHES (BLEACHED EFFECT)** | | |
| Bleached mahogany | Prima vera | |
| Bleached walnut | Butternut | |

Note: Prima vera and butternut take a good finish from platinum, blond, light tan, medium brown to dark finishes of mahogany and walnut

| 1 | CAUSES OF FINISH FAILURES |
|---|---|

1—Inferior or defective lumber

2—Excessive moisture in wood

3—Dents, scratches, tool marks, glue spots and stains on work

4—Insufficient or improper sanding of wood before finishing

5—Presence of sanding dust on surfaces when finishing

6—Dust in air settles on surfaces of work while and after finishing

7—Wrong temperature and humidity

8—Inadequate illumination

9—Finishing in direct sunlight

10—Poor grade of finishing materials

11—Old, spoiled finishing materials

12—Incompatibility of materials

13—Wrong type of brush

14—Improperly cleaned brushes

15—Poor brushing technique causing brush marks, skipped areas, runs, sags, and pileup in corners

16—Air bubbles in shellac, sealer, varnish, and lacquer

17—Faulty spray-gun technique

18—Wrong spraying consistency

19—Improper adjustment of spray gun

20—Insufficient drying between coats

21—Improper sanding between coats

22—Wrong rubbing and polishing materials

23—Faulty rubbing and polishing

# YOU *CAN* FINISH FURNITURE

*Haste trips up most beginners when finishing furniture. Passing over important little steps in surface preparation is the biggest mistake. Take it easy and you'll find that you can finish furniture beautifully the very first time*

### By E. R. HAAN

ADDING THE BEAUTIFUL finishes which give that store-bought look to home-built furniture is a part of furniture making that throws the average home craftsman for a loop. And yet, it actually requires far less skill than the cabinetry. The cause of most finish failures on the part of the home craftsman is haste. In his eagerness to complete the piece and put it in use, the tendency is to overlook many seemingly unimportant little steps and, consequently, his efforts to produce a fine piece of furniture, finish-wise, result in disappointment. In addition to impatience, other causes of finish failures that plague the beginner are given in Fig. 1.

### Starting Out Right

A transparent finish emphasizes both the beauty and the defects of wood. Therefore, when building fine furniture to be so finished, select each piece of wood carefully and avoid that which has undesired knots, mineral streaks, sap and heartwood. As it is impossible to obtain lumber without any defects at all, enough should be purchased so that undesired areas can be cut out as waste. For exacting standards in fine cabinet work this may mean a waste of 30 to 40 percent. Where economy must be considered, it is possible to cut costs by using certain substitute woods as listed in Fig. 2, and finish them to resemble the more expensive ones.

Finishing nails should be set below the wood surface and the holes filled with wood putty as in Fig. 3. Sunken screwheads can be concealed with "boat plugs" which show surface grain as in Fig. 4. You can cut these from relatively thin wood by using a "hole punch" of proper size to assure a perfect fit. Such plugs should match the wood grain around the holes. Glue them in place and sand them flush after the glue has dried.

Take care to avoid glue stains as they prevent uniform staining. Remove unavoidable glue drops with a sharp wood chisel or scraper, then sand the surface smooth. To eliminate shallow dents, moisten them and then apply a warm iron as in Fig. 5. If the dent does not raise enough, make several razor slits with the grain and then repeat the process.

### Sanding Prior to Finishing

Much time and effort can be saved by using power sanders, a belt sander, Fig. 6, for heavy cutting, and a reciprocating pad sander, Fig. 7, for fine finishing. The pad sander is better for cutting off fine ends of wood fibers but is not intended for heavy work. Three grades of sandpaper, coarse, medium and fine, as recommended by the machine manufacturers, are used successively to produce a perfectly smooth and scratch-free surface.

When hand-sanding wood, you also use three grades of open-coat aluminum-oxide abrasive paper, Fig. 8, detail A. Use No. 1/0 to remove tool marks and light glue spots, No. 3/0 to level and smooth and No. 6/0 to produce the final smooth finish. For flat surfaces you should hold the sandpaper on a wooden block or other type of holder. The block or holder shown in detail B, has a felt

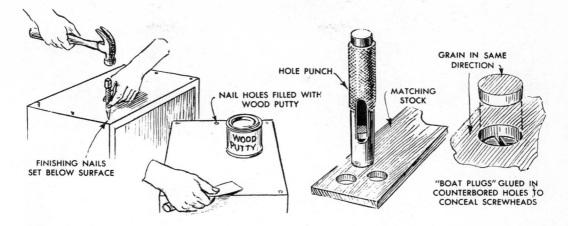

FINISHING NAILS SET BELOW SURFACE

NAIL HOLES FILLED WITH WOOD PUTTY

WOOD PUTTY

HOLE PUNCH

MATCHING STOCK

GRAIN IN SAME DIRECTION

"BOAT PLUGS" GLUED IN COUNTERBORED HOLES TO CONCEAL SCREWHEADS

**3   WAYS TO CONCEAL NAILHEADS**

**4   AND FLATHEAD WOOD SCREWS**

backing. For curved surfaces, hold the sandpaper on a ½-in.-thick felt pad as in detail C. For small-radii molding always use a finger behind the paper to make it conform to the curvature. For sanding many pieces of similar molding you can make a sanding block having the same contour, as in detail D.

Always sand with the wood grain to avoid cross scratches that are hard to remove. Pressure should be light, letting the grit do the work. Slightly bevel, or break, all sharp edges with two or three strokes of No. 6/0 sandpaper, but not more than this as the edge then will become noticeably rounded. A sharp edge causes finishing material to build up on either side of it but prevents good coverage on the edge itself.

Fuzzy grain that remains on some woods after sanding is removed by first applying a glue size (glue, 1 oz. and water, 1 pt.), letting it dry for 24 hours and then sanding. After the bare wood on any furniture job has been completed, dust off all surfaces with a soft brush or use a vacuum cleaner with a small brush attachment.

### Room Conditions for Finishing

Many home craftsmen do their finishing under adverse room conditions of temperature, humidity, air circulation, cleanliness and illumination. Temperature should be 70 deg. F. or more. Humidity should not exceed 90 percent as this greatly prolongs drying time and much more dust than normal will settle and spot the finish.

There should be a constant change of air. This equalizes inside and outside humidity and eliminates volatile vapors that may be harmful to breathe and are a fire hazard as well. Too fast a change of air should be avoided as it raises dust. When using a spray gun, a discharge fan and a respirator for the worker are necessary.

Lighting above and on the side of the work as in Fig. 9 (top) should be adequate so that the application of finishing materials can be seen by slight reflection, and thus can be controlled. Finishing and drying should never be done in direct sunlight as this may cause haze and discoloration. The room should be as free as possible of dust. A room that is separate from the workshop is best. Fine finishing never should be attempted outdoors or in an open garage or workshop that is exposed to even a slight wind. This invariably results in a ruined, dust-speckled finish.

Plan on using only the best finishing materials available. Price often is a good criterion. Use fresh materials, avoiding the temptation to economize by using the contents of an opened can over three months old. Old material may never dry,

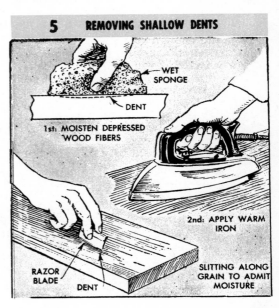

**5   REMOVING SHALLOW DENTS**

WET SPONGE

DENT

1st: MOISTEN DEPRESSED WOOD FIBERS

2nd: APPLY WARM IRON

RAZOR BLADE

DENT

SLITTING ALONG GRAIN TO ADMIT MOISTURE

**6  BELT SANDER FOR HEAVY CUTTING**

Skil photo

**7  PAD SANDER FOR FINE FINISHES**

Miller Falls photo

may contain dust deposited in it by a previously used brush, may be oxidized and covered with a skin, may have undergone chemical changes so that a resulting finish will be cloudy.

One kind of finishing material may have a formulation not compatible with another. For example, the solvent of a sealer or top coat applied on a stain or primer may cause the stain to bleed or prevent it from drying. A lacquer top coat should never be applied over a pigmented oil stain, nor over varnish, although varnish can be applied over lacquer. Some materials serve as both sealer and top coat, and are not compatible with regular varnishes and lacquers.

### Tips on Brushes and Spray Guns

Using the right kind and size of brush contributes to better work. A soft, long-bristle brush, 2 to 3 in. wide, is best to apply sealer, varnish and lacquer. An inexpensive soft brush, 2 or 3 in. wide, is adequate for applying stain. A stiff-bristle brush, 3 to 4 in. wide is best for applying filler. Get good quality brushes.

Many finish failures are caused by improper cleaning and storage of brushes. They should be cleaned immediately after using them. Brushes used for stain and filler are cleaned with turpentine, benzine or white gasoline. Those used for varnish are cleaned with turpentine or special solvent used for some varnishes, but never with benzine or white gasoline, which causes the varnish to curdle and form small particles that come off in subsequent jobs. Brushes for shellac are cleaned with wood

**8    SANDING BLOCKS AND PADS FOR FLAT AND CONCAVE SURFACES**

SANDPAPER (4½" X 5")

FOR SANDING WOOD PRIOR TO FINISHING

No. 1/0      No. 3/0      No. 6/0

A

B

½" FELT PAD AND SANDPAPER FOR LARGE-RADII CONCAVE SURFACES

C

4½"

1½"

3"

½" FELT PAD GLUED TO BLOCK

SANDPAPER GRIPPED IN GROOVE

TACKS

4½"

MATCHING CURVATURE OF BLOCK FOR MOLDING

D

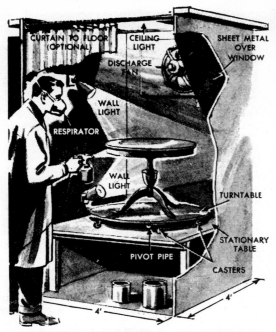

**9  SPRAY BOOTH AND SPRAYING TECHNIQUES**

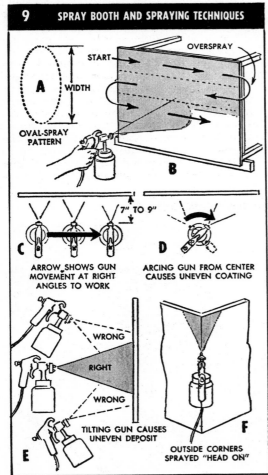

A
OVAL-SPRAY PATTERN

WIDTH

START

OVERSPRAY

B

7" TO 9"

C
ARROW SHOWS GUN MOVEMENT AT RIGHT ANGLES TO WORK

D
ARCING GUN FROM CENTER CAUSES UNEVEN COATING

WRONG

RIGHT

WRONG

E
TILTING GUN CAUSES UNEVEN DEPOSIT

F
OUTSIDE CORNERS SPRAYED "HEAD ON"

alcohol, and those for lacquer and lacquer sealer are cleaned with lacquer thinner.

To clean a brush properly, submerge it in solvent suitable for material in the brush, working this well into the bristles with your fingers as in Fig. 10. Repeat the process with fresh solvent until the brush is cleaned thoroughly. Shake the brush to throw out dirty solvent each time. Then straighten out the bristles by combing with a wire brush and wrap the brush in aluminum foil for storage as in Fig. 11.

The same solvents are used for cleaning a spray gun, which should be cleaned immediately after use. Clean the cup first, then pour in fresh solvent and spray this through the nozzle. Next, unscrew the nozzle to inspect it and the orifices for cleanliness. If the orifices are clogged, disassemble the gun and submerge the parts in solvent until the orifices are clean. Don't push wire through the orifices.

Any finishing materials should be stirred to mix the ingredients and produce the right consistency. Shellac, sealer, varnish and lacquer are stirred carefully to avoid forming air bubbles which are transferred to the work surface and may cause tiny craters. The brush is dipped into the liquid about one third of its bristle length, and then is drawn over the can rim to remove the excess. In large half-empty cans the brush can be slapped against the inside to do this.

Shellac, varnish and lacquer are "flowed" on with a full brush, first with long and slightly overlapping strokes in the grain direction, then with light cross strokes for uniform spreading, and finally with light finishing strokes with the grain.

### Spraying Technique

A spray booth equipped with a fan to discharge the fumes, a turntable and suitable lighting, as shown in Fig. 9, is highly desirable. The average home spray gun op-

859

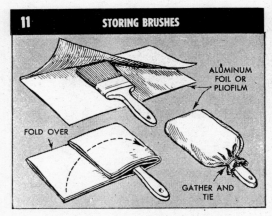

**11** STORING BRUSHES

ALUMINUM FOIL OR PLIOFILM

FOLD OVER

GATHER AND TIE

erates on a pressure of about 35 lbs. p.s.i., which permits spraying of liquids having about 20 percent solid material. Spray guns working on 90 to 110 lbs. of pressure can spray from 35 to 45 percent solid material in liquids. Finishing materials are brought to proper spraying viscosity by adding solvent. Then they are strained through a 60-mesh wire screen before being used.

The gun nozzle is adjusted to spray a fan pattern 5 to 6 in. wide, detail A, Fig. 9, when holding the gun from 7 to 9 in. from the surface. For each 10 lbs. of additional pressure, the gun is held 1 in. farther away. Holding the gun too close results in an uneven coating that has ripples and runs. Holding it too far away results in a dry, sandy spray with excessive dusting.

Always start spraying a vertical surface at the top and work downward with successive cross strokes as in detail B. Pull the gun trigger just before the spray hits the work, and release it just after it passes the work. You can spray the two vertical edges before making the horizontal strokes to minimize over-spraying. Always spray full wet coats just short of running.

Keep the spray axis at right angles to the work and at a uniform distance from it as in detail C. Arcing the gun from a central position, detail D, results in a heavier deposit at the center frequently causing runs. Holding the gun downward produces a heavier deposit at the upper fringe of the spray pattern, and holding it upward will make a heavy deposit at the lower fringe, detail E.

In spraying horizontal surfaces, you start at the edge nearest you and proceed to the farthest edge with successive horizontal strokes. Then the spray dust that lands on the uncoated surface will be dissolved by a full spray stroke. Reversing this procedure will cause spray dust to settle on the finished surface. Outside corners are sprayed head-on as in Fig. 9, detail F, with the nozzle set horizontally to produce an even deposit.

AFTER PREPARING the surfaces of a piece of furniture for finishing as described earlier, you are ready to apply the finishing materials. As mentioned before, proceed slowly. At this point, especially, many home craftsmen make the mistake of hurrying. Producing an exceptionally fine finish often requires more time than building the project.

### Clear Finishes on Furniture

The procedure for finishing close-grain and open-grain wood, as given in Fig. 15, is the same except that open-grain wood requires filling. Complete drying of each application is of utmost importance, as well as light sanding and scrupulous cleaning between all coatings.

Transparent top coats are applied after stain, toner and filler have been sealed. This prevents the solvent of the top coat from softening the material underneath and allowing it to bleed. Many pigmented stains and toners are self-sealing, but are intended for use under varnish or shellac, not under brushing lacquer, which softens them. Most sealers are similarly affected by brushing lacquer. Therefore, if a lacquer top coat is desired, the procedure to prevent the above trouble consists of "fogging" a lacquer sanding-sealer over the stain, toner or filler with a spray gun. So applied, this sealer dries before it can affect the underlying material. When dry, the sealer coat is followed by lacquer coats sprayed on, not brushed on, as brushing lacquer has a retarded drying time and may dissolve the sealer coat. Lacquer cannot be applied over varnish, but in refinishing work, varnish can be applied over lacquer.

Staining or toning tends to add color beauty to wood and, in some cases, helps accentuate the grain

## Stains and Staining

Wood is tinted by staining or toning as in Fig. 12. Getting the right color and shade is first done experimentally on scrap wood of the same kind as the furniture to be finished. Types of stains are given in Fig. 13. A pigmented stain does not have the color clarity of penetrating stain, which contains a dye. Pigment stain usually is applied by brush or cloth and is allowed to stand for 5 to 10 min. before the excess is wiped off with a clean, soft cloth. The time varies with the wood and the shade desired. If the stain gets dry or gummy before wiping, the cloth is dampened with benzine or turpentine. The stain should dry from 3 to 4 hrs. before the next finishing step. Pigment stain is more effective on softwood than on hardwood. On some softwoods, which absorb stain unevenly, it is best to first use a wash coat of ½-lb. cut shellac, which is allowed to dry, and then sand before applying the stain. Penetrating stains are most effective on hardwoods. Penetrating sealer-stains have become highly popular, as they stain and seal in one operation. Varnish stains should not be used on new work where the grain is to be left visible.

Stains having high-color clarity and permanence can be made by dissolving aniline dye in powder form in water, wood alcohol or lacquer thinner as in Fig. 14. These can be used under lacquer. The mixing proportions are powder, 1 oz., to wood alcohol, 1 qt., or the same amount of hot water just below boiling temperature. For lighter or darker shades the amount of the solvent is varied. After preparing this stain it should be passed through a fine strainer. Using alcohol makes a nongrain-raising stain, but if water is used, the resulting stain raises wood grain, which then requires resanding. After application, the stain is wiped to produce a uniform tone. Water stain requires from 12 to 24 hrs. of drying time. The alcohol stain dries very fast and must

Ready-mixed stains are of three general types: pigmented, penetrating and combination sealer-stain

Mix-your-own stain consists of dissolving powdered aniline dye in water or in wood alcohol

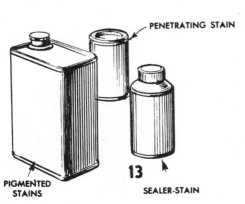

PENETRATING STAIN

PIGMENTED STAINS

**13**

SEALER-STAIN

POWDERED ANALINE DYE

**14**

**15**       **10 BASIC STEPS IN FINISHING**

**0** — Surface sanded for finishing
Sometimes requires wash coat for uniform staining

**1**   STAIN OR TONER

Stains
- Sealer-stain
- Pigmented or penetrating oil-base stains
- Aniline dye dissolved in water or alcohol

Toners: Semitransparent or opaque

DRYING TIME — SEE TEXT

**2**   SANDING — Lightly with No. 6/0 open-grain sandpaper

**3**   FILLER — For open-grain wood (oil-base stain is sealed first)

DRYING TIME — 12 to 24 hrs.

**4**   SANDING — No. 6/0 or 8/0 open-grain sandpaper

**5**   SEALER — 2-lb. cut shellac or less, or other prepared sealer under shellac or varnish
Lacquer sanding sealer sprayed on for lacquer top coat

DRYING TIME — 2 to 6 hrs. (Doubled or tripled for high humidity)

**6**   SANDING — No. 8/0 open-grain sandpaper

**7**   TOP COATINGS
- Shellac, 3 to 5 coats of same
- Varnish, high sheen, 3 or 4 coats
- Lacquer, high sheen, 2 or 3 coats (sprayed)

DRYING TIME
- Shellac, 4 hrs.
- Varnish, 24 hrs.
- Lacquer, 4 to 6 hrs.

**8**   SANDING
- For shellac, No. 280 waterproof sandpaper
- For varnish or lacquer, No. 8/0 partly worn sandpaper

**9**   FINAL TOP COATING
- Shellac on shellac
- Gloss or rubbed-effect varnish on varnish
- Gloss or rubbed-effect lacquer on lacquer
- (Final coat included in number of top coats in step 7)

DRYING TIME
- Shellac, 12 to 24 hrs.
- Varnish, 48 hrs.
- Lacquer, 12 to 24 hrs.

**10**   RUBBING OR POLISHING
- Semiluster, FFF pumice stone and rubbing oil on felt pad
- High sheen, FFF pumice stone and water on felt pad
- Medium sheen, No. 4 steel wool
- (Not applicable to rubbed-effect top coat)

be applied rapidly, preferably by spraying, to assure uniformity. When brushed on large surfaces it should be applied in two half-strength coats with a wide brush, working fast for quick and uniform coverage. A drying time of 2 to 3 hrs. is allowed.

In using any stain, the light-colored mineral streaks in wood are first darkened, using a small brush, after which the over-all surface is stained. Stain will not penetrate glue spots, or many other spots, which should be removed previously. Bleaching new wood generally is not recommended. Instead, it is better to use lighter wood or to use toners for lightening dark wood.

### Toning or Glazing

This process is practically the same as staining with pigmented stain. Colored pigments reduced to a thin paint are used to partly or wholly obscure the wood grain. By so changing the appearance of wood, less-expensive kinds often can be used.

To produce bleached or frosted effects the pigment is white, which may be tinted. It is applied over the entire surface as in Fig. 16. When the color starts to dull, the toner is delicately wiped in the direction of grain with a clean, lint-free, soft cloth, folded to suit as in Fig. 17. The amount of wiping largely controls the degree of transparency obtained although the toner itself is thin and semitransparent after it has been applied.

For contrasty grain effects in open-grain woods, such as oak, walnut or mahogany, toning is more opaque, with little or no wiping, and after the coating has dried, the wood grain is filled with a contrasting paste wood filler as in Fig. 18.

Toners may be pigmented sealers applied over a sealer-stain or over ordinary stain. They may consist of colors ground in japan and thinned with turpentine, or they may consist simply of flat enamel or enamel undercoater, 1 part, and turpentine, 2 parts. Toners should dry from 12 to 24 hrs., or according to the manufacturer's recommendations.

### Paste Wood Filler

To make the surface of open-grained wood smooth, it is filled with paste wood filler. This is never done directly on bare wood or over an oil-base stain without a wash coat of ½-lb. cut shellac or other sealer. The shellac wash coat consists of 4 or 5-lb. cut shellac, 1 part, dissolved in wood alcohol, 8 parts. Filling can be done directly on sealer-stain after this has dried. The sealer or sealer-stain is sanded with No. 8/0 sandpaper before filler is applied.

The filler is reduced to the consistency of a heavy cream for large pores, and to

Light, semitransparent toner being brushed on. Lower part of photo shows the untreated surface

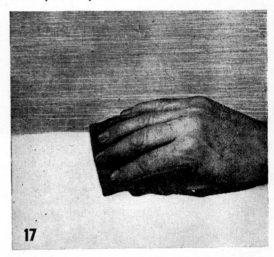

Above, toner partly wiped off, giving frosty effect.

Below, wiping off filler applied over dark toner

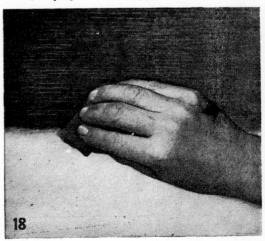

19

Lacquer is best sprayed on. Work should be mounted on turntable in a spray booth, or taken outdoors

that of milk for small pores. Two thin coats applied 12 hrs. apart are better than a single thick coat. A solvent may be recommended on the can for reducing the filler, or equal parts of benzine and turpentine can be used. A variety of colors can be obtained by adding stain or pigment to the filler, pigment being reduced with benzine before it is added.

Filler is brushed well into the grain, covering an area not greater than can be wiped before the filler turns flat. The excess is wiped off first across the grain with burlap, then with the grain, using a soft cloth. This is done carefully to avoid pulling the filler out of the pores. If excess filler is not all removed, the subsequent finish will appear blotchy. Rags used for wiping off filler are disposed of immediately as they are subject to spontaneous combustion. A stiff stencil brush is used to clean filler from moldings, carvings and scrollwork. Dried filler is picked off with a sharpened dowel. When dry, the filled surfaces are sanded with No. 8/0 sandpaper.

Pad sander fitted with felt shoe helps reduce the work of polishing, as well as the work of sanding

20

## Sealing

Where sealer-stain was used and no filler over it, the separate step of sealing is eliminated. Ordinary stain is sealed before applying filler. Filler, when dry, also is sealed. Sealers should not be applied thickly, as they are brittle and tend to check.

Shellac is the most-common sealer for use under varnish. It should be a 2-lb. cut or less. A lacquer sanding sealer is used under a lacquer top coat sprayed on. Some synthetic sealers also serve as top coats. Most sealers dry in 2 to 6 hrs., but this time is doubled or tripled when humidity is high, especially for shellac. A sealer should be so dry that it can be sanded with No. 8/0 sandpaper to a powder without clogging the sandpaper. Sealers can be applied with a soft, long-bristle brush, or sprayed. Lacquer sealers are sprayed—not brushed—over any undercoat that may bleed.

## Shellac Top Coat

Although a shellac top coat is damaged easily by water and alcohol. such damage is simply repaired by recoating with shellac. A wax coat over shellac will retard the action of water and alcohol. White shellac is used on lightwood and on walnut. Orange shellac may be used on mahogany and other dark woods, but tends to darken them further. Shellac tends to discolor in a few months after having been exposed to air. It should not be applied heavier than a 2-lb. cut, and only wood alcohol is used to thin it. A good top coat of shellac is built up by three to five applications, each being allowed to dry fully and then sanded. Drying time for shellac top coats is given in Fig. 15. For sanding shellac, No. 280 wet-or-dry paper is best, applying a little light machine oil to the surface to minimize heating from friction.

## Varnish and Lacquer Top Coats

A substantial top coat consists of three or four applications of varnish, or two or three applications of lacquer. The lacquer coats are sprayed on, Fig. 19. All coats should have a hard, high-sheen surface, but the final coat may be one that gives a rubbed-effect or stain finish. The stain finish should not be used for undercoats as it then will produce a cloudy appearance.

Most varnishes are thinned with turpentine, but the so-called plastic finishes require special thinners. Varnish should not be shaken or stirred before application as this produces air bubbles which are transferred to the work. Varnish is brushed on in a full-flowing coat. See Fig. 15 for drying time. Lacquer is clearer than varnish. When thinning lacquer for spray-gun application the best grade of thinner is used. Lacquers are applied in full wet coats and can be sanded and recoated in 4 to 6 hrs. but the final coat should dry from 12 to 24 hrs. before it is rubbed.

### Sanding Between Coats

Light sanding with partly worn No. 8/0 sandpaper between coats is done to cut the glaze and to make the next coat adhere better. It also removes dust specks and high spots. Care is taken to avoid cutting through the coats, espcially at corners and sharp edges. Heavy runs should not be sanded until a 48-hr. period has elapsed. Care is taken to avoid heating which results in gumming and peeling. After surfaces are sanded, the dust is brushed off and the surfaces wiped with a tack rag to remove all traces of dust before applying the next coat. A tack rag is a lint-free rag dampened slightly with thinned varnish, and used when nearly dry.

### Rubbing and Polishing

Proper rubbing of thoroughly dry varnished or lacquered surfaces produces a smooth, satin finish. Rubbed-effect or satin-finish varnish or lacquer should never be rubbed as they do not have sufficient hardness for this. Rubbing always is done with the grain of the wood, using light pressure. A pad sander can be used for this purpose as in Fig. 20.

Where a real fine finish is not required No. 4/0 steel wool may be used. A higher sheen is obtained by lubricating the work with soapy water. A dull satin finish is produced by rubbing with FFF pumice stone and rubbing oil, using a ½-in. felt pad about 2½ by 4 in. in size. No other oil than rubbing oil should be used. The pad is first dipped in the oil, then in the pumice stone, which is repeated as necessary, keeping enough oil on the pad to prevent rubbing dry. All traces of oil and pumice are wiped off after rubbing. A highly polished finish is produced by rubbing with FFF pumice stone and water, using the same procedure of wetting the pad. After cleaning off the work, a rubbing with rottenstone and water on the following day will bring out a high luster. ★ ★ ★

# Valuable Advice From Master Craftsman on Refinishing Antiques

A master craftsman, wise in the ways of refinishing antiques to the smoothness of old ivory and with a gleaming, rich luster, gave me the following tips: First, clean the work with a good paint and varnish remover, using a cheap brush to apply a generous coat over a small area. Let the remover stand about 15 min. and, without wiping it off, apply a second coat. Then mix a gallon of warm water with a cup of household ammonia and use the mixture with a stiff-bristled brush to scour the treated surface. Dip a rough cloth (an old towel is excellent) into the ammonia water and wipe the area. Rinse at once with clear water, removing all traces of ammonia and the work should be good and clean. Remember to clean only a small area at a time, for if varnish remover is applied over too large an area, it will harden into a cement-like finish. Should that happen, apply more remover—several coats, 15 min. apart—until you can wipe the surface clean. Before further refinishing is done, make any necessary repairs to the work. Then sand with 1/0 or 2/0 garnet or sandpaper until very smooth. Wipe clean and apply the first coat of shellac, using a 4-lb. cut. Thin a pint of shellac with a pint of denatured alcohol. Use orange shellac on dark woods, such as mahogany, cherry and walnut, and white shellac on the lighter woods. Using a pure bristle brush, apply two coats of shellac with the grain of the wood, allowing 4 or 5 hrs. between coats. Between succeeding coats, allow 24 to 48 hrs. drying time. Sand after each coat using 6/0 or 7/0 garnet paper. Never apply shellac in damp or humid weather, and if the shellac gums up on the sandpaper, allow more drying time. When you have built up the desired number of coats, mix 3 heaping tablespoonfuls of fine pumice with paraffin oil to attain a creamy mixture. Then dip a pad of 000 steel wool in the mixture and rub the work briskly with the grain. When finished, wipe the surface with a soft cloth. Repeat this process twice.—Ray Wilkie, Lexington, Ky.

# HAND-RUBBED FINISH

**On home-shop furniture projects the final touch of the craftsman is best expressed in a hand-rubbed finish**

THAT GLASS-SMOOTH satiny finish you see on high-grade furniture is still done by skillful hand-rubbing with powdered abrasives. What happens to the surface of the finish during the rubbing process is shown graphically in Fig. 1. Rubbing the dry finish removes brush marks, orange peel (the wavy effect caused by spraying lacquers without the proper retarders), dust specks and bubbles. All are common defects and are almost impossible to avoid in some degree unless the finish can be applied under ideal conditions of dust-free air and rigid temperature control. The first rubbing removes defects and levels the finish, giving it a dull, flat appearance. Then the surface is brought to varying degrees of sheen, or gloss, with a flour-fine abrasive and a final polishing. In current practice the finish is left dull flat on antiques. For period furniture a semigloss is preferred but on modern designs the finish usually is rubbed to a high satin polish.

Although rubbing may be done with a cloth pad, a thick felt pad is best. Felt has just enough "give" to follow slight irregularities without danger of cutting through the finish. Powdered pumice, FFF grade or finer, is commonly used for the first rubbing. Pour the powder into a tumbler of water as in Fig. 2 and allow it to settle before pouring off the water. Mix the sediment to a creamy paste. Some finishers

BEFORE RUBBING

AFTER RUBBING

**Pour abrasive powder into a glass tumbler about two thirds full of water and allow to settle. Then pour off most of the water and mix to a creamy paste**

**Brush the paste onto the surface to be rubbed, applying it in a thin film of uniform thickness. Be sure that the brush used is clean and free from grit**

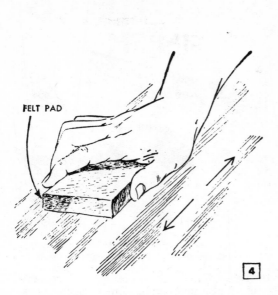

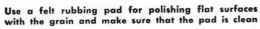

4

Use a felt rubbing pad for polishing flat surfaces with the grain and make sure that the pad is clean

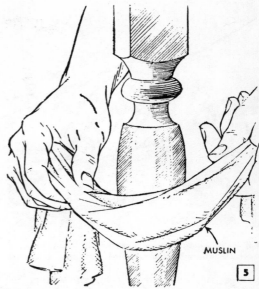

5

Turnings can be polished with a clean cloth charged with abrasive cream. Use only light polishing pressure

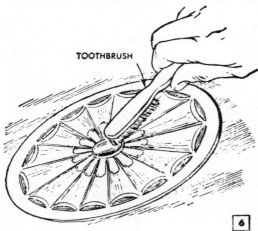

6

Above, paint small carvings with abrasive cream and polish with a toothbrush. Below, some finishers apply wax with a cloth pad to get a uniform coating

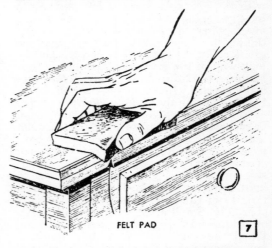

7

Above, be careful not to cut through finish when sanding or rubbing corners and edges. Below, some finishers prefer to apply paste wax with a steel-wool pad

8

9

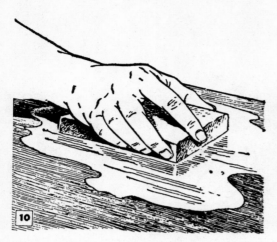

Before polishing certain types of work, finishers go over it lightly with 8/0 wet-or-dry sandpaper and oil

Expert finishers often polish varnished work simply by rubbing the surface with the palm of the hand

prefer rubbing oil instead of water. In either case, mix the powder and liquid to a creamy paste and pour or brush it on the surface to be rubbed, Fig. 3. In rubbing with the abrasive-charged felt pad, use a long sweeping stroke, Fig. 4, each stroke overlapping the previous one about half the width of the pad. Always rub with the grain on straight-grained woods and the long way of the surface on panels or tops having a burled or butt graining. Be especially careful when working near the edge, Fig. 7, allowing the pad to overlap the edge on only one or two strokes at the most. Otherwise the abrasive may cut through the finish and expose a narrow line of bare wood. Check the progress of the work occasionally by wiping a spot clear of abrasive and examining it carefully in a good light. An easy way to determine the uniformity of the surface is to look across it obliquely. Small areas that are still rough or untouched are easily spotted in this way. When the surface is uniformly flat and feels smooth to the touch of a finger, it is ready for final polishing.

Turned legs, pressed or carved moldings and both overlay and relief carvings require a different treatment. Turnings are rubbed by means of an abrasive-charged muslin cloth as in Fig. 5, special care being taken not to rub the finish off the high places. Small carvings are rubbed with an old toothbrush after painting the surface with the abrasive cream. On large carvings a worn scrubbing brush is often used to advantage. In finishing carvings be careful to brush as much as possible lengthwise of the high places, not across them. This often will require brushing in several directions. As a rule, carvings and the short-radius portions of turnings are left in a

dull gloss finish. When a lathe turning is the project, rubbing can be done with the work turning at slow speed, Fig 15.

In polishing a finer abrasive is used. Also, it should be noted that if nothing but water is added to the 3F pumice slush, Fig. 13, continued rubbing will grind the abrasive finer and finer. A thorough rub with pumice will produce a medium-low sheen. Leave the spent rubbing slush on the work. Then make a final rub with clean cotton waste.

For a polished finish, let the work stand overnight and then continue the rubbing process, using rottenstone and rubbing oil or water. Rottenstone does not actually cut like pumice but it will bring up a polish quickly if the work has been pumice-rubbed absolutely level. After rubbing, clean thoroughly with a damp rag.

Lacquer presents a harder surface than varnish and is often rubbed with wet-or-dry abrasive papers which cut faster than pumice. Even if you prefer the soft action of pumice, a quick cut-down with 8/0 paper lubricated with water or oil, Fig. 10, will greatly lessen the labor of pumice rubbing. The paper should be soaked a few minutes in water, Fig. 12, as the backing is weak and brittle when dry. A satisfactory satin finish can be obtained with 8/0 paper alone, but can be followed by rottenstone or rubbing compound for higher gloss if desired.

Rubbing compounds are available in a variety of types and grits for coarse or fine polishing. In all types of rubbing, they are preferred by many finishers to the older pumice and rottenstone abrasives. Compounds are supplied in paste form and may be used with or without a lubricant, depending on type.

Within the scope of rubbing technique, French polishing is worth considering.

Wet-or-dry abrasive paper should be soaked in water for flexibility and strength. Right, in the final stages of pumice rubbing, add water to the spent slush to reduce cutting action

Don't try this with homemade mixtures of shellac and alcohol—buy a good ready-made product and you will be surprised how easily and quickly you can give any varnish or lacquer surface a high gloss. First, give the finish a good rub with 8/0 paper and water. Dry thoroughly. Pour a little of the polish on a soft cloth or gauze pad, and apply to the work with a circular motion, Fig. 14. Add more polish as needed. Make a final wipe with long sweeping strokes with the grain.

Frenching with a ready-made polish is an easy and fast way to build a high polish. Left, turned projects can be rubbed or polished while revolving in the lathe

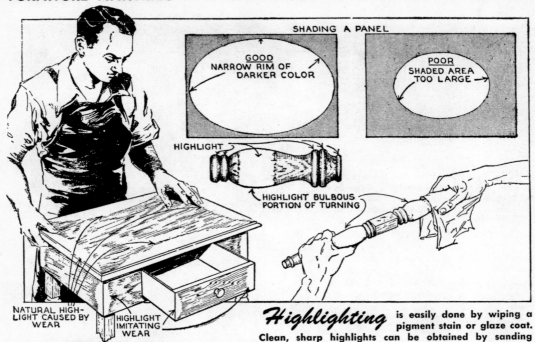

SHADING A PANEL

GOOD
NARROW RIM OF
DARKER COLOR

POOR
SHADED AREA
TOO LARGE

HIGHLIGHT

HIGHLIGHT BULBOUS
PORTION OF TURNING

NATURAL HIGH-
LIGHT CAUSED BY
WEAR

HIGHLIGHT
IMITATING
WEAR

*Highlighting* is easily done by wiping a pigment stain or glaze coat. Clean, sharp highlights can be obtained by sanding

*Shading* certain areas darker with stain or a different color with enamel is easily done with the spray gun, using a small pattern for good atomization to produce even blending

# ANTIQUING

SHADING plays an important part in the finishing of period furniture, and also has a considerable role in the decoration of other projects in both wood and metal. Briefly, the technique is simply a matter of lightening or darkening certain areas of the work to contrast with the general tone of the piece. Related terms include highlighting, glazing, antiquing, smutting, etc.

**Spray shading:** The spray gun is an excellent tool for shaded effects, and is capable of either sharp or soft shading. Sharp shading is confined largely to colored enamels, an example being the shading of a cream-colored chair with blue enamel, as shown in the photo at left. The color separation is strong and sharply defined—it is a kind of shading that is plainly visible. On the other hand, soft shading, as done on the average piece of furniture, is hardly apparent at first glance.

Various methods are used in spray shading. Most direct is to shade the work during the application of the stain coat, spraying lightly on some parts, heavy on others. Again, a first coat of stain, considerably diluted, can be allowed to dry, after which a second coat can be sprayed for shaded areas. Shading can also be done at any time during the finishing schedule by using special shading stains. These can be purchased ready-mixed or made by mixing powder stain with thin shellac or lacquer. Soft

*Glazing* is the term for a shading medium or technique. In the example above, the ground coat is blue, left photo. The white glaze is brushed on, center, and then wiped to expose the highlights, as shown in right photo

spray shading should be done with a small spray pattern and with the gun held 10 to 20 in. from the work.

**Highlighting:** If you don't have a spray gun—or perhaps even if you do—you can do shaded work by the reverse technique of highlighting. This is easily done with pigment oil stain, penetrating oil stain, and to some extent is practical with almost any type of stain. Cleaner wiping for highlights can be obtained if done on a second coat of wiping stain applied over a sealer. That is, you stain first for a uniform body color, not too dark. Then apply a sealer coat. Over the sealer coat brush on a second coat of pigment wiping stain. Clean this off rather thoroughly with a rag to leave the stain only on areas which are to appear darker.

Highlighting can also be done mechanically on the first stain coat after it is dry by using fine sandpaper or steel wool, as shown in the photo. This is sometimes useful to obtain a few very sharp highlights. It has the fault that if overdone, patching by restaining is not always easy.

**Glazing:** Glazing is the term which most nearly describes the whole art of using a wiped, translucent shading medium. You can glaze a piece of work and then wipe it for highlights. You can glaze the work with the idea of antiquing it. Or you can use a glaze coat for a textured ground or to imitate wood grain. The glaze itself can be any wiping stain, any thin paint, etc., but is specifically a product called glazing liquid. This can be purchased ready made or can be made with varnish, 4 parts, boiled linseed oil, 2 parts, and turpentine, 1 part. Pigment colors in oil or japan are added as needed to obtain desired colors. The glaze coat is applied over a foundation coat of sealer or colored enamel. It is sprayed or brushed over the whole area and is immediately wiped with a cloth or blended out with a dry brush. It can also be applied with a cloth and wiped with the same cloth, a kind of rubbing-on process.

A soft-brown glaze on an off-white enamel ground (bone-white finish) is effective. The same on a cream ground gives a pleasing soft, shaded effect. For a clear finish, the glaze coat should be somewhat darker than the wood or the stained color of the wood. For colored enamel finishes, any of hundreds of color combinations can be used. An example is shown in the photos.

For most work, the glaze should be wiped rather thoroughly. Graining effects can be obtained by wiping the glaze coat with a dry brush, whisk broom, combs and other gadgets. You can use your finger for tricky texture effects and designs. If a glaze coat becomes too tacky for clean working, it can be wiped with a cloth moistened with naphtha.

**General technique:** Regardless of how you do this shading, highlighting or antiquing, the work should not be overdone. On clear finishes especially, any shading or highlighting should be soft. A combination of methods is sometimes useful. For example, it is nearly impossible to spray-shade carvings, but it is very easy to apply pigment stain or glaze and then expose highlights by wiping. On the other hand, the spray gun is excellent for shading panels and table tops. Turnings are best treated by wiping since a simple run-over with a rag from end to end will automatically highlight the bulbous portions.

OIL FINISHING

ROTTENSTONE

LINSEED OIL

BOILED LINSEED OIL

SPAR VARNISH

TURPENTINE

PASTE FILLER

ALKANET ROOT

MULE-HIDE LEATHER FACING

BUFFING BLOCK

BUFFING STICK

① MATERIALS AND TOOLS NEEDED

② 

③ After sanding, the wood is moistened with water, using either a sponge or cloth pad

④ Then the surface is steamed by playing the flame of a blowtorch over the dampened wood

⑤ This raises the grain which is removed by sanding lightly with very fine sandpaper

MANY articles made of wood, particularly of walnut, cherry and mahogany, can be given a beautiful soft finish with linseed oil. Unlike most finishes, the oil finish is in the wood, not on it, making the surface proof against ordinary wear and scratching and the wood itself highly moisture-resistant.

**Materials needed:** Few materials are needed, and only two tools—a buffing stick and a buffing block, as shown in Fig. 1. The stick is used somewhat like a file to buff off legs, spindles and other rounded surfaces, while the block is used on table tops and other flat surfaces. Both tools are covered with leather, the time-honored material being mule hide, but other leathers, canvas or cloth are all acceptable rubbers. The No. 1 material is boiled linseed oil. Then, depending on the job and working schedule, you may need some raw linseed oil, turpentine, rottenstone, spar varnish, dark paste filler (walnut), and a handful of alkanet root. The latter makes a staining red oil when steeped in linseed oil, producing a reddish tinge which enhances the appearance of most brownish woods. Any dark red oil stain in powder form can be used.

**Surface preparation:** One of the key features in oil finishing is that the work must be dead smooth. Final sanding paper should be 5/0 aluminum oxide or garnet. After the wood is perfectly smooth, wipe it with a damp cloth or sponge, Fig. 3, and dry quickly. Some experts use a blowtorch for drying, Fig. 4, but equally good results can be obtained with an electric heater. After the wood is dry, you will find it covered with whiskers. Cut these off with new, sharp sandpaper applied very lightly, Fig. 5. Some workers like 2/0 steel wool for this job because it slices off the very fine fuzz which sandpaper tends merely to flatten.

**Oiling:** A number of different procedures are used in applying the oil. Simplest but also the most work is straight coats of boiled linseed oil. Each coat is applied by hand or with a cloth or brush. It is immediately rubbed into the wood with the heel of the hand. More oil can be added until it seems as if the wood has reached its absorption limit. The rubbing continues until the surface oil disappears—don't leave a skin of oil on the surface. The gunsmith's rule is to rub once a day for a week, once a week for a month, once a month for a year and once a year for life. Additional sanding with 8/0 paper can be done at any time as needed.

For furniture work on open-grain wood, the work should be filled with paste wood filler. This can be done on bare wood, or, a coat of raw linseed oil can first be applied as a staining medium, Fig. 6. Filler kills some of the excessive suction of bare wood, allowing the oil coats to build faster with less labor.

A third method starts off with a coat of raw linseed oil, 3 parts, mixed with turpentine, 1 part, Fig. 6. Let this stand 30 min., wipe off clean and let stand overnight. Next, apply paste wood filler, well-rubbed into the end grain. Tow this off in the usual manner and allow 24 hrs. dry. Then you swing into the "once a day for a week" with boiled linseed oil. Before the fourth rub, sand with 8/0 garnet. Before the seventh rub, use 3/0 steel wool. For the eighth coat, add japan drier half-and-half to linseed oil. Let this coat stand until it is tacky and then rub off with burlap or other coarse material, Fig. 9. Now, inspect the pores of the wood. If not filled nearly level, apply a thin mix of paste wood filler.

**Final rubbing:** The work has now reached the final-rubbing stage. Take your buff stick and rub the leather surface several times over a lump of rottenstone, Fig. 12. Use the buff stick just like you would a file; use the buffing block for flat surfaces. This step of the procedure removes any gummy oil deposit on the surface of the work. The leather will become slick and shiny from the oil it picks up, and should be scraped clean with a knife, Fig. 13. More rottenstone is then applied. A second result of rottenstone rubbing is that fine particles of the stone will embed in the wood, building the pores up perfectly flush. Just one rottenstone rub is enough, but it should be thorough.

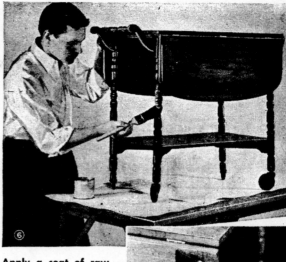

Apply a coat of raw linseed oil and turpentine to the sanded work, wipe off after 30 min., and then let the work stand overnight to dry completely

Next, seal the surface against further absorption of oil with a coat or two of paste filler well rubbed into the wood end grain

After 12 hrs., apply from three to six coats of boiled oil 24 hrs. apart, rubbing each coat into the wood with the bare hands

Follow the oil treatment with a coat of boiled oil and drier and let dry until tacky; then rub the oil off across the wood grain

| ⑩ POLISH FORMULA | |
|---|---|
| Heavy boiled linseed oil | 16 oz. |
| Turpentine | 2 oz. |
| Japan drier | 1½ oz. |
| Venice turpentine | 4 teaspoonfuls |
| Carnauba wax | 400 grains |

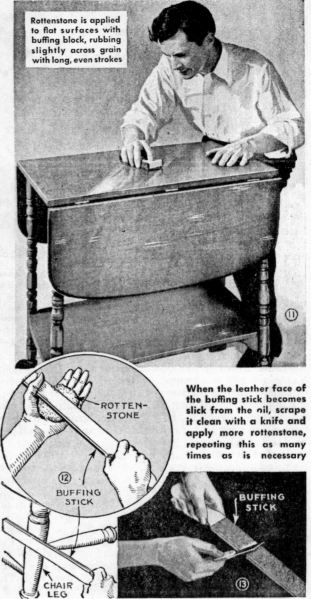

Rottenstone is applied to flat surfaces with buffing block, rubbing slightly across grain with long, even strokes

ROTTEN-STONE

⑫ BUFFING STICK

CHAIR LEG

When the leather face of the buffing stick becomes slick from the oil, scrape it clean with a knife and apply more rottenstone, repeating this as many times as is necessary

BUFFING STICK

⑪

⑬

**Polishing:** After the rottenstone rub, additional coats of oil mixed with one-third turpentine should be applied. While this is as good as anything, gunsmiths have numerous pet formulas, such as given in Fig. 10. To make this, melt the carnauba wax with the Venice turpentine in a double boiler. Add the oil and drier and let simmer for about 10 min. Then add the gum turpentine and stir until cool. Either this or the simpler oil-turp mix makes a good furniture polish for any surface.

**French polish:** A fourth method of oil finishing calls for the addition of spar varnish, 1 part, to boiled oil, 4 parts, making what is essentially a thin French polish. This takes about 48 hrs. between coats, but builds much faster than plain oil.

**Oil finish for pine paneling:** Pine paneling is attractive with a simplified oil finish. Mix gum turpentine, 1 part, with boiled linseed oil, 2 parts, and brush on like paint. The first coat will soak right in. After drying, apply a second coat. This will give a slight sheen to the work, which can be renewed as needed with additional coats. A single coat of the oil-turpentine mixture is often used as a stain under shellac or varnish. This is effective on aromatic red cedar and walnut as well as pine. The oil finish provides a perfectly satisfactory foundation for later coats of enamel or varnish—simply wipe with a rag moistened with turpentine or naphtha to remove any gummy residue, and then go ahead with the new finish.

**Linseed oil:** The oil used for the hand-rubbed oil finish should be pure, boiled linseed oil. Do not use substitute products. Linseed oil is crushed from flaxseed. The basic product is raw linseed oil, which is thin, dark and slow-drying. Allowed to season several years in the sun, raw linseed oil becomes clearer, heavier-bodied and tacky, making what is known as "stand oil." A short cut to stand oil is kettle-boiled oil, which is thickened by the direct application of heat. Although these heavy oils were popular at one time, they are poor finishing materials, tending to produce a gummy surface film rather than impregna-

tion deep into the pores of the wood.

In modern methods, pure linseed oil is reinforced by the addition of polymerized or heat-treated linseed oil, plus driers. This product has all the toughness of the raw oil film, plus faster drying. This kind should be used wherever linseed oil is indicated; the cheaper sort can be used where drying time is not important.

The hand-rubbed oil finish is a labor of love. If you want a quicker finish with about the same features, you can do the job with penetrating floor sealer. Don't forget that one coat of paste filler is worth 10 coats of oil for building up the surface.

# EIGHT OCCASIONAL PIECES YOU CAN MAKE

**Includes drop-leaf table for combination living-dining room and sectional wall ensemble with versatile units**

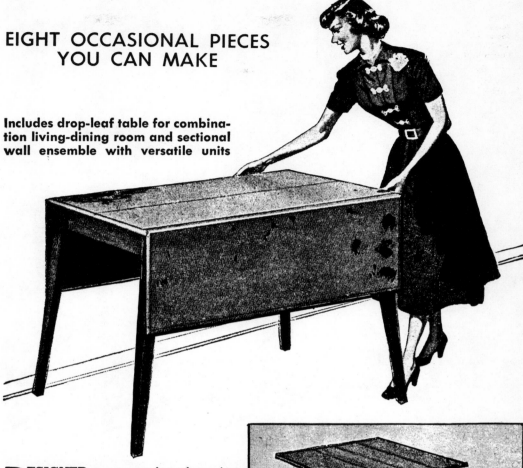

DESIGNED as companion pieces to harmonize with dining and living-room furniture of almost any style, these smart occasional pieces can be used to augment other pieces you already have or used by themselves in any particular arrangement you desire. The drop-leaf table pictured above is designed especially for a dining alcove where limited space does not permit room for even a small dinette set. Such is the case in the latest trend toward eliminating a separate dining room in favor of a combination living-dining room. This table is also ideal for the one-room or one-and-a-half-room-apartment dwellers. This piece adequately fills the requirement for a table that takes little space against the wall when not in use, and yet has big-table capacity when needed. To seat four persons comfortably, the leaves of the table are raised to a horizontal position and the whole top is rotated 90 deg. on a center pivot. In this position, the base of the table supports the drop leaves as

**1** **TABLE OPEN**

**2** **TABLE FULLY EXTENDED**

shown in Fig. 1. Retractable brackets in each end of the table pull out to support the leaves when the table is fully extended. A lazy-tong mechanism, taking the place of the usual extension slide, extends to permit insertion of two extra leaves, Fig. 2, providing a top surface 40 x 74 in. When the table is fully extended, you can accommodate six to eight dinner guests. You can either make your own dining chairs for the table or purchase suitable unfinished ones, to which you can apply a finish to match the table. In selecting the type of dining chairs you want, it is suggested that one which is not too bulky be chosen to stay in keeping with the compact table. Actual construction of the table, detailed in Figs. 12, 13 and 14, will be explained step by step later in the article.

The pieces of the functional wall ensemble pictured above are coordinated in size to fit together in a number of separate sectional arrangements in addition to the complete grouping shown. The arrangement pictured above is ideal for a rectangular-shaped room. The window unit can be shifted so that it is positioned correctly in front of the window. Here are other ar-

rangements. For the first example, the secretary, which is pictured in use at the bottom of the opposite page, may be combined with an open-end bookcase at each side. Likewise, the three-shelf unit, with doors at the bottom, may be grouped in the same way. An attractive corner grouping is had by flanking the corner bookcase with end bookcases. Still another arrangement is to place the window unit between two end bookcases. These are but a few of the attractive arrangements that are possible with these sectional pieces. If desired, any one of the three basic units, namely, the secretary, three-drawer chest and two-door chest, may be used individually.

**The secretary** features a pull-out writing shelf which looks like a drawer when closed. This piece, in the closed position, is shown second from the left. The "drawer" front is hinged with special fixtures and lets down to become part of the writing surface, as illustrated at the right on the facing page. The secretary, like the other pieces, is made primarily from plywood, with solid stock being used for the drawers, base and edging. The edging is used here to give a

hopper-front effect and at the same time to conceal the laminations of the plywood. Figs. 3 and 4 detail the construction of the secretary. In comparing its construction with that of the other pieces you will notice that much of the construction is duplicated. The bases are all the same, as are the drawers and, in most cases, even the manner in which the plywood panels are fitted. The exception is noted in the window, corner and end units which are designed to be flanked by other pieces. Here, the plywood is placed on the inside instead of the outside of the framework. Plywood, ¼ in. thick, is used to cover the sides and back of the secretary, while a heavier stock of ¾-in. plywood is used for the top.

Make the base assembly first. The members are mitered at all four corners, the rear member having a rabbet cut in the top edge to take the plywood back. A small, ⅛-in. cove is run along the top edges of the other pieces, which can be done either before or after gluing and nailing the base together. The hopper edging which frames the front of the cabinet is shaped according to the sectional details included with the

cutaway drawing, Fig. 4. The center and bottom shelves can be of plywood, or glued up from solid stock. These should be cut 31½ in. long and the front edge of the bottom shelf rabbeted for the hopper edging. Then the bottom shelf is glued and nailed

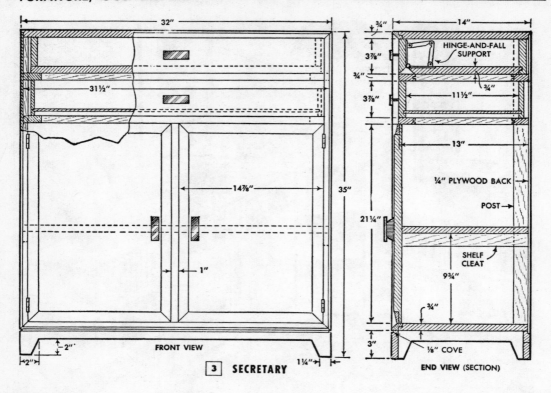

**32"**
**31½"**
**14⅞"**
**1"**
**35"**
**2"**
**2"**
**FRONT VIEW**
**1¼"**

### 3 SECRETARY

**¾"**
**14"**
**3⅞"**
**HINGE-AND-FALL SUPPORT**
**¾"**
**11½"**
**¾"**
**3⅞"**
**13"**
**¼" PLYWOOD BACK**
**POST**
**21¼"**
**SHELF CLEAT**
**9¾"**
**¾"**
**3"**
**⅛" COVE**
**END VIEW (SECTION)**

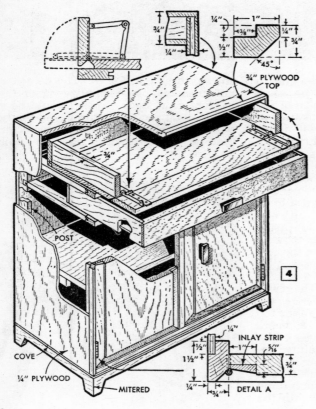

**¾"**
**¼"**
**1"**
**¼"**
**3⅜"**
**¼"**
**¾"**
**¼"**
**½"**
**45°**
**¾" PLYWOOD TOP**
**¾"**
**POST**
**COVE**
**¼" PLYWOOD**
**MITERED**
**4**
**¼"**
**1½"**
**INLAY STRIP**
**1"**
**3/16"**
**1½"**
**¾"**
**¼"**
**¾"**
**DETAIL A**

to the base assembly. The ¾-in. top, including the edging, should have the same over-all measurements as the base. This is rabbeted on all four edges. Note at the ends that the rabbets are cut ¼ in. deep and to the thickness of the top ply of the wood. The top is supported at the rear corners by posts and at the front by the hopper edging. Frames for the drawer and writing shelf are typical open frames, being assembled from ¾ x 1¾-in. stock. Inner edges of the front and rear members are grooved to take tenons formed on the ends of the side members. The frames are fitted into notches cut in the rear posts and supported at the front by nailing into them through the edging rabbet. The ¼-in. side panels will probably overlap the edge of the plywood back and are cut to fit accurately in the rabbets of the top and in the edging strips. The writing shelf is made similarly to a drawer except that the front is hinged. Note in the sectional detail, Fig. 4, that the bottom edge of the front piece is beveled to match a similar cut made on the front edge of the shelf. A stop should be fitted in the underside of the top to prevent the shelf from being pulled all the way out, and a bullet friction catch installed to hold the drop front closed. Construction of the drawer is apparent from the drawing. Plywood is best for the two doors, but solid stock can be used. In producing the raised-panel effect in plywood, an inlay strip is used to conceal the plies as indicated in detail A, Fig. 4. The door and drawer handles pictured are made up special from ¼-in. brass. Fig. 11 shows how these are soldered together T-shaped and then drilled and tapped for attaching with machine screws. The edges are rounded slightly with a fine file and then the brass is buffed to a high polish. A thin coat of clear lacquer will keep the handles bright.

The three-drawer chest is

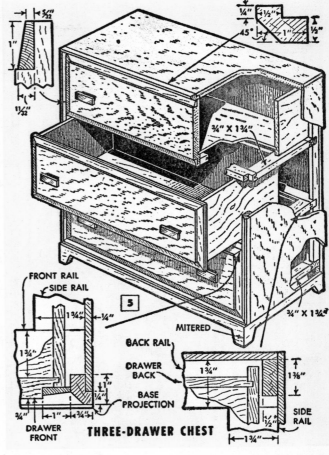

**THREE-DRAWER CHEST**

FRONT RAIL
SIDE RAIL
¾" X 1¾"
MITERED
BACK RAIL
DRAWER BACK
BASE PROJECTION
DRAWER FRONT
SIDE RAIL

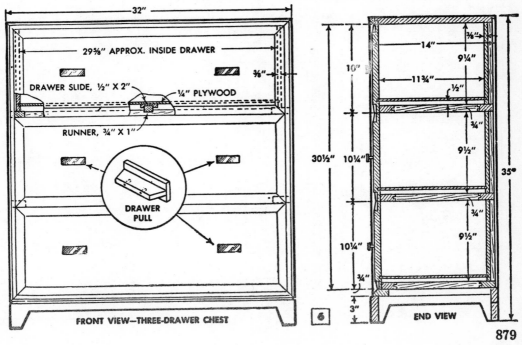

29⅝" APPROX. INSIDE DRAWER

DRAWER SLIDE, ½" X 2"     ¼" PLYWOOD

RUNNER, ¾" X 1"

DRAWER PULL

FRONT VIEW—THREE-DRAWER CHEST

END VIEW

# FURNITURE, OCCASIONAL

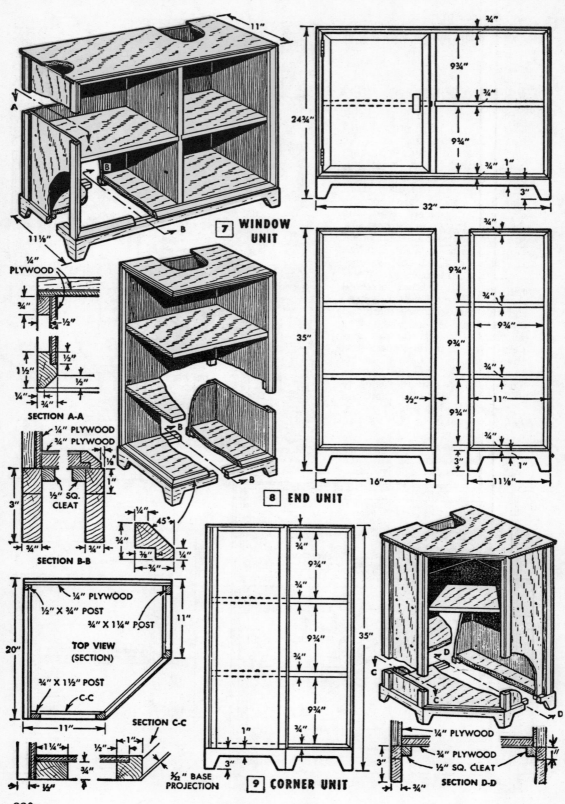

**7 WINDOW UNIT**

**SECTION A-A**

¼" PLYWOOD

**SECTION B-B**

**8 END UNIT**

¼" PLYWOOD
½" X ¾" POST
¾" X 1¼" POST

**TOP VIEW (SECTION)**

¾" X 1½" POST
C-C

**SECTION C-C**

³⁄₃₂" BASE PROJECTION

**9 CORNER UNIT**

¼" PLYWOOD
¾" PLYWOOD
½" SQ. CLEAT

**SECTION D-D**

basically of the same construction. The cutaway drawing in Fig. 5 and the front and side views in Fig. 6 give the necessary details. Typical chest construction is employed with frames supporting each drawer. Hopper edging is applied as explained before and the drawer fronts are inlaid around the edges. The front view, Fig. 6, details the drawer runners. The strip nailed to the frame engages a wooden channel which is glued and bradded to the bottom of the drawer. This same type of runner is used for the drawer of the secretary. The lower details, Fig. 5, show plan views of the drawer at the front and rear corners.

**Window, end and corner units,** Figs. 7, 8 and 9, differ basically in construction in that the plywood side panels are placed on the inside of the cabinets instead of the outside. Whether this should be done on the side of the corner unit depends upon the grouping arrangement. If placed next to the window unit as pictured on page 877,

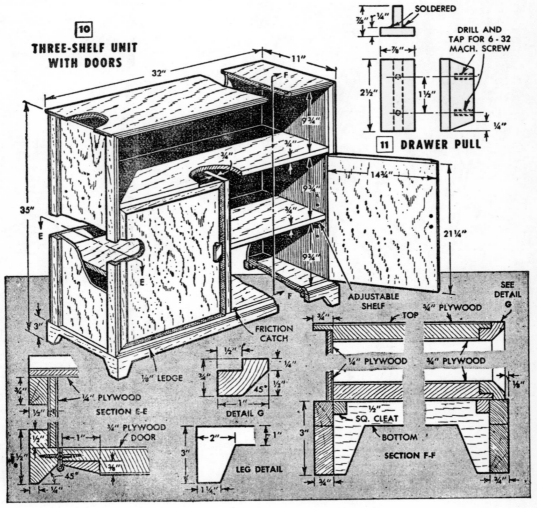

**10 THREE-SHELF UNIT WITH DOORS**

**11 DRAWER PULL**

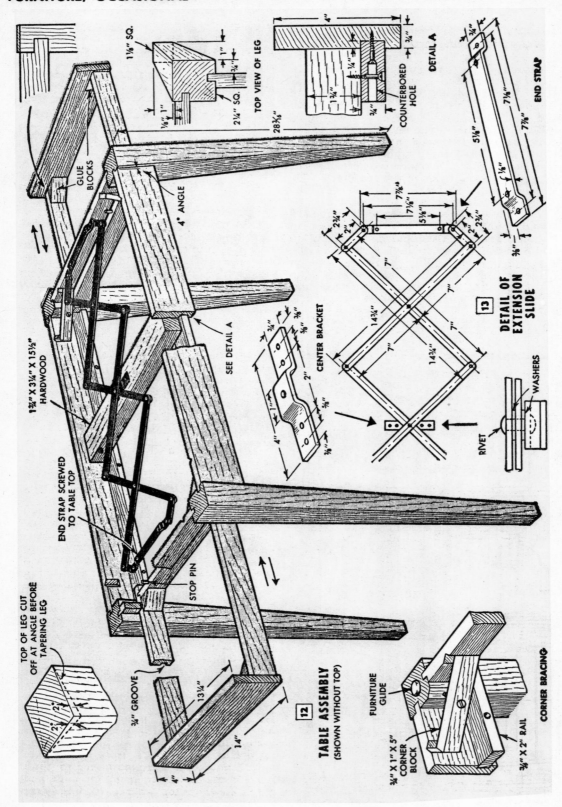

1⅛" SQ.

1"

¾"

2¼" SQ.

⅛" 1"

TOP VIEW OF LEG

4"

¾"

¼"

1¾"

COUNTERBORED HOLE

¾"

DETAIL A

GLUE BLOCKS

4° ANGLE

28⅞"

1¾" X 3¼" X 15½" HARDWOOD

SEE DETAIL A

END STRAP SCREWED TO TABLE TOP

STOP PIN

TOP OF LEG CUT OFF AT ANGLE BEFORE TAPERING LEG

2" 2"
2"

¾" GROOVE

13¼"

14"

4"

**12**

**TABLE ASSEMBLY**
(SHOWN WITHOUT TOP)

¾"

¾"

1"

2"

⅜"

4"

⅜"

CENTER BRACKET

¾"

¾"

⅜"

7⅞"

7⅞"

END STRAP

⅜"

7¾"

7⅛"

5⅝"

2¾"
2"

2¾"
2"

7"

7"

14¾"

7"

7"

14¾"

**13**

**DETAIL OF EXTENSION SLIDE**

RIVET

WASHERS

FURNITURE GLIDE

¾" X 1" X 5" CORNER BLOCK

¾" X 2" RAIL

**CORNER BRACING**

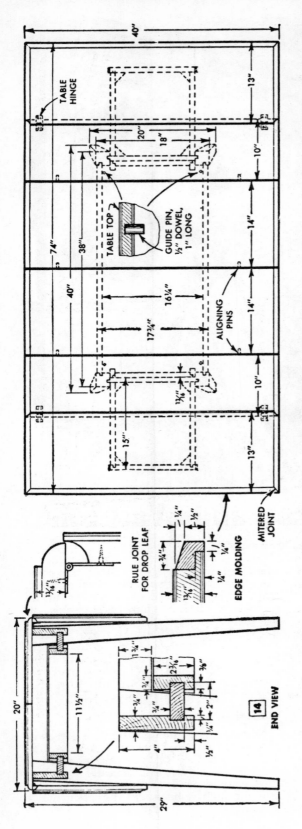

the plywood will have to be applied to the outside. Remember in cutting duplicate parts that the end units will have to be right and left-hand assemblies.

**The three-shelf unit,** shown fitted with doors in Fig. 10, can be made entirely open, in which case the partition is eliminated and the middle shelf brought out even with the one above it. The sectional details accompanying the cutaway drawing in Fig. 10 show how the ¼-in.-plywood side panels fit in rabbets cut on the inner edge of the hopper edging.

**The drop-leaf table,** Figs. 12, 13 and 14, has flared, tapered legs which assume the correct slant by making a compound cut at the top and bottom. This is done before tapering the legs in one of two ways: Either set the miter gauge 2 deg. and tilt the saw table 2 deg., or, support the work horizontally on one corner and make the cut with the gauge set at 2 deg. and the table at 90 degs. Only the adjacent inner faces of each leg are tapered, as indicated in the top-view detail, Fig. 12. The leg tapers from a full 2¼-in. square at the top to 1⅛ in. at the bottom. The two side aprons of the table are angle-cut to match the slant of the legs and the ends are rabbeted to fit open mortises cut in the tapered faces of the legs. Note in detail A that the side aprons are grooved along the lower edge to take strips on which the retractable end brackets slide. Half-width aprons are fitted across the ends of the table and then corner blocks are applied in the manner shown in the corner-bracing detail. Notice that a furniture glide is driven into the top of each leg t  make the table top pivot easily. The pull-out brackets are made to slide under the end aprons and are corner-blocked for rigidity. A stop pin is provided at each side.

The lazy-tong extension slide is assembled from flat iron and riveted together as indicated in Fig. 13. This is pivoted to a center bracket which in turn is screwed to a hardwood center member installed between the side aprons. Each end of the extension slide is screwed to the underside of the two top leaves of the table. Fig. 14 shows an end view and a plan view of the table top including the two extra leaves. Outer edges of the plywood top are fitted with a mitered edge molding set in a rabbet, and a rule joint is run on the drop leaves for hinging them with regular drop-leaf hinges. When cutting the rule joints, be sure to allow sufficient clearance between the male and female members so that the joints will not bind after the finish has been applied to the surfaces. Note in the plan view that steel dowel pins forced in blind holes in the underside of the top align and guide the table top when extending it for inserting extra leaves.

# Queen Anne Mirror and Wall Shelf

### By C. W. Woodson

EARLY QUEEN ANNE is the period represented by the graceful design of this mirror and companion wall shelf. Mahogany-faced ¼-in. plywood is used throughout for the shelf, and also for the jigsawed panels above and below the mirror. The frame around the mirror glass is made from ornamental picture-frame molding that you buy.

### Mirror

Start construction of the mirror by making the frame, which has mitered corners. Before assembling, saw a groove in the upper and lower members to accommodate the plywood panels, as indicated in the lower left-hand detail. Next, make a pattern of the upper and lower panels by enlarging the squared drawings in the detail. Trace the patterns on the plywood and cut them out with a jigsaw. Sand the edges smooth and glue the panels to the mirror frame. Now, set the glass mirror in the frame and glue and nail narrow cleats to the inside edges of the frame to keep the mirror in place. Cleats also are glued to the plywood panels as indicated in the lower left-hand detail and a piece of ³⁄₁₆-in. plywood is glued and nailed over the mirror back as indicated, both to protect and to stiffen the plywood panels.

### Wall Shelf

Both sides of the wall shelf are jigsawed at the same time to assure that they are identical. The sides then are mortised to receive tenons cut on the shelf ends and the assembly is glued together. A pattern is made for the back, cut out, then nailed to the back edges of the sides. ★ ★ ★

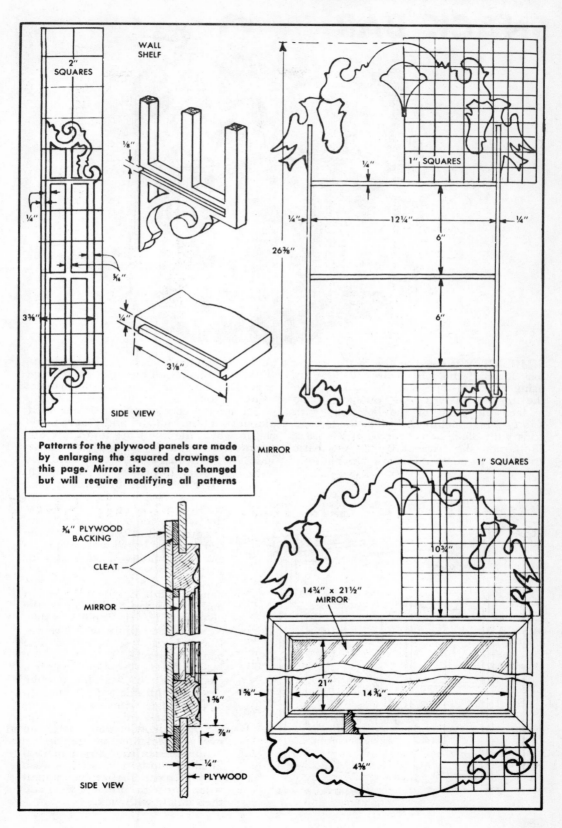

2"
SQUARES

WALL
SHELF

1/8"

1/4"

3/16"

1/4"

3 3/8"

SIDE VIEW

1/4"

3 1/8"

1" SQUARES

1/4"

1/4"

12 1/4"

1/4"

6"

26 3/8"

6"

MIRROR

Patterns for the plywood panels are made by enlarging the squared drawings on this page. Mirror size can be changed but will require modifying all patterns

3/16" PLYWOOD
BACKING

CLEAT

MIRROR

1" SQUARES

10 3/4"

14 3/4" x 21 1/2"
MIRROR

1 5/8"

21"

14 3/4"

1 5/8"

7/8"

4 3/8"

1/4"

PLYWOOD

SIDE VIEW

# SNACK BAR

SIMPLICITY is the keynote of this snack bar, for half the job is already done by using an open-type bookshelf to provide the interior shelves. All you have to do is face the front of the bookcase with knotty-pine paneling and cover the top and ends with plain 1-in. boards. A 9 x 36 x 36-in. bookshelf was used as the basic structure to make the snack bar pictured above. If you don't happen to have a bookshelf, you'll be ahead by purchasing an inexpensive, unpainted one at a department store. Figure out the number of boards you'll need to cover your particular shelf picking out select tongue-and-groove material in which the knots are uniformly distributed. The cutaway drawing shown below at left indicates how the end boards are allowed to project at the front to cover the edges of the knotty-pine boards. Use boards of uniform width or at least space them so that the two outside boards are of nearly equal width. The tongue on the starting face board will have to be cut off to make a flush, butt joint with the piece covering the end. Allow the snack-bar top to overhang the ends and the front, and in nailing the top and ends to the bookshelf, use short nails so they do not extend all the way through. Beveled edges on the knotty-pine paneling provide V-joints on the face of the bar to relieve the plain front. The top of the bar may be covered with oilcloth or linoleum and the edges trimmed with regular stainless-steel counter-top edging. A piece of decorative laminate may be cemented to the top for a durable surface. For a natural finish of knotty pine, apply a wash coat of clear shellac, rubbing it when dry with fine steel wool and then follow with wax.

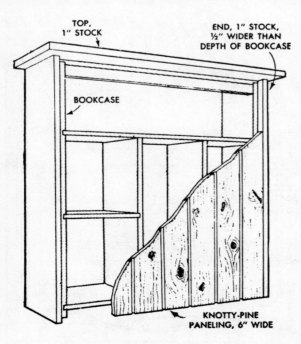

TOP, 1" STOCK

END, 1" STOCK, ½" WIDER THAN DEPTH OF BOOKCASE

BOOKCASE

KNOTTY-PINE PANELING, 6" WIDE

# Patio Lounge

## By Hi Sibley

LOTS OF LAZY COMFORT is built into this contour patio lounge, and it's a fairly simple thing to make if you have a bandsaw to cut out the curved parts. Staves from nail kegs, which are used to cover the top, add to its body-conforming comfort. Except for the wheels and the member to which they are attached, all parts are cut from ¾-in. material. The side rails are cut from 1 x 10 boards and consist of two separate pieces butted together and held securely by screws in the rear legs. The drawing shows at a glance how the other parts go together. Give it two coats of exterior paint, add a padded cushion and lean back in solid comfort.

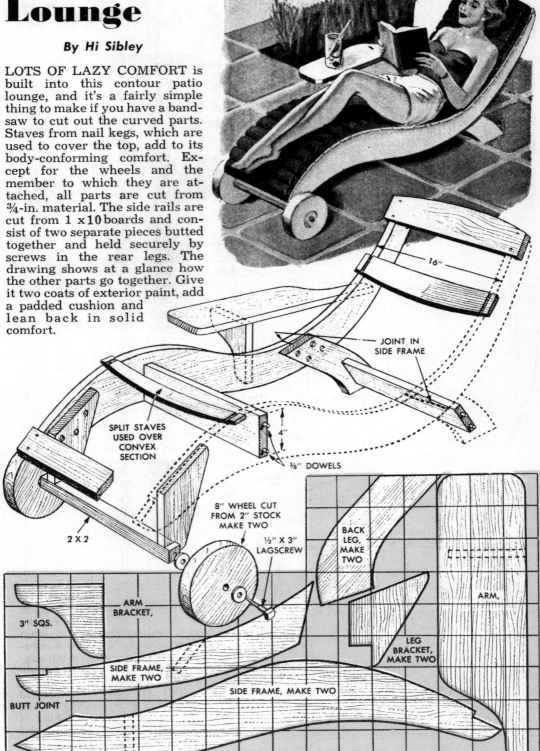

16"

JOINT IN SIDE FRAME

SPLIT STAVES USED OVER CONVEX SECTION

4"

⅜" DOWELS

2 X 2

8" WHEEL CUT FROM 2" STOCK MAKE TWO

½" X 3" LAGSCREW

BACK LEG, MAKE TWO

ARM,

ARM BRACKET,

3" SQS.

LEG BRACKET, MAKE TWO

SIDE FRAME, MAKE TWO

SIDE FRAME, MAKE TWO

BUTT JOINT

# Bent-Tube

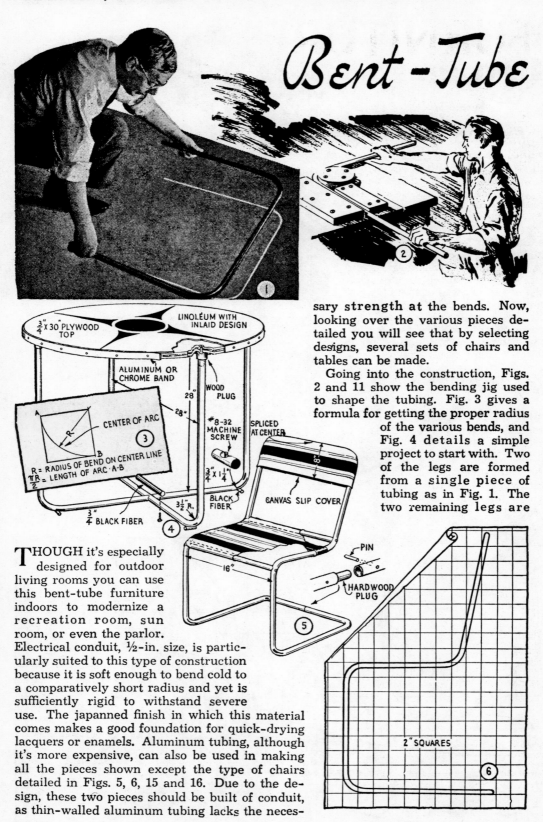

**Fig. 3 labels:**
A
CENTER OF ARC
R
B
R = RADIUS OF BEND ON CENTER LINE
πR/2 = LENGTH OF ARC·A-B

**Table/figure labels:**
¾" X 30" PLYWOOD TOP
LINOLEUM WITH INLAID DESIGN
ALUMINUM OR CHROME BAND
WOOD PLUG
28"
28"
#8-32 MACHINE SCREW
SPLICED AT CENTER
¾" X 1¼"
3½" R.
BLACK FIBER
¾" BLACK FIBER
CANVAS SLIP COVER
16"
PIN
HARDWOOD PLUG
2" SQUARES

sary strength at the bends. Now, looking over the various pieces detailed you will see that by selecting designs, several sets of chairs and tables can be made.

Going into the construction, Figs. 2 and 11 show the bending jig used to shape the tubing. Fig. 3 gives a formula for getting the proper radius of the various bends, and Fig. 4 details a simple project to start with. Two of the legs are formed from a single piece of tubing as in Fig. 1. The two remaining legs are

THOUGH it's especially designed for outdoor living rooms you can use this bent-tube furniture indoors to modernize a recreation room, sun room, or even the parlor. Electrical conduit, ½-in. size, is particularly suited to this type of construction because it is soft enough to bend cold to a comparatively short radius and yet is sufficiently rigid to withstand severe use. The japanned finish in which this material comes makes a good foundation for quick-drying lacquers or enamels. Aluminum tubing, although it's more expensive, can also be used in making all the pieces shown except the type of chairs detailed in Figs. 5, 6, 15 and 16. Due to the design, these two pieces should be built of conduit, as thin-walled aluminum tubing lacks the neces-

# FURNITURE

## MADE FROM ELECTRICAL CONDUIT

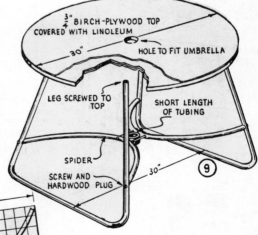

bent separately and the lower ends are filed concave to fit the first member and form a neat right-angled joint. A short length of ¾-in. round black fiber is fastened over the joint with screws driven through the tubing. This holds the joint and further carries out the modern design. The four feet are of the same material. Hardwood plugs, turned to a tight fit, are driven into the top end of each leg, and screws, which hold the circular plywood top, are driven through the top into these

plugs. Linoleum, of whatever design you choose, is cemented to the top. A chrome or aluminum band around the edge finishes the job.

Now, to build the other two tables, shown in Figs. 7, 8, 9 and 19, you follow the same general procedure in bending the tubing and joining parts together. When you bend thin-walled aluminum tubing, it's best to fill the tube with sand, ramming it hard, and plug the ends as in Figs. 17 and 18. Also, it's a good idea to turn a concave groove in the edge of the bending disk on the jig,

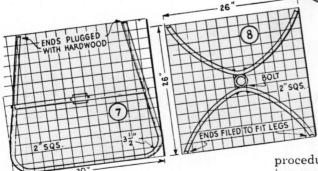

*A table just suited to use in the outdoor living room for refreshments, card parties, etc. It's arranged to hold a lawn umbrella which can be anchored with a pin driven into the ground. The inlay design shown in Fig. 4 can be used on this table top, if desired*

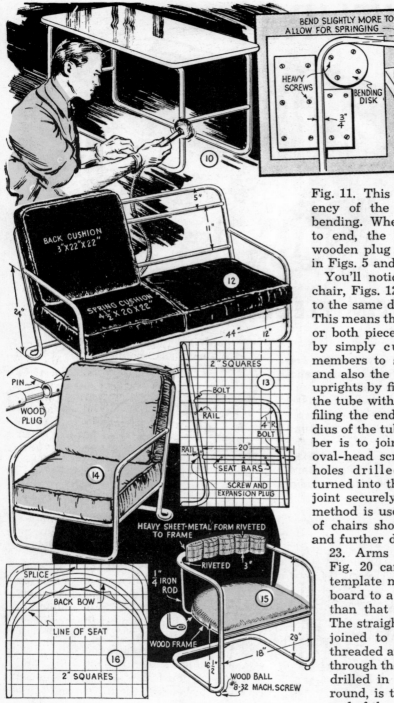

Fig. 11. This will prevent any tendency of the tube to flatten when bending. Where the tubing joins end to end, the joint is made with a wooden plug and two metal pins as in Figs. 5 and 12.

You'll notice that the settee and chair, Figs. 12 and 14, are fashioned to the same dimensions as in Fig. 13. This means that you can build either or both pieces from the same plan, by simply cutting the lengthwise members to suit. Here these parts and also the arms are joined to the uprights by first plugging the end of the tube with a hardwood plug, then filing the end concave to fit the radius of the tube the horizontal member is to join. A chromium-plated oval-head screw inserted through holes drilled in the upright and turned into the wood plug holds the joint securely. Practically the same method is used in joining the parts of chairs shown in Figs. 20 and 22 and further detailed in Figs. 21 and 23. Arms of the chair shown in Fig. 20 can be shaped around a template made by band-sawing a board to a slightly shorter radius than that required on the tube. The straight rails of this chair are joined to the legs with a rod, threaded at both ends and passing through the rail and through holes drilled in the legs. A nut, filed round, is then turned up on each end of the rod. Another way is to simply use the rod as a long rivet, peening over the projecting ends. If you countersink the hole before inserting the rod, the ends can be peened over and the excess filed

*By halving the width, the settee in Fig. 12 becomes the chair shown in Fig. 14, as the end dimensions are the same. Spring-cushioned backs and seats can be made by purchasing the spring assembly ready-made, padding it lightly with cotton and sewing on a covering of cloth or artificial leather. The metal frames can be made of conduit, enameled in color, or polished aluminum tubing*

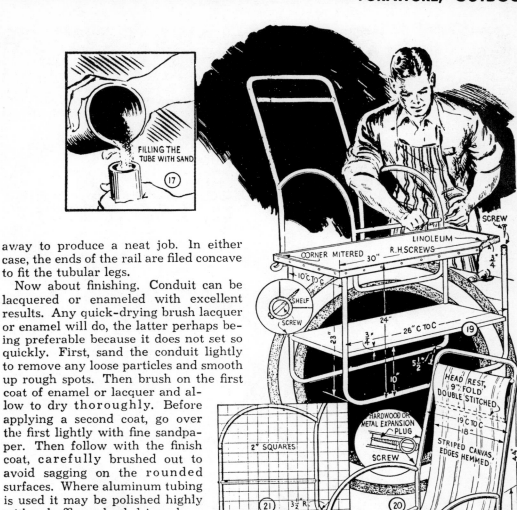

away to produce a neat job. In either case, the ends of the rail are filed concave to fit the tubular legs.

Now about finishing. Conduit can be lacquered or enameled with excellent results. Any quick-drying brush lacquer or enamel will do, the latter perhaps being preferable because it does not set so quickly. First, sand the conduit lightly to remove any loose particles and smooth up rough spots. Then brush on the first coat of enamel or lacquer and allow to dry thoroughly. Before applying a second coat, go over the first lightly with fine sandpaper. Then follow with the finish coat, carefully brushed out to avoid sagging on the rounded surfaces. Where aluminum tubing is used it may be polished highly with a buffing wheel driven by a flexible shaft as in Fig. 10. A coat of clear metal lacquer will help to preserve the high polish.

*Metal frames for any of these three pieces can be made of either polished aluminum tubing or electrical conduit finished in quick-drying colored lacquer or enamel. By combining these and other designs shown, several sets of attractive porch and garden furniture can be made*

# LAWN FURNITURE

HERE IS THE "new look" in outdoor furniture, designed by a well-known furniture stylist who has come up with some original and exciting pieces which feature knock-down construction to lick the problem of winter storage. By building these easy-to-make pieces of furniture yourself, the budget for your home grounds need not be unreasonably stretched to include outdoor furnishings. Gay, comfortable and easy to dismantle, this striking lawn furniture incorporates the use of ready-made waterproof cushions. These can be purchased from department stores in sizes to fit the various pieces of the group. The complete back yard ensemble features six pieces, including an Adirondack-type chair, porch chair, serving cart, garden lounge, porch glider and a table-and-bench set. Several of the pieces, such as the porch chair, lounge and glider, also can be used during the winter on an enclosed porch or in a sunroom. Both the lounge and the Adirondack chair have tilting

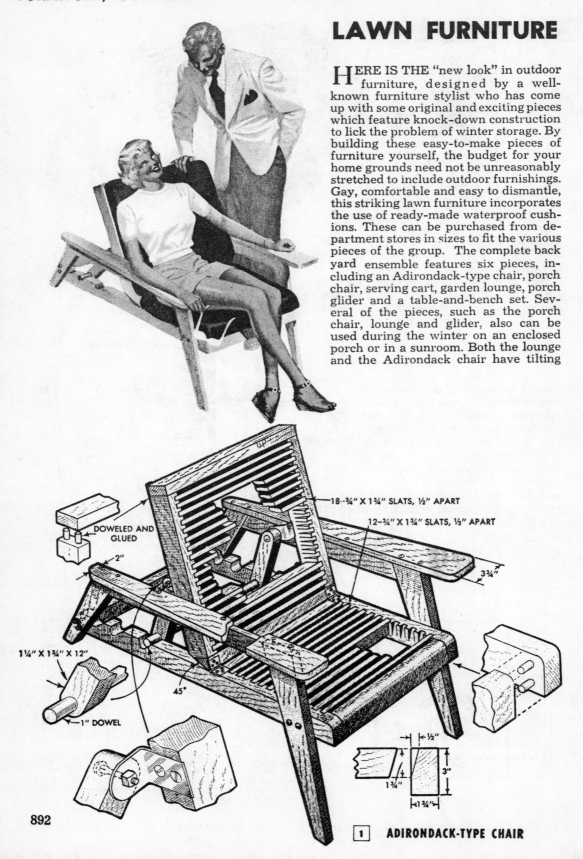

DOWELED AND GLUED

2"

18-¾" X 1¾" SLATS, ½" APART

12-¾" X 1¾" SLATS, ½" APART

3¾"

1¼" X 1¾" X 12"

1" DOWEL

45°

½"

3"

1¾"

1¾"

**1** ADIRONDACK-TYPE CHAIR

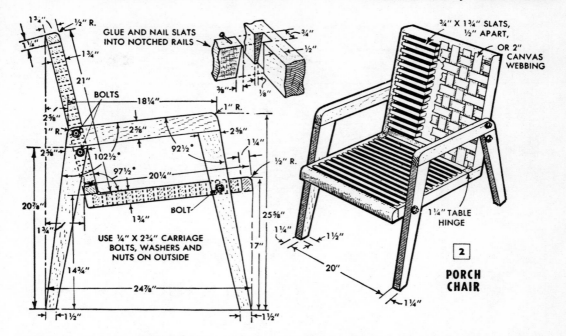

GLUE AND NAIL SLATS INTO NOTCHED RAILS

BOLTS

USE ¼" X 2¾" CARRIAGE BOLTS, WASHERS AND NUTS ON OUTSIDE

BOLT

¾" X 1¾" SLATS, ½" APART, OR 2" CANVAS WEBBING

1¼" TABLE HINGE

**2**

**PORCH CHAIR**

backs that can be adjusted to suit the comfort of the individual. Except in the case of the garden table-and-bench set, a choice of slats or webbing is given in constructing the seats and backs of the furniture. Both types are partially indicated in most of the drawings, and this should not be confused with actual construction details.

While redwood and cypress are two of the most durable woods, especially suitable for outdoor furniture, common lumberyard stock, such as yellow pine or fir, is perfectly satisfactory if the pieces are kept well painted.

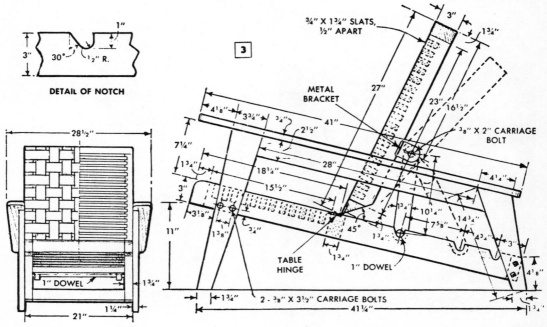

**DETAIL OF NOTCH**

METAL BRACKET

¾" X 1¾" SLATS, ½" APART

⅜" X 2" CARRIAGE BOLT

**3**

TABLE HINGE

1" DOWEL

2 - ⅜" X 3½" CARRIAGE BOLTS

1" DOWEL

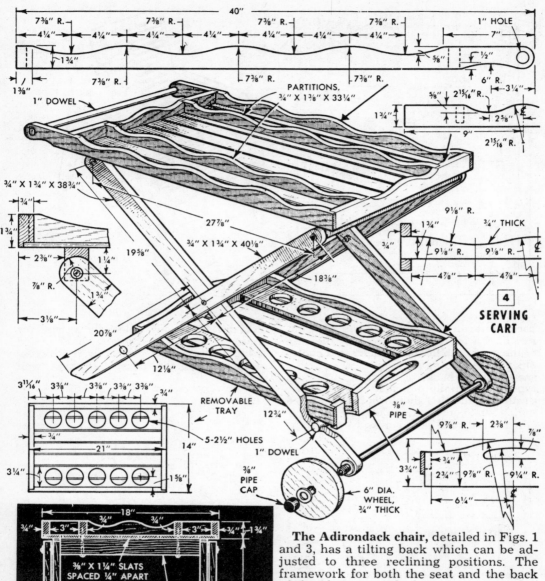

40"

7⅜" R.   7⅜" R.   7⅜" R.   7⅜" R.   1" HOLE   7"

4¼"  4¼"  4¼"  4¼"  4¼"  4¼"  4¼"

1¾"   ⅝"   ½"

1⅜"   7⅜" R.   7⅜" R.   7⅜" R.   6" R.   3¼"

PARTITIONS.
¾" X 1⅜" X 33¼"

⅝"  2¹⁵⁄₁₆" R.

1" DOWEL

1¾"   2⅝"

9"

2¹⁵⁄₁₆" R.

¾" X 1¾" X 38¾"

¾"

1¾"

2⅜"   1¼"

19⅝"

7⅞" R.   1¾"

3⅛"

27⅞"

¾" X 1¾" X 40⅛"

18⅜"

¾"

9⅛" R.   ¾" THICK

1¾"

9⅛" R.   9⅛" R.

4⅞"   4⅞"

**4**

**SERVING
CART**

20⅞"

12⅛"

3¹¹⁄₁₆"  3⅜"  3⅜"  3⅜"  3⅜"   ¾"

REMOVABLE
TRAY

12¾"

¾"

1" DOWEL

5-2½" HOLES

⅜"
PIPE

21"

14"

3¼"   1⅝"

⅜"
PIPE
CAP

6" DIA.
WHEEL,
¾" THICK

9⅞" R.   2⅜"   ⅞"

¾"

3¾"   2¾"  9⅞" R.   9¼" R.

6¼"

18"   ¾"

¾"   3"   3"   ¾"  1¾"

⅜" X 1¼" SLATS
SPACED ¼" APART

1¼" X 1¾"

⅛"   ¾"   ¾"   ⅛"

¾"   ¾"

WASHER

28⅜"

14"

½" X 3¼"

¾"   ¾"

⅜" X 1¾" SLATS, ¼" APART

⅜"
PIPE   **END VIEW**

14½"

17¾"

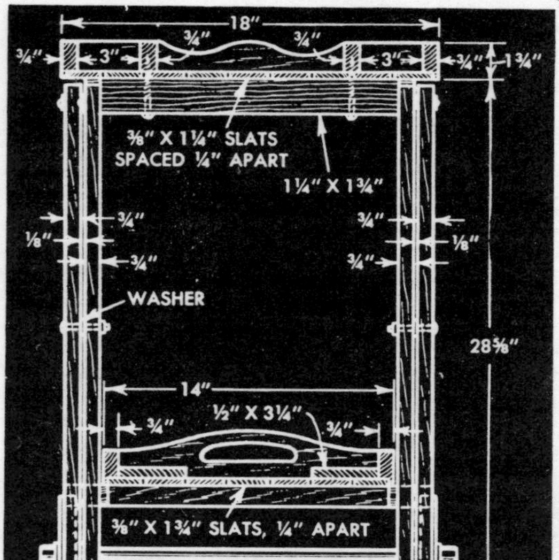

**5**

**The Adirondack chair,** detailed in Figs. 1 and 3, has a tilting back which can be adjusted to three reclining positions. The framework for both the seat and the back of the chair is made from 2 x 4 material, while the legs and the rails which support the arms can be of 1⅛ or 1¼-in. stock. Each framework is made as a separate unit and the back is hinged to the seat with 1¼-in. table hinges, set flush. If slats are used instead of webbing, the slanting notches for them must be made before the frames are doweled and glued together. These can be cut with a ¾-in. dado head on a circular saw by utilizing a narrow strip tacked temporarily to the face of the work along the rear edge. The strip is positioned to tilt the work at an angle that will produce a notch 1¾ in. long. The slats are cut from common 1 x 2 lumber, the ends being sawed off at an angle to fit the slanting notches and then nailed in place, flush with is pivoted to it with sheet-metal brackets in the manner shown in Fig. 1. If webbing is preferred to the slats, use either nylon parachute webbing or common canvas webbing and interlace it as shown. The ready-made cushions will hide the tacks used in fastening webbing to the frames.

**The porch chair,** Fig. 2, is somewhat similar in construction. The seat and back are hinged together to fold flat for storing, while the legs and arms can be taken off as single units by removing only six nuts and washers. Frames for the seat and back are assembled from 1¼ x 1¾-in. stock, notched if slats are used, before doweling and gluing together.

**The serving cart,** Figs. 4 and 5, can be wheeled about and features a removable beverage tray which rides on two rungs

fitted between the crossed legs. Each pair of legs are duplicates, and registering holes for the pipe axle, dowel rungs and screw fastenings are bored at one time through each set. The upper ends of the legs are pivoted with wood screws to 1¼ x 1¾-in. cleats which support the upper tray.

**The garden lounge,** Figs. 6 and 7, like the Adirondack chair, has a tilting back which is supported in the same manner except that it is adjustable to four positions. The bed frame of the lounge, including the tilting back, is made of 2 x 4 material, with a second frame of lighter stock being bolted to the underside. This second frame carries the wheel axle and also the notches which engage the tilting back support. The end-view detail shows how the pipe axle is bolted in place with lag screws. The arms of the

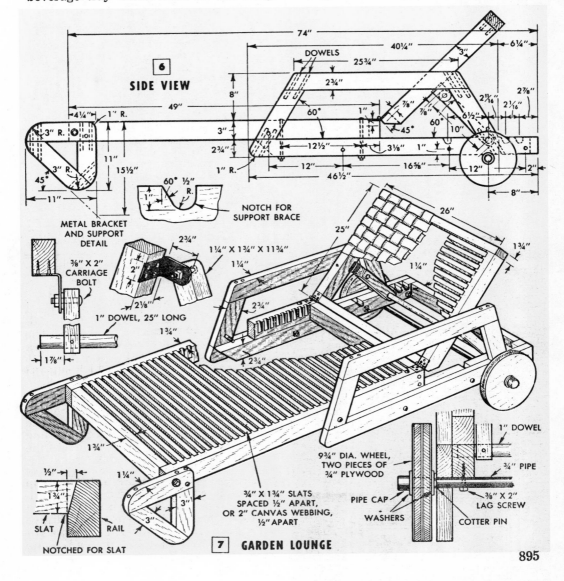

**6** SIDE VIEW

METAL BRACKET AND SUPPORT DETAIL

NOTCH FOR SUPPORT BRACE

⅜" X 2" CARRIAGE BOLT

1¼" X 1¾" X 11¾"

1" DOWEL, 25" LONG

SLAT    RAIL

NOTCHED FOR SLAT

¾" X 1¾" SLATS SPACED ½" APART, OR 2" CANVAS WEBBING, ½" APART

9¾" DIA. WHEEL, TWO PIECES OF ¾" PLYWOOD

PIPE CAP

WASHERS

1" DOWEL

¾" PIPE

⅜" X 2" LAG SCREW

COTTER PIN

**7** GARDEN LOUNGE

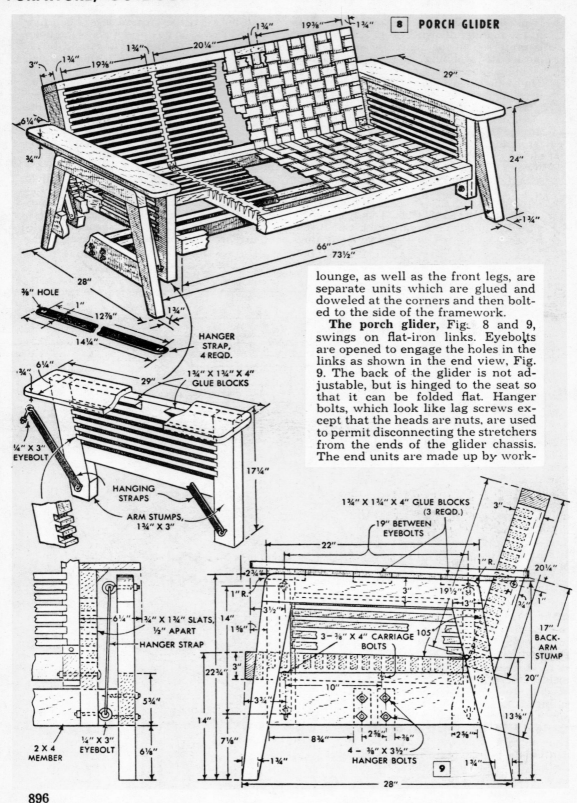

**8** PORCH GLIDER

lounge, as well as the front legs, are separate units which are glued and doweled at the corners and then bolted to the side of the framework.

**The porch glider,** Fig. 8 and 9, swings on flat-iron links. Eyebolts are opened to engage the holes in the links as shown in the end view, Fig. 9. The back of the glider is not adjustable, but is hinged to the seat so that it can be folded flat. Hanger bolts, which look like lag screws except that the heads are nuts, are used to permit disconnecting the stretchers from the ends of the glider chassis. The end units are made up by work-

⅜" HOLE

1"

12⅞"

14¼"

1¾"

HANGER STRAP, 4 REQD.

¾"

6¼"

28"

29"

1¾" X 1¾" X 4" GLUE BLOCKS

¼" X 3" EYEBOLT

HANGING STRAPS

ARM STUMPS, 1¾" X 3"

17¼"

1¾" X 1¾" X 4" GLUE BLOCKS (3 REQD.)

19" BETWEEN EYEBOLTS

3"

22"

1" R.

20¼"

1"

19½"

3"

¾"

17" BACK-ARM STUMP

2¾"

1" R.

3½"

1⅝"

3"

3"

3 – ⅜" X 4" CARRIAGE BOLTS

105°

14"

22¾"

3"

3¾"

10"

20"

13⅜"

14"

7⅛"

8¾"

2⅝" ⅜"

2⅝"

4 – ⅜" X 3½" HANGER BOLTS

1¾"

1¾"

28"

6¼"

¾" X 1¾" SLATS, ½" APART

HANGER STRAP

5¾"

2 X 4 MEMBER

¼" X 3" EYEBOLT

6⅛"

**9**

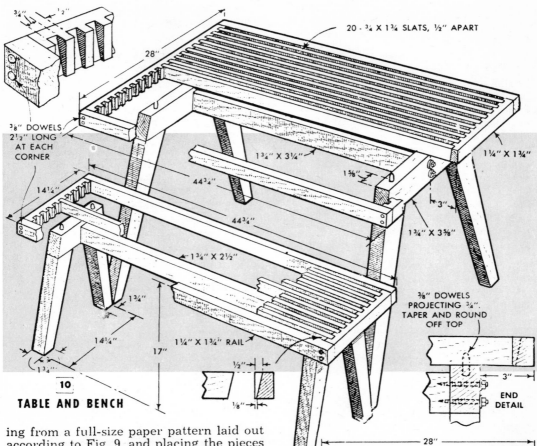

20 - ¾ X 1¾ SLATS, ½" APART

28"

¾" DOWELS 2½" LONG AT EACH CORNER

14¼"

44¾"

44¾"

1¾" X 3¼"

1⅝"

1¾" X 2½"

1¾"

14¼"

17"

1¾"

1¼" X 1¾" RAIL

½"

⅛"

1¼" X 1¾"

3"

1¾" X 3⅝"

**10**
**TABLE AND BENCH**

⅜" DOWELS PROJECTING ¾". TAPER AND ROUND OFF TOP

3"

END DETAIL

ing from a full-size paper pattern laid out according to Fig. 9, and placing the pieces right over the pattern to obtain the correct slant for the legs and top arm rails.

The picnic table-and-bench set, Fig. 10, also can be taken completely apart for storing. The tops of both the table and benches lift off, being held in place merely by stub pins which engage registering holes. Hanger bolts in the ends of the center stretchers permit the U-shaped legs to be removed in a jiffy. Except for size, the construction of the three pieces is exactly alike. As the slats are spaced ½ in. apart, it is best to paint them before they are nailed in place. Note that here the tapering notches are cut the full width of the end rails. This can be done with a small dado head by gluing a strip of beveled siding temporarily to the inside face of the work to bring the line of cut parallel with the saw table. The siding strip is glued with paper between it and the work so that it can be pried off easily when all the notches have been cut. However, to simplify the job, the notches can be cut straight through and the 1 x 2 slats glued in place and nailed from the outside face. The legs are cut from 2 x 4 material and glued and doweled to the apron pieces. Screws can be used instead of dowels at the corners of the bench tops.

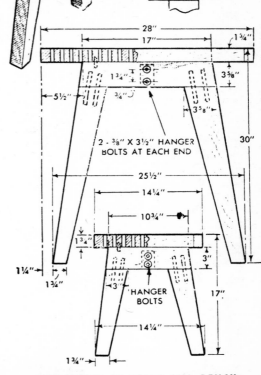

28"

17"

1¾"

3⅝"

5½"

1¾"

¾"

3⅝"

2 - ⅜" X 3½" HANGER BOLTS AT EACH END

30"

25½"

14¼"

10¾"

1¾"

1¼"

1¾"

3"

3"

HANGER BOLTS

17"

14¼"

1¾"

**END VIEWS OF TABLE AND BENCH**

## LUMBER LIST FOR LAWN FURNITURE

### ADIRONDACK CHAIR

2 pcs. 1¾ x 3 x 42 in.—Side seat rails
1 pc. 1¾ x 3 x 21 in.—Front seat rail
1 pc. 1¾ x 3 x 17½ in.—Center seat rail
1 pc. 1¼ x 3 x 17½ in.—Back seat rail
2 pcs. 1¾ x 3 x 27 in.—Side back rails
1 pc. 1¾ x 3 x 21 in.—Top back rail
1 pc. 1¾ x 2¼ x 17½ in.—Bottom back rail
30 pcs. ¾ x 1¾ x 18½ in.—Seat and back slats
2 pcs. 1¼ x 3¾ x 22 in.—Front legs
2 pcs. 1¼ x 3¾ x 14⅝ in.—Back legs
2 pcs. 1¼ x 2½ x 29⅞ in.—Arm aprons
2 pcs. ¾ x 3¾ x 41 in.—Tops of arms
2 pcs. 1¼ x 1¾ x 12 in.—Back stays
1 pc. 1-in. dia. x 20 in. long—Dowel rung
33 yds. 2-in. canvas webbing—Seat and back covering

### PORCH CHAIR

2 pcs. 1¼ x 1¾ x 20¼ in.—Side seat rails
1 pc. 1¼ x 1¾ x 20 in.—Front seat rail
1 pc. 1¼ x 1¾ x 17½ in.—Back seat rail
2 pcs. 1¼ x 1¾ x 21 in.—Side back rails
1 pc. 1¼ x 1¾ x 20 in.—Top back rail
1 pc. 1¼ x 1¾ x 17½ in.—Bottom back rail
27 pcs. ¾ x 1¾ x 18½ in.—Seat and back slats
2 pcs. 1¼ x 2⅝ x 23½ in.—Front legs
2 pcs. 1¼ x 2⅝ x 21¾ in.—Back legs
2 pcs. 1¼ x 2⅝ x 19 in.—Arms
20 yds. 2-in. canvas webbing—Seat and back covering

### SERVING CART

2 pcs. ¾ x 1¾ x 40 in.—Top side rails
2 pcs. ¾ x 1¾ x 17 in.—Top end rails
2 pcs. ¾ x 1⅜ x 33¼ in.—Partitions
7 pcs. ⅜ x 1¾ x 33¾ in.—Bottom slats
2 pcs. ⅜ x 1⅝ x 33¾ in.—Bottom slats
1 pc. 1¼ x 1¾ x 14½ in.—Brace
1 pc. 1¼ x 1¾ x 16½ in.—Brace
2 pcs. ¾ x 1¾ x 38¾ in.—Legs
2 pcs. ¾ x 1¾ x 40⅛ in.—Legs
4 pcs. ¾ x 6 x 6 in.—Wheels
2 pcs. ¾ x 1¾ x 21 in.—Tray sides
2 pcs. ¾ x 3¾ x 13½ in.—Tray ends
7 pcs. ⅜ x 1¾ x 20 in.—Tray bottom
2 pcs. ½ x 3¼ x 19½ in.—Glass holders
1 pc. 1-in. dia. x 17½ in.—Dowel
1 pc. 1-in. dia. x 17 in.—Dowel
1 pc. 1-in. dia. x 17¾ in.—Dowel

### GARDEN LOUNGE

2 pcs. 1¾ x 3 x 49 in.—Seat side rails (front half)
2 pcs. 1¾ x 3 x 22½ in.—Seat end rails (front half)
1 pc. 1¼ x 3 x 22½ in.—Seat end rail (back half)
2 pcs. 1¾ x 3 x 23¼ in.—Seat side rails (back half)

1 pc. 1¾ x 3 x 26 in.—Top rail for back
1 pc. 1¾ x 2½ x 22½ in.—Bottom rail for back
2 pcs. 1¾ x 2¾ x 44¾ in.—Back side rails
2 pcs. 1¼ x 2¾ x 29 in.—Tops of arms
2 pcs. 1¼ x 2¾ x 46⅜ in.—Bottoms of arms
2 pcs. 1¼ x 2¾ x 14¼ in.—Front arm stumps
2 pcs. 1¼ x 2¾ x 11⅛ in.—Back arm stumps
2 pcs. 1¼ x 1¾ x 11¾ in.—Back supports
2 pcs. 1¼ x 3 x 15½ in.—Front leg horizontals
2 pcs. 1¼ x 3 x 8 in.—Front leg uprights
2 pcs. 1¼ x 3 x 17½ in.—Front leg diagonals
53 pcs. ¾ x 1¾ x 23½ in.—Seat and back slats
4 pcs. ¾ x 9¾ x 9¾ in.—Wheels
1 pc. 1-in. dia. x 25 in. long—Dowel rung
60 yds. 2-in. canvas webbing—Seat and back covering

### PORCH GLIDER

4 pcs. 1¾ x 3 x 20⅜ in.—Legs
2 pcs. 1¾ x 3 x 22¾ in.—Top leg rails
2 pcs. 1¾ x 5¾ x 22 in.—Lower leg rails
2 pcs. 2 x 4 x 73½ in.—Leg stretchers
2 pcs. ¾ x 6¼ x 29 in.—Arms
2 pcs. 1¾ x 2½ x 20¾ in.—Top arm rails
2 pcs. 1¾ x 3 x 18 in.—Lower arm rails
2 pcs. 1¾ x 3 x 17¼ in.—Front arm stumps
2 pcs. 1¾ x 3 x 17¾ in.—Rear arm stumps
1 pc. ¾ x 1¾ x 108 in.—Arm slats
1 pc. 1¾ x 1¾ x 4 in.—Arm glue blocks
1 pc. 1¾ x 3 x 66 in.—Front seat rail
1 pc. 1¾ x 3 x 62½ in.—Rear seat rail
2 pcs. 1¾ x 3 x 23 in.—Side seat rails
2 pcs. 1¾ x 3 x 19½ in.—Center seat rails
1 pc. 1¾ x 3 x 66 in.—Top rail for back
1 pc. 1¾ x 3 x 62½ in.—Lower rail for back
2 pcs. 1¾ x 3 x 22⅝ in.—Side rails for back
2 pcs. 1¾ x 3 x 16¾ in.—Center rails for back
56 pcs. ¾ x 1¾ x 20⅜ in.—Side back and seat slats
28 pcs. ¾ x 1¾ x 21¼ in.—Center back and seat slats
105 yds. 2-in. canvas webbing—Seat and back covering

### TABLE-AND-BENCH SET (table)

2 pcs. 1¼ x 1¾ x 44¾ in.—Top side rails
2 pcs. 1¼ x 1¾ x 25½ in.—Top end rails
20 pcs. ¾ x 1¾ x 43¼ in.—Slats
4 pcs. 1¾ x 3⅝ x 25⅜ in.—Legs
2 pcs. 1¾ x 3⅝ x 18-1/16 in.—Leg rails
1 pc. 1¾ x 3¼ x 35¼ in.—Brace

### (Material per bench)

2 pcs. 1¼ x 1¾ x 44¾ in.—Top side rails
2 pcs. 1¼ x 1¾ x 11¾ in.—Top end rails
9 pcs. ¾ x 1¾ x 43¼ in.—Slats
4 pcs. 1¾ x 3 x 11¾ in.—Legs
2 pcs. 1¾ x 3 x 11½ in.—Leg rails
1 pc. 1¾ x 2½ x 35¾ in.—Brace

# ..Suitcase Picnic Bench

Have you ever packed a picnic basket and hurried off to the park only to find all the tables and benches taken? Such a situation will be of little concern when you have your own picnic table packed away in a compact "suitcase" measuring only 4½ x 14 x 36 in. It's small enough to fit nicely in the car and light enough to carry easily. Set up, the unit provides a 28 x 36-in. table flanked by two attached benches. The whole thing is designed so that the benches nest in the two halves of the table top. Regular card-table leg braces are used on the benches to permit the legs to fold flat inside the bench tops. Wooden links pivot the benches to the table, and strap webbing provides check straps to keep the bench tops level with table.—John Bergen, Chicago

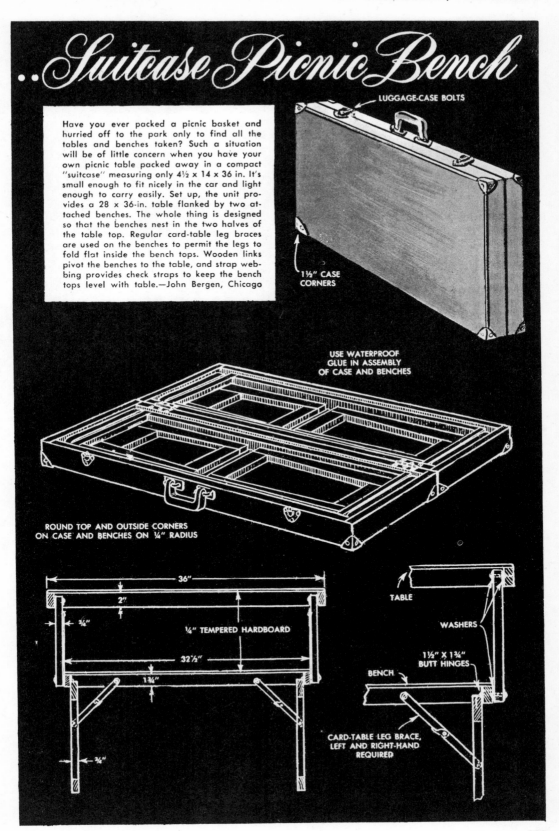

LUGGAGE-CASE BOLTS

1½" CASE CORNERS

USE WATERPROOF GLUE IN ASSEMBLY OF CASE AND BENCHES

ROUND TOP AND OUTSIDE CORNERS ON CASE AND BENCHES ON ¼" RADIUS

36"

2"

¾"

¼" TEMPERED HARDBOARD

32½"

1¾"

¾"

TABLE

WASHERS

1½" X 1¾" BUTT HINGES

BENCH

CARD-TABLE LEG BRACE, LEFT AND RIGHT-HAND REQUIRED

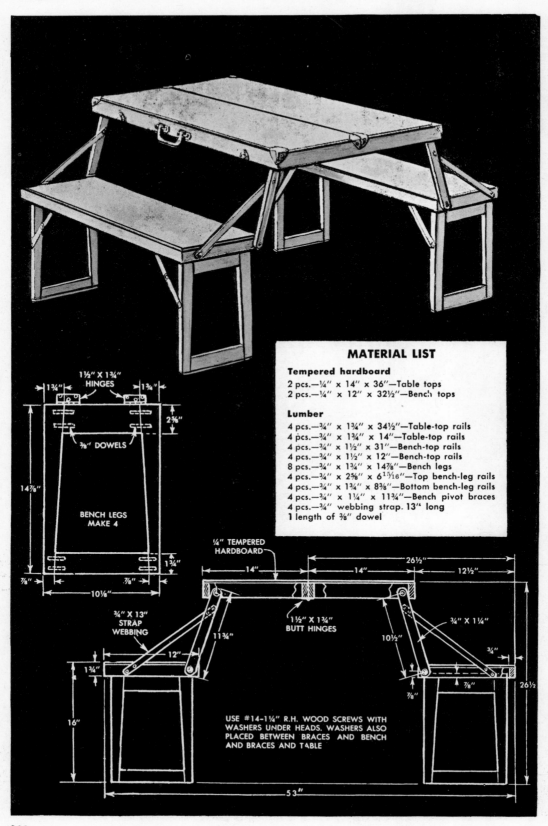

**MATERIAL LIST**

**Tempered hardboard**
2 pcs.—¼″ x 14″ x 36″—Table tops
2 pcs.—¼″ x 12″ x 32½″—Bench tops

**Lumber**
4 pcs.—¾″ x 1¾″ x 34½″—Table-top rails
4 pcs.—¾″ x 1¾″ x 14″—Table-top rails
4 pcs.—¾″ x 1½″ x 31″—Bench-top rails
4 pcs.—¾″ x 1½″ x 12″—Bench-top rails
8 pcs.—¾″ x 1¾″ x 14⅞″—Bench legs
4 pcs.—¾″ x 2⅝″ x 6¹⁵⁄₁₆″—Top bench-leg rails
4 pcs.—¾″ x 1¾″ x 8⅜″—Bottom bench-leg rails
4 pcs.—¾″ x 1¼″ x 11¾″—Bench pivot braces
4 pcs.—¾″ webbing strap. 13″ long
1 length of ⅜″ dowel

1½″ X 1¾″ HINGES

1¾″  1¾″

2⅝″

⅜″ DOWELS

14⅞″

BENCH LEGS MAKE 4

1¾″

⅞″  ⅞″

10⅛″

¼″ TEMPERED HARDBOARD

26½″

14″  14″  12½″

¾″ X 13″ STRAP WEBBING

1½″ X 1¾″ BUTT HINGES

¾″ X 1¼″

11¾″

12″

10½″

¾″

1¾″

⅞″  ⅞″

26½

16″

USE #14-1¼″ R.H. WOOD SCREWS WITH WASHERS UNDER HEADS. WASHERS ALSO PLACED BETWEEN BRACES AND BENCH AND BRACES AND TABLE

53″

# COURT LAYOUTS

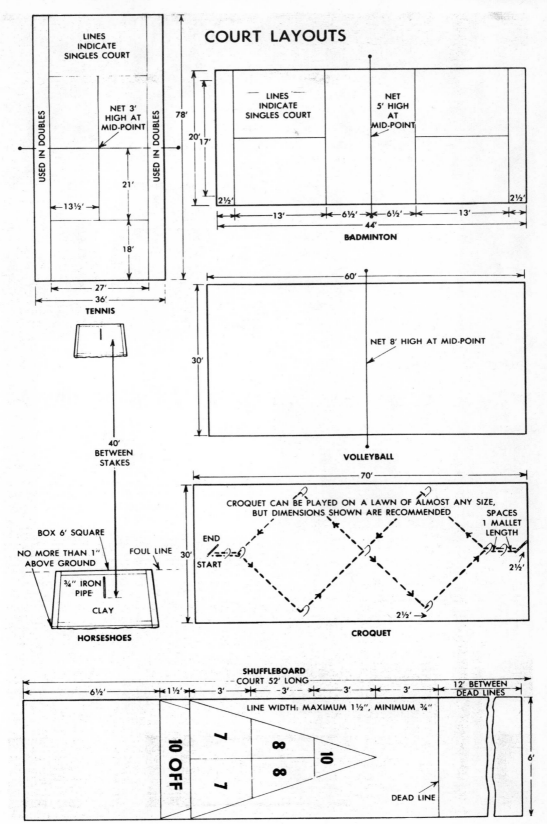

**TENNIS**

LINES INDICATE SINGLES COURT

NET 3' HIGH AT MID-POINT

USED IN DOUBLES

USED IN DOUBLES

78'

21'

18'

13½'

27'

36'

**BADMINTON**

LINES INDICATE SINGLES COURT

NET 5' HIGH AT MID-POINT

20' 17'

2½'

13'

6½'

6½'

13'

44'

2½'

**VOLLEYBALL**

60'

30'

NET 8' HIGH AT MID-POINT

**HORSESHOES**

40' BETWEEN STAKES

BOX 6' SQUARE

NO MORE THAN 1" ABOVE GROUND

FOUL LINE

¾" IRON PIPE

CLAY

**CROQUET**

70'

30'

CROQUET CAN BE PLAYED ON A LAWN OF ALMOST ANY SIZE, BUT DIMENSIONS SHOWN ARE RECOMMENDED

SPACES 1 MALLET LENGTH

END
START

2½'

2½'

**SHUFFLEBOARD**

COURT 52' LONG

6½'

1½'

3'

3'

3'

3'

12' BETWEEN DEAD LINES

LINE WIDTH: MAXIMUM 1½", MINIMUM ¾"

10 OFF

7

7

8

8

10

DEAD LINE

6'

# Expanded Garage Houses Second Car and Boat

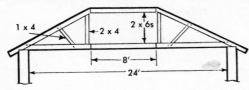

IF A WIDER late-model car is crowding your one-car garage; if you need room for a second car, or simply require more storage space, then do as Everett Hedgcock of East Peoria, Ill., did and expand the garage. First step is to pour a new footing level with the old. The roof is shored up and separated at the ridge. Front and side walls then are pulled down, the loose half of the roof being supported on the back wall and shores, and new walls are built on the new footings. The free half of the roof now is moved to position on the new walls. In the original job, 2 x 4 rafters were spaced on 2-ft. centers as were the roof beams. A 2 x 6 was spiked to each rafter, and lengths of 2 x 4s joined them to the separated roof sections. Between the roof sections a length of 2 x 6 was positioned horizontally. The result is a sort of truss. An advantage of this type of construction is that an 8-ft.-wide deck is formed between the roof halves. Using a "haymow type" door at the front of the garage permits this deck to be used for storage of a boat. A doubled 2 x 8 header, set on edge and even with the top course of blocks, is used across the door opening to support the end truss.

# GARAGE ENLARGING

NEW CARS and old garages just don't go together. Whether the rear bumper extends an inch or a foot beyond the wall line, the problem is essentially the same—how to gain the extra space needed to close the doors. In some cases, the doors will close but the short length of the building leaves no room for walking around the car to the side door. Easing into such a restricted space without knocking out the rear wall of the building is an added inconvenience, especially when the car is used every day.

There are several ways of stretching an old garage so that new car will fit in it with room to spare. The method used will depend on the construction of the building, the type of doors used, and the amount of room needed. If, for example, the doors swing outward and it happens that the car bumper extends only 3 or 4 in., building out the door jambs, as in Fig. 1, will give the required space. To do this, the doors are removed and two 2 x 4s are spiked or bolted to the sides and across the top of the doorframe directly over the trim boards, as shown in the detail. This arrangement gives the maximum space. Provide a wide sheet-metal drip cap across the top to prevent leakage. Then paint all the new woodwork and rehang the doors. It may be necessary or desirable to build out the ramp

to close an open space under the doors. When an overhead door has been installed or where the doors are of the folding type that rolls on an overhead track along the inside of one wall, about the same amount of space can be gained at the rear wall of the building by using the methods shown in Figs. 2 and 4. Where still more room is required, the lean-to structure detailed in Fig. 3 is the most practical solution. This is built high enough to clear the car hood. Use of waterproof plywood sheathing and flooring simplifies and speeds up this job.

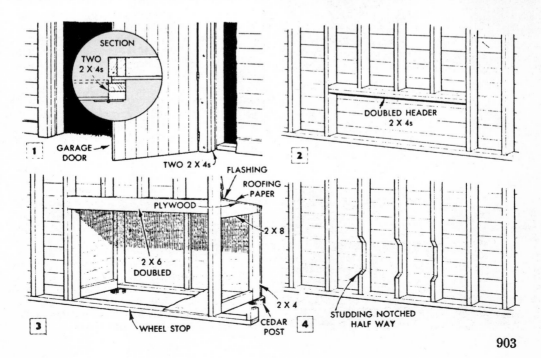

**HANGING PLANTER** is coconut half-shell with bottle cap over drain hole drilled in bottom

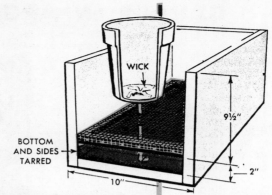

**SELF-WATERING PLANTER** made by nailing hardware cloth to cleats inside box and tarring bottom. Wick nailed to bottom and inserted in pot carries water to plants by capillary action

# Gardening

**SUB-IRRIGATED PLANTER** is assembled with marine glue and screws. Inner surfaces are coated with tar to seal the joints

**WATER PISTOL** is handy for spraying insecticide on undersides of plant leaves. Thoroughly rinse inside of pistol with water immediately after using

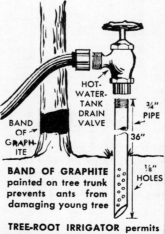

**BAND OF GRAPHITE** painted on tree trunk prevents ants from damaging young tree

**TREE-ROOT IRRIGATOR** permits watering of root system for fast growth. It is made of galvanized steel pipe, coupling and hot-water tank drain valve

**FLOWERPOT** placed on coffee can for painting, can be rotated without touching pot for fast smudge-free paint job

904

**PARCEL-SIZE RURAL MAILBOX** mounted on post in garden provides convenient storage for frequently used garden tools

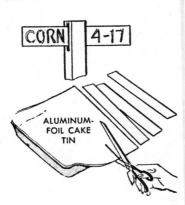

**PERMANENT PLANT MARKERS** can be made by cutting strips from aluminum pan of type used for frozen foods. Plant names and dates planted are lettered on with ball-point pen

CORN 4-17

ALUMINUM-FOIL CAKE TIN

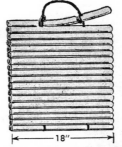

18"

**LENGTHS OF GARDEN HOSE** strung on heavy cord make soft kneeling pad for garden use. Lengths are held in place by tying loops around end pieces

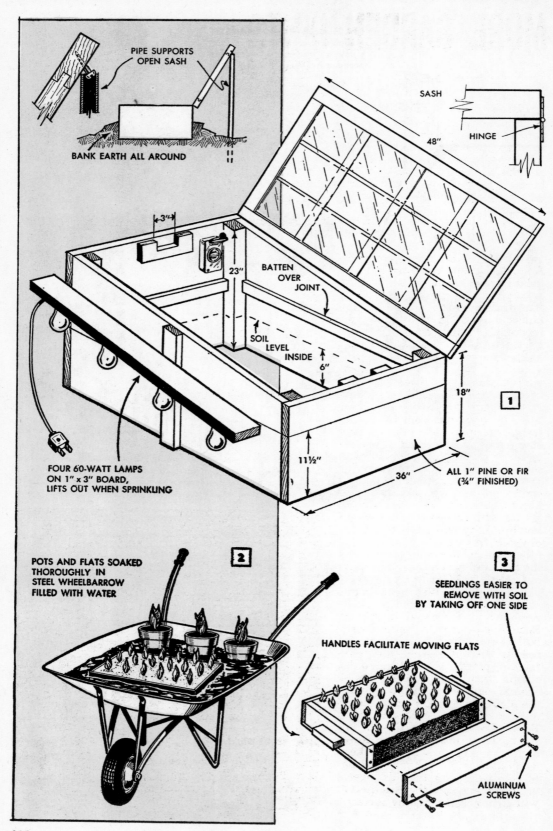

PIPE SUPPORTS OPEN SASH

BANK EARTH ALL AROUND

SASH

HINGE

48"

3"

23"

BATTEN OVER JOINT

SOIL LEVEL INSIDE

6"

18"

11½"

36"

ALL 1" PINE OR FIR (¾" FINISHED)

FOUR 60-WATT LAMPS ON 1" x 3" BOARD, LIFTS OUT WHEN SPRINKLING

**1**

**2**

POTS AND FLATS SOAKED THOROUGHLY IN STEEL WHEELBARROW FILLED WITH WATER

**3**

SEEDLINGS EASIER TO REMOVE WITH SOIL BY TAKING OFF ONE SIDE

HANDLES FACILITATE MOVING FLATS

ALUMINUM SCREWS

# MORE GARDEN HINTS

### By Hi Sibley

SPRING IS THE TIME not only for planning a garden, but for getting a head start with seedlings so your "crops" are ready for the table weeks ahead of time. It also is time to consider how to keep birds away from the newly planted seedlings, and how to support plants, such as tomatoes, when they are full of heavy, ripe fruit.

For growing young plants from seed, a cold frame, Fig. 1, is the answer if you have enough room. A stock window sash, available at most lumber dealers, is hinged to a box built of creosoted lumber. An underground cable brings house current to a weathertight receptacle which furnishes electricity to a "lift out" board that holds four 60-watt lamps to provide heat on chilly nights and sunless days. The weather-tight receptacle is closed when plants in the frame are sprinkled.

If you have no room for a cold frame, wooden flats, Fig. 3, and clay pots can be located in a basement or utility room for starting seedlings. It is best to give the seedlings a good soaking once a week, rather than a daily sprinkling. This is true especially in homes with forced-air heat where low humidity will cause fast evaporation. A metal wheelbarrow filled with water will permit giving flats and pots a thorough soaking, Fig. 2. Whether you make your own flats or buy them, fix one side of each unit so that it can be removed as indicated in Fig. 3. Each seedling, with its necessary ball of soil, then can be removed readily. After setting out each tomato plant, drive three laths, strung with heavy cord, Fig. 4, around each one for support when the plant is mature. Pole beans require a fence of cord and laths, Fig. 5. For all plants, tin-can lids strung as indicated in the lower detail in Fig. 5 will help keep away hungry birds. Every whisper of wind will blow the lids together noisily and spin them so the sun will glitter on their shiny surfaces.

★ ★ ★

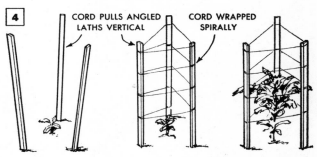

**4** | CORD PULLS ANGLED LATHS VERTICAL | CORD WRAPPED SPIRALLY

Supports shown above for tomato plants require only a few laths and some heavy cord. The same materials are used for a "fence" on which pole beans can grow. Lids saved from food tins are strung in pairs to frighten away hungry birds

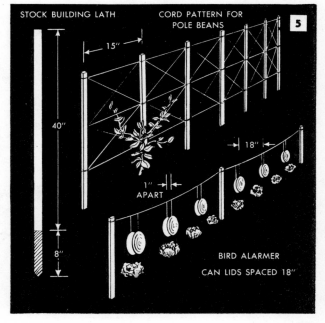

STOCK BUILDING LATH | CORD PATTERN FOR POLE BEANS | **5**

15"

40"

1" APART

18"

8"

BIRD ALARMER
CAN LIDS SPACED 18"

# TOOLS FOR YOUR YARD AND GARDEN

## GARDEN TOOLS YOU SHOULD OWN

**Power Mowers**
Rotary or reel, both save work. Reel shears, makes smooth lawn; rotary cuts weeds, tough grass

**Wide Trowel**
Helpful for taking up and planting larger bulbs, potted plants. Proper handle is very important

**Round-Point Shovel**
Helpful for digging in hard or clay soils. Blade should be made of tough and tempered steel

**Hand Cultivator**
Lightweight, about 18 inches long, for close work in weeding and tilling soil around plants

**Spading Fork**
Sharp tines penetrate soil easily; more efficient than spade except in soils that are sandy

**Weed Knife**
Also called dandelion knife. Blade slides under plant crown to remove weeds or wild grass

**Rakes**
Garden rakes spread fertilizer, soil. Lawn rakes need flexible teeth that won't harm roots

**Hose**
Larger diameter moves water faster. Some plastic hose sensitive to sunrays, temperature

**Narrow Trowel**
Makes rows for seeds, small holes for small plants; can be used as weeder in flower beds

**Sprinklers**
Consider water pressure, land contour, soil type. New lawns, some flowers require fine spray

## EQUIPMENT YOU CAN RENT OR SHARE

**Lawn Roller**
Helps you maintain a smooth lawn, levels frost upheavals, improves germination, rooting

**Wheelbarrow**
For heavy duty hauling jobs around yard. Usually has more capacity than a garden cart

**Aerator**
Permits moisture, air, nutrients to penetrate soil freely by making soil porous and loose

**Lawn Spreader**
Distributes commercial fertilizer, grass seed or top dressing on lawn quickly and accurately

**Power Tiller**
Prepares soil for lawn seeding or gardening. Pulverizes old plants and soil into fine mulch

**Pressure Sprayer**
Holds several gallons of spray to control weeds, insects and plant diseases in your yard

**Lawn Sweeper**
Removes sticks, stones before mowing, stands grass shoots up for even cut, gathers clippings

**Hedge Trimmer**
Cuts woody growth, controls shape and size of shrubs. Also trims grass missed by mower

**Garden Cart**
Moves small loads of soil, sand or fertilizer. Dip front down and scoop leaves into hopper

**Pruners**
Cut back stems of tender flowers as well as tree branches. Long pole type is for tree tops

# SUB-SURFACE IRRIGATION FOR FLOWER BED

### By Lee G. Braunstein

FOR A TIMESAVING method of watering a flower bed without puddling the surface soil, excavate the bed to the required depth and bury lengths of eaves trough and fittings in the inverted position in it as illustrated. A depth of 1 ft. is about right for perennials; 6 to 8 in. for annuals. The irrigator units also serve to aerate the soil, and make an easy job of applying plant food. The latter is simply poured into the open rain pipe extending aboveground at the head of each row and carried directly to the plant roots by flushing the pipe with a garden hose.

When preparing a flower bed for this type of irrigation, excavate it 1 in. deeper than required if the soil is heavy. Then spread a 1-in. layer of sand on the bottom before assembling the eaves trough and fittings in the bed, as indicated in the drawing below. The strip of screening on which each irrigator unit is placed prevents the earth from filling the trough. Do not omit it. The rain-pipe length on each unit should extend from the drop-outlet section to 1 in. above grade level of a completed bed. Irrigator units may be assembled from galvanized or aluminum parts, but do not mix metals in the same installation. To do so would create an electrolytic situation, resulting in rapid destruction of one of the metals.

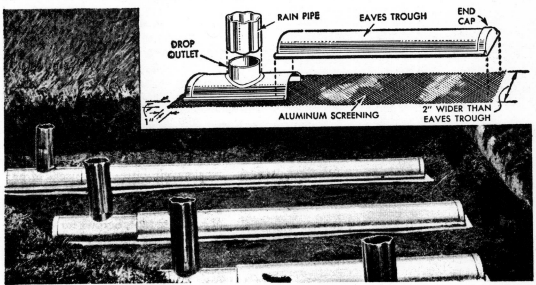

RAIN PIPE     EAVES TROUGH     END CAP

DROP OUTLET

ALUMINUM SCREENING

2" WIDER THAN EAVES TROUGH

1"

# *Better* WATERING

## *By* ROBERT STAHLER

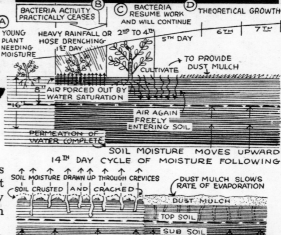

Most gardeners agree that generous flooding several times a week or a light sprinkling almost every evening is very harmful to sturdy growth of many common plants and grasses.

Now for some of the reasons why: First look over Fig. 1, which charts a cycle of theoretical growth from one heavy hosing or rainfall to another, with added details on capillary rise and consumption of moisture. Growing on the outer reaches of the smaller feeding roots of the plant are myriads of tubular, microscopically fine root hairs, Fig. 3. These root hairs take up moisture by a process which agrono-

ROOT SPREAD IS EQUAL TO PLANT HEIGHT

WATER-FORCED TO HIGHEST GROWTH

SEEDLING

SAME ROOT YEARS LATER

FEEDING ROOT

WATER-CONVEYING ROOTS IN THIS AREA

HARD CAP.

HAIRS DYING OFF

TIP END OF FEEDER ROOT WITH ROOT HAIRS ENLARGED

FEEDING ROOTS AND THEIR ROOT HAIRS ARE FOUND IN THIS AREA

③

SECTION OF SOIL GREATLY ENLARGED

ROOTLET ROOT HAIR

mists call osmosis. Applied to plant growth, this is the absorption through a thin membrane of a lighter liquid into a heavier one. Thus is moisture, the lighter liquid, drawn through the thin walls of the root hairs by the sugary sap (the heavier liquid) which they contain. A few hours after a drenching rain, try squeezing a handful of wet soil. Not a drop of water will come forth, because the water now surrounds the soil particles in microscopically thin films, and the humus (decayed vegetable and animal matter) is now minute reservoirs which will release their stored moisture to the plants as needed. Feeding roots receive moisture from distances several feet away from the tip ends. This is due to capillary movement of water and to osmosis. Capillary movement is the movement of water from soil particles to other particles and on to others which have lost part of their moisture. This is the reason plants thrive in a comparatively dry soil.

In the section B, Fig. 1, the soil air, vitally necessary to the roots and as a means of escape for the foul gases formed by decaying vegetation, is forced out of the soil by rainfall or hosing, but is soon entering again and bacteria resume activity. As the top soil gradually loses moisture, the roots grow longer and curve downward for moisture now coming up to them by capillary movement, which brings with it plant food washed into low levels by winter and spring rains. In the last section, Fig. 1, notice the abrupt upsweep of theoretical growth. This is due not wholly to the re-

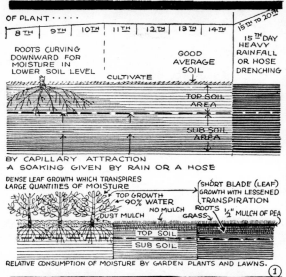

RELATIVE CONSUMPTION OF MOISTURE BY GARDEN PLANTS AND LAWNS. ①

So, contrasting the two cycles, the following method of watering appears to be best: A heavy soaking (2 to 3 in. of water applied to the garden or lawn) at 10-day to 3-week intervals governed by temperature, texture of soil, and water-holding ability. Then cultivate immediately when top soil is sufficiently dry, with one or more cultivations before the next soaking. In time, density of growth makes impossible further cultivation. So, after the final one, some gardeners apply a 1-in. mulch of peat. This mulch applied to freshly cultivated soil will act as a cushion, preventing hard rains from packing the soil, and permitting air to pass in, and foul gases to escape. Naturally, the mulch will obviate the need of frequent waterings and also lessen the danger of foliage diseases.

There are also certain plants which have special, seasonal water requirements. For example, you should keep peonies well watered throughout August for this is the season that new eyes are formed. Immediately after flowering, the foliage of early spring bulbs such as tulips, hyacinths, etc., continue to grow, and store within the bulb next season's foliage and bloom.

Many evergreens have no true dormant season, and are likely to be in active growth in fall and early winter. Thus they may winter-kill if these seasons are dry. Fig. 4 shows how to water tall-growing ornamentals such as shrubs and evergreens. As there are few feeding roots inside the spread of the foliage, Fig. 3, the area outside should be watered as shown in Fig. 4. In all cases, ground soaking is the best method, for it directs the water where needed without waste and reduces chances of foliage diseases.

freshing benefits of the applied moisture, but is the result of bacteria—those working in the dryer soil levels above the roots where they have been making available plant food, which was washed into the immediate vicinity of the roots and rapidly taken up by them. Occurring in uncounted numbers in each tablespoonful of rich garden soil, these bacteria, which are single-cell micro-organisms, break down complex compounds into simple elements and render them as food available to plant life. Were it not for their work, the soil would become lifeless and unproductive.

Now suppose you were to keep your garden and lawn top soil soaked during this theoretical 14-day cycle. As a result the soil would be without air, to the detriment of aerobic (air-loving) bacteria and much of the root system of the plants would perish, while the sparse remainder would function too close to the soil surface. The soil would become sour, full of poisonous gases, and the plant foliage would take on a sickly, yellowish-green color.

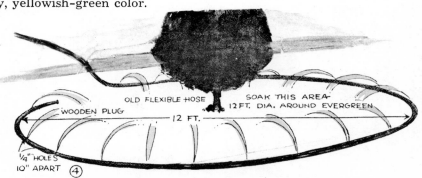

# "Overcoats" for Tender Shrubs

Pole fence on the windward side protects the taller-growing shrubs from severely cold winds

Pieces of corrugated cardboard cut from packing boxes and nailed to stakes make a good windbreak

For low-growing shrubs a combination windbreak and sunshade can be made from burlap and stakes

Sunshades made by tying long grass or cornstalks in bundles and supporting them with a frame

# Shrubs

Most high and low-growing shrubs exposed to winter winds and reflected sunlight need additional protection

MANY valuable shrubs, plants and small ornamental trees require some protection from cold winds and drifting snows if they are to survive the winter without damage. Species which are hardy in protected locations during average winters will often winterkill when fully exposed to cold winds for long periods. Others suffer from freezing and thawing of the bark when exposed alternately to bright sunlight in daytime and the cold of long winter nights. Some plants, particularly evergreens, which are located close to white walls that reflect the sunlight on the foliage while the roots are still frozen in the ground, often suffer from "winter-burn," which dries and withers foliage and twigs.

Single shrubs may be protected by driving stakes around the plant and covering these with burlap as in Fig. 3. The purpose of the burlap "fence" is not to keep out the cold, but to keep the temperature more nearly uniform. Tender shrubs, such as English boxwood, need this protection in the colder climates. Sheets of cardboard cut from large packing cartons and arranged about the plants as in Fig. 2 make a good windbreak or a sunshade when necessary. Other materials suitable for making windbreaks are coarse straw, tall grass and dry cornstalks. Small trees may be wrapped with a thick covering of tough grass, Fig. 6, or a long windbreak may be made by using posts and supporting strips to hold the material in place as in Fig. 4.

Low ornamental trees can be wrapped with burlap and the top pruned back to such an extent that it also can be covered with a protecting layer of the same material, Fig. 5. Heavy paper may be used for this purpose, but it must be tied securely in place. When wrapping shrubs, be careful not to break the tender twigs or stems.

Rustic pole fences, Fig. 1, snow fences or latticed frameworks make good two or three-sided windbreaks. Where a low shrub planting covers considerable area, an open board fence along the windward side will offer some protection and also will help to drift protective snow over the planting. Often a pole fence, such as that in Fig. 1, along one side of a hedge or other planting will be sufficient protection. A thin coating of dry straw spread uniformly and held down with light woven wire or poultry netting makes a good covering for hedges or other low growth which require protection from wind and cold. In some locations a sunshade is more important than a covering or even a windbreak. This is especially true on the south side of a white wall or on any southern slope or exposure where heat from the midday sun raises the temperature above freezing for several hours during the day. Evergreens of most varieties never become entirely dormant; some growth takes place the year 'round. After a dry fall water evergreens before the ground freezes. If soil around the roots freezes "dry" the plant is very apt to suffer.

Spring bulbs should be taken from the ground in fall and potted for forcing. Pot them about the second or third week in October and store in cold frames so they remain dormant until removed in January

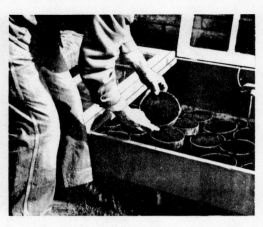

In January the potted spring bulbs are removed from the cold frames and taken indoors or into a hothouse to artificially induce them to start their spring growth. Bulbs treated this way will bloom in March

# *Winter Insurance for Your Garden*

*Given a little assistance, your flowers will winter well, bloom early.*

Dead leaves and grass clippings can be made into valuable mulch by treating them with commercial compost-producing preparations

ABOUT THE MIDDLE OF OCTOBER is the time to dig up and pot spring bulbs if you want to force them for early blooming. Store the potted plants in cold frames until January, then move them indoors or into a hothouse. They will bloom in March. Annual plants should be dug up before the first frost, potted and taken indoors. Replant them outside in spring. To assure vigorous peony bushes, prune the stalks down to within a few inches of the ground in fall. Cover the root area with several inches of mulch, such as peat moss, composted material or a blanket of straw 2 or 3 in. thick.

Annuals that would be destroyed by winter weather should be taken out of the ground before the first frost and placed in pots. The plants will grow all winter indoors and then can be replanted outdoors

Peony bushes have fresh growth every spring and the old stalks must be cut down to provide room for the new growth. Prune the old stalks down to within a few inches of the ground as shown in the photograph

Requiring especially good care if they are to last through the winter are rosebushes. To protect these plants, pile soil around the roots and about halfway up the main stem of the plant. Rosebushes are not pruned in the fall, but in the early spring

To make sure that the dirt piled around the rosebush does not thaw, once it has frozen, straw or hay is piled over the dirt to insulate it. This is done after the ground has frozen thoroughly. Straw also is piled around the rosebush to protect it

 *Trees and shrubs, although hardier than flowers, also require protection.*

Freezing does not hurt most plants, rather it protects them. Alternate thawing and freezing is what does the damage, breaking the roots and sometimes heaving the plants above ground level. Insulation by mulching, therefore, is required. Pile soil about 8 in. high around a rosebush, then completely surround the bush with straw. Some trees, such as figs, are unusually sensitive and should be wrapped completely with waterproof paper, as well as having their roots protected with a heavy layer of mulch. Soft trees, such as rose trees, should be wrapped in straw or hay of the type that has long strands, which provides a "blanket" around the tree. Older trees are hardy enough to go through a winter with no assistance, but young trees, because their roots are close to the surface, can be killed by freezing. For this reason, the roots should be insulated with mulch.

Fig trees and some dwarf fruit trees are extremely sensitive to weather extremes and must be wrapped completely in waterproof paper and the roots well mulched

Soft trees, such as rose trees, should be wrapped completely in straw or hay that has long strands, permitting it to be tied around the tree like a blanket. The straw protects the tree against winter weather and early buds against the spring frosts

Roots of young trees should be protected against the damage that can be caused by alternate thawing and freezing, which may break them or heave them out of the ground. Insulate around the root area with a layer of mulch after the ground has frozen

Winterizing treatment for a lawn begins late in the fall with the application of fertilizer and lime, distributed evenly over the lawn with a spreader

Next operation after fertilizer and lime are spread on lawn is to aerate it with one of a number of devices to assure that air and food reach grass roots

After the entire lawn has been aerated thoroughly, spread a top-dressing, such as peat humus, over it

*"Scalp treatment" for lawn readies it for winter.*

Preparation of your lawn in the fall will have much to do with its health the following spring. The first step in winterizing a lawn is to spread fertilizer and lime, making sure the materials are evenly distributed. A spreader designed for this purpose will give the best results. After the fertilizer has been spread, aerate the lawn with a spiked disk, plate or roller to assure that both air and food reach the grass roots. After aerating the lawn, apply a top-dressing; peat humus is excellent. A month after the top-dressing has been applied, sweep the lawn thoroughly to remove any debris. Mechanical sweepers, mounted on wheels and fitted with rotating brushes make this job a simple one, but an ordinary straw broom will do just as well, although requiring more time. The lawn now is ready for winter. To further guarantee a healthy lawn, there is a precaution to take during the winter. If possible, avoid piling snow very high on a lawn when cleaning walks and drives. The weight of banked snow seems to encourage "snow mold," which often causes large areas of grass to turn brown and die. ★ ★ ★

About a month after applying the top-dressing, sweep the lawn to remove debris. Mechanical sweeper pictured makes this job a simple one

# PLANT PROTECTORS

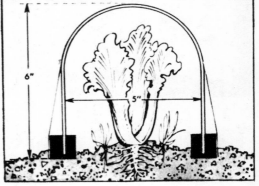

TO PROTECT newly germinated sweet corn from predatory birds, and to prevent frost damage to seedlings, cover them with fabricated plastic protectors as illustrated. Made in 6-ft. lengths, the lightweight units are easy to store and use since they nest when stacked and in use are simply placed on the ground over the row of plants. Each unit consists of two 6-ft. lengths of 1 x 1-in. wood strips drilled to take U-shaped frames formed from clothes-hanger wire. The stringers are spaced 5 in. apart, the wire frames about 6 in. Next, plastic-coated fabric or wire mesh, such as is used for covering a storm door, porch enclosure, or window openings, is stretched over the frames and tacked to the stringers. In a warm climate, where protection from only predatory birds is needed, window screening may be used instead.

Strips of aluminum foil do a good job of keeping birds away from ripening raspberries when hung on a line stretched over the bushes between stakes as shown at the right. Strips 1½ x 9 in. are cut from heavyweight aluminum foil and are threaded on a length of heavy cord. Spaced about 1 ft. apart, the strips are kept apart by tying knots in the cord on both sides of them. They should be crimped so that the wind will make them flutter and sparkle in the sun.—Hi Sibley, Nuevo, Calif.

# "Picture Frame" Gate

## By Hi Sibley

THIS DECORATIVE "picture frame" gate will make any yard more attractive. It is practical as well as beautiful. Children and pets are kept inside the yard, wandering stray dogs are kept out. Crimson roses climbing the trellis around the gate give it added beauty.

Four 78-in. lengths of 2 x 3 stock are used as corner posts for the gate, the lower ends being set in concrete. These lower ends are creosoted or treated with wood preservative before being centered in holes dug to the shape indicated. When concrete is poured into these holes, it is "keyed" into the ground when it hardens, assuring that the posts will not loosen easily. To further assure solid anchoring of the posts, drive a number of nails into the lower ends as indicated, so the posts are "locked" into the concrete. The top arches of the trellis frame, and of the gate halves, are sawed in three segments, then screwed together as indicated. The lower ends of the trellis arches, and the corner posts, are half-lapped. To keep out smaller animals, the lower section of each gate half is latticed horizontally with lengths of flat steel, that also offer protection against damage by toddlers' wheeled vehicles.

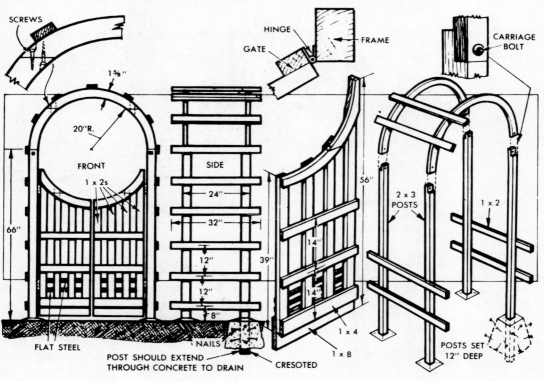

1

"Sasheen" Ribbon photo

*Gift wrapping as the experts do it is neat and conservative, and often symbolizes the occasion or the hobby, vocation or personality of the recipient*

# SECRETS OF ATTRACTIVE PACKAGES

IT'S THE GIFT that counts, of course, but it's the wrapping that makes the first impression and sets the stage for lively anticipation. Two important factors to keep in mind when gift wrapping are neatness and simplicity of design. It is better to be "awfully simple than simply awful." Notice in the examples given that the

**Creasing the paper at the edges squares the wrapping**

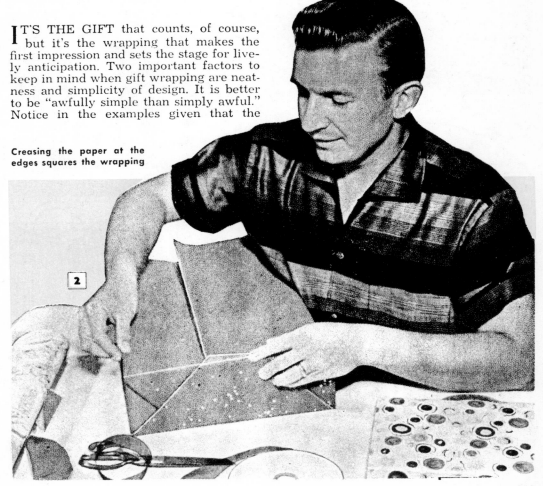

2

919

**3**

designer depends on the paper for coloring and not on ribbon decoration. Also notice that mostly metallic papers are used, their plain colors being highlighted by simple decorations of ribbon bows or practical, useful objects peculiar to the occasion, or to the personality, hobby or vocation of the recipient.

Figs. 3, 12, 14 and 15 are good examples of wrappings designed for the occasion. In Fig. 3, Dad's birthday gift is wrapped with paper in a conservative color. A little ribbon decoration and lettering done with cigarettes completes the package. For a bridal shower or wedding-anniversary gift of silverware, three pieces of silverware stitched to the wrapping and augmented with a ribbon bow definitely key the gift package to the occasion.

What could be more appropriate for a baby-shower gift than a stork decoration as in Fig. 12? The stork is shaped from a

**Above, silverware gift personalized by using three pieces as decoration. DAD spelled with cigarettes**

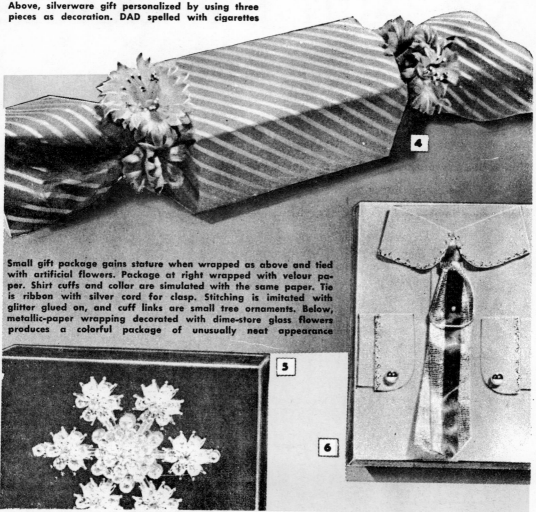

**4**

**5**

**6**

Small gift package gains stature when wrapped as above and tied with artificial flowers. Package at right wrapped with velour paper. Shirt cuffs and collar are simulated with the same paper. Tie is ribbon with silver cord for clasp. Stitching is imitated with glitter glued on, and cuff links are small tree ornaments. Below, metallic-paper wrapping decorated with dime-store glass flowers produces a colorful package of unusually neat appearance large safety pin. Bits of stiff ribbon through the eye of the pin simulate wings; a round toothpick takes care of the beak from which is hung the paper diaper carrying a tiny doll or the name card.

A wrapping symbolic of his hobby or vocation will tickle the vanity of any man. Such a wrapping is not intended to give an inkling as to what's inside nor represent the gift itself. Examples given in Figs. 1, 6, 8 and 10 should start you off. The "candy cane" saw decoration pictured in Fig. 1 is ideal for the handyman. It is a keyhole saw wrapped in red paper and then wound spirally with narrow white ribbon. A ribbon poinsettia adds the floral effect.

**Tree decoration at right formed with Hawaiian lei glued on and ornamented with small tree ornaments and silver cord with star at top. Below, artificial fishing fly symbolizes recipient's hobby. Hook should be shielded**

7

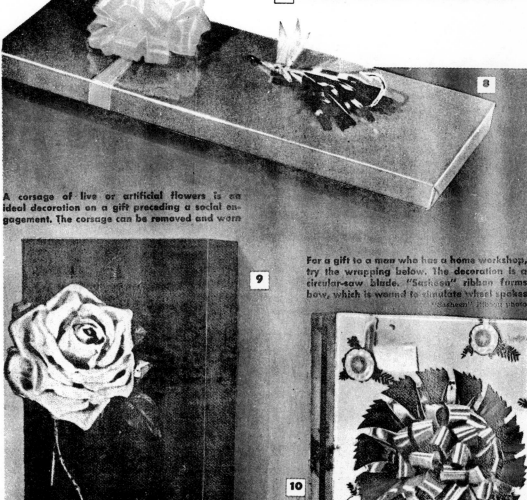

8

**A corsage of live or artificial flowers is an ideal decoration on a gift preceding a social engagement. The corsage can be removed and worn**

9

**For a gift to a man who has a home workshop, try the wrapping below. The decoration is a circular-saw blade. "Sasheen" ribbon forms bow, which is wound to simulate wheel spokes**

*"Sasheen" Ribbon photo*

10

Metallic paper, a Santa Claus head and a wide ribbon band combine to produce the neat, attractive wrapping above. What could be more appropriate for the baby-shower gift than the stork decoration at the right? The stork is bent from a safety pin, wings are stiff ribbon and the beak a round toothpick. Paper diaper holds a tiny doll

Aleen's Floral Supply photo

Packages above show what can be done with colorful paper and simple decorations. Left-end package is decorated with Puffed Wheat and ribbon, while the one at the right end is done with Styrofoam and artificial leaves. Wrappings below are ideal for Christmas packages

Aleen's Floral Supply photo

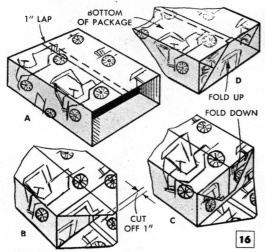

**Steps in wrapping packages to get neat square ends**

**Amount to cut off varies with different packages**

For the sport-shirt fancier, try the wrapping shown in Fig. 6, which also gives the key to the shirt inside. The package is wrapped in velour crepe paper or similar material, after which collars and cuffs are simulated with the same material and glued in place. Stitching is imitated with glitter glued on, and cuff links are tiny ornament balls glued in place. The tie is ribbon with gold cord for the clasp.

The standard, but welcome, necktie gift shown in Fig. 8 becomes more personalized when decorated with a practical symbol of the receiver's hobby—in this case a colorful fishing fly. Point of the hook should be shielded with several wrappings of cellulose tape.

Fig. 10 is a wrapping for the "Big Wheel" with a power saw in his home shop. Done in a wheel motif complete with ribbon spokes, the decoration on this package is a circular-saw blade. Cellulose tape is

folded over the saw teeth to prevent possible injury.

Your "precious things come in small packages" type of gift that always seems so inconspicuous in size will increase in stature if wrapped as in Figs. 4 and 18. Paper or other artificial flowers are used as ties at the ends. Other ties suitable to the occasion may be used.

For a gift preceding a social engagement the package in Fig. 9 depicts a dual-purpose decoration. The package is wrapped in metallic paper and decorated with a corsage of live or artificial flowers, which are removed and worn by the recipient.

When wrapping Christmas gifts it is hard to beat the simplicity and good taste of the wrappings shown in Figs. 7, 11, 14 and 15, and the right and left-hand packages of Fig. 13. The white tree, Fig. 7, is shaped with a Hawaiian lei glued in place

**This method of wrapping makes small package larger**

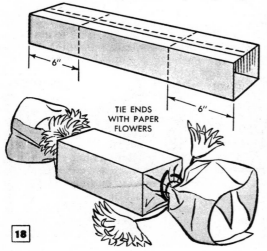

TIE ENDS WITH PAPER FLOWERS

**Using folded strip of wrapping paper as name card**

Word NOEL spelled out on base-metal trays. Metal is available at most hobby shops. Letters are outlined with glue, then sprinkled with glitter. Ribbon streamers complete this unusual wrapping

Aleen's Floral Supply photo

and ornamented with small tree ornaments, silver cord and a small gold star. In Fig. 11, a Santa head and white ribbon contrast with a blue metallic paper to produce a neat effect. Notice in Fig. 19 how a folded strip of the paper serves as the name card.

The two Christmas packages of Fig. 13 are very easy to wrap. The snowman is made of Puffed Wheat kernels and decorated with a marshmallow hat and red cinna-mon-candy buttons. Arms, ear muffs and hat top are chenille, all glued in place. The lantern dec oration in the right-hand detail is shaped from half-round pieces of Styrofoam, sprayed with gold glitter and completed with dime-store leaves and ribbon. Candle flame is a piece of red chenille.

Notice in the two center wrappings of Fig. 13 how simple ribbon decorations relieve the lines of striped paper.

Fig. 14 shows what can be done with gold metallic paper, Styrofoam eggs, gold cord, sequins and evergreen sprigs. The eggs are shaped to resemble tree ornaments, colored and then decorated with pearl-headed pins and sequins.

Green metallic paper, artificial snow and small pine cones are combined to produce the wrapping in Fig. 15. The green-fern effect is achieved by using a flattened fern as a stencil and spraying the snow over it.

The word NOEL is spelled out on the package in Fig. 20 on base metal, obtainable from hobby shops. The metal is formed into trays. Each letter is first drawn on a tray with glue, then sprinkled with glitter and the surplus shaken off, allowing a little to adhere to the wrapping paper. Trays and ribbon are glued to the wrapping.

When designing a gift wrapping remember the plainer the paper the more elaborate the decoration may be, and the busier the design the more conservative must be the decoration. But no matter how well the design is worked out, the whole effect will be lost if the package is not wrapped neatly.

Fig. 16 shows one method of wrapping. First, size the wrapping carefully to the package, allowing 1 in. overlap in width, and letting the ends project an amount equal to the thickness of the package plus ¼ in. Then proceed as indicated by steps A, B, C, D, cutting off one flap as in Fig. 17.

The wrapping method illustrated in Fig. 21 shows how to fold a wrapping without cutting the ends, but requires accuracy to produce a neat package.

After folding and securing one end of the wrapping, creasing the edges as in Fig. 2, especially on metallic papers, squares the package for neater appearance. ★ ★ ★

Steps in wrapping gift without cutting the ends of the paper

# RIBBON BOWS

YOU PROBABLY HAVE been delighted, at one time or another, to receive a gift-wrapped package that was made especially attractive by having one or more ribbon bows on it. Quite likely you wished that you, too, could tie such bows, but hesitated to try because they seemed so intricate. As with many things that seem complicated, the bows actually are fairly easy to make. They do require time and patience, and not all the first few attempts will be completely satisfactory, but you soon will find yourself proficient enough to be able to place fancy bows on all the packages you gift wrap.

In Fig. 1 is shown the step-by-step method of making a "magic" bow. First, a length of ribbon is formed into a fairly large loop. Second, the loop is flattened in such a manner that the loose end of the ribbon is even with the end of the flattened loop. The third step requires the flattened loop to be folded in half and a diagonal cut made across each corner at the fold. A narrow ribbon or cord then is tied around the resulting V-notches when the ribbon is unfolded, as shown in the fourth step. The ribbon is refolded, and the open loops are pulled through each other for the fifth step. The pulled-through loops then are shaped with your hands and positioned to result in the flower-like bow shown in the sixth step in Fig. 1.

The French bow in Fig. 2 is formed by "piling" a number of loops one on top of the other, then tying the loops at the center with the loose ends of the ribbon. The resulting pattern of loops is pulled out to form the bow as shown in the right-hand detail. The elongated bow, shown below in Fig. 2 is started in the same manner as the French bow, but some of the loops of the bow are cut so there are a number of loose ends. The dahlia bow, lower, right-hand detail, Fig. 2 also is formed in the same way as the French bow. Then all the loops are cut diagonally at their centers to provide a leaflike appearance.

The tailored bow at the top of Fig. 3 is formed much like the French bow, with loops being piled one on the other, but each succeeding loop is made slightly shorter than the preceding one. The free ends of the ribbon are spread out as shown and the bow tied at the center with a small

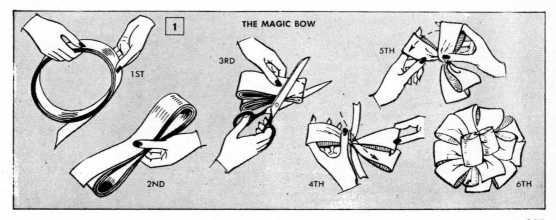

1   THE MAGIC BOW

1ST   2ND   3RD   4TH   5TH   6TH

TAILORED BOW

CARNATION BOW

DAISY BOW

TWO-IN-ONE BOW

INFORMAL BOW

ribbon, or with a cord. The latter is available with strands of silver, gold and other colors woven into it, so it adds to the attractiveness of the bow. The carnation bow in Fig. 3 is started like the magic bow in **Fig. 1.** After the loops are pulled through each other they are grasped in the hand and cut with the scissors to simulate the petals of a carnation. For the daisy bow, fairly wide ribbon is used. The bow is started by piling a number of loops, which then are tied at the center. The loops are pulled through each other and the finished bow is held at the center by a thumbtack or a small hatpin. The latter is best when attaching the bow to a package. As shown in the detail, the two-in-one bow is simply a flattened roll of ribbon that then is folded off-center and cut across the corners to form V-notches, as for the magic bow. Being off-center, the notches, when tied, cause the bow to have one end longer than the other. The loops of this bow also can be pulled apart for a different effect. Tying the informal bow starts by looping the ribbon around your thumb. Loops then are formed as shown. The bow can be left loose and fastened to a package with cellulose tape, or the ends of the ribbon can be pulled through the loop formed on the thumb, and the bow tied firmly.

After you have tied a number of the bows shown here, you might design some of your own. Using two different colors of ribbon for one bow is one method of modifying the designs shown. Bows of the same type tied with narrow ribbon will appear to be different when tied with wide ribbon. Using both wide and narrow ribbon, as well as two colors also makes for different appearance.

The bows presented here were reproduced from an instruction sheet issued by Minnesota Mining and Mfg. Co. ★ ★ ★

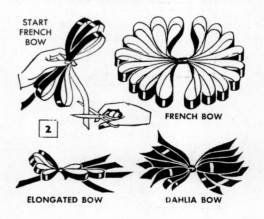

START FRENCH BOW

FRENCH BOW

ELONGATED BOW

DAHLIA BOW

# *Easier Way To Install*
# GLASS-BLOCK
# "WINDOWS"

HOMEOWNERS planning to install small decorative glass-block panels in an exterior wall will be happy to know that the manufacturers of structural glass block have developed a simplified method of installation which eliminates the need of expansion strips and wall ties. Instead, an asphalt emulsion is used, and an expansion space is allowed above the top row of blocks as in the upper detail. The opening must be framed in the same way as for a double-hung window, with adequate lintel support at the head, and it should be not more than 5 ft. wide or 7 ft. high, including a maximum of 25 sq. ft. The first step is to brush a heavy coat of asphalt emulsion onto the wooden frame, applying it in a strip about 3½ in. wide across the sill, lower detail, and up the jambs, center detail. The blocks are laid up in ¼-in.-thick mortar joints consisting of portland cement, 1 part, hydrated lime (high-calcium type), 1 part, and graded plastering sand, 4 to 6 parts. Trowel the joints neatly and, when finished, scrub the panel to remove all excess mortar. Scrape out any loose mortar from the expansion space at the head and finally run a line of calking completely around the opening.

Apply a heavy coating of asphalt emulsion to the sills and jambs. The coating should be at least 3½ in. wide

Above, lay the blocks in mortar joints troweled to a uniform thickness of ¼ in. Below, run a line of calking compound all around the completed panel

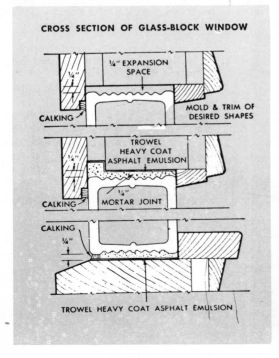

CROSS SECTION OF GLASS-BLOCK WINDOW

¼" EXPANSION SPACE

¼"

MOLD & TRIM OF DESIRED SHAPES

CALKING

TROWEL HEAVY COAT ASPHALT EMULSION

¼"

CALKING

¼" MORTAR JOINT

CALKING

¼"

TROWEL HEAVY COAT ASPHALT EMULSION

# DRILLING AND

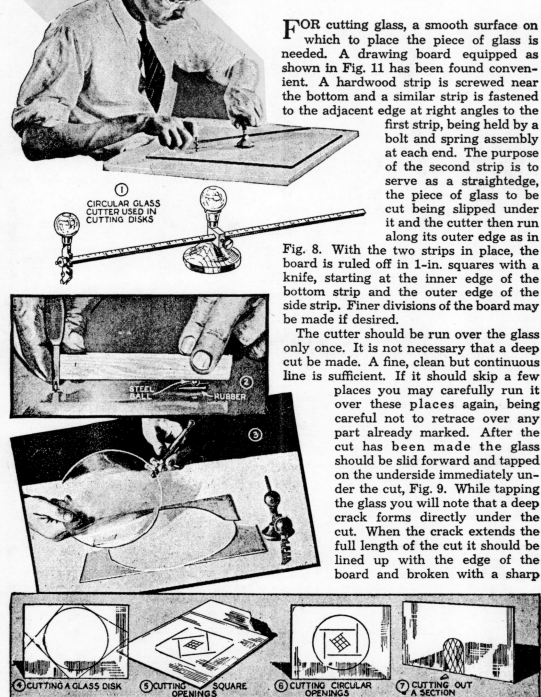

① CIRCULAR GLASS CUTTER USED IN CUTTING DISKS

② STEEL BALL — RUBBER

③

FOR cutting glass, a smooth surface on which to place the piece of glass is needed. A drawing board equipped as shown in Fig. 11 has been found convenient. A hardwood strip is screwed near the bottom and a similar strip is fastened to the adjacent edge at right angles to the first strip, being held by a bolt and spring assembly at each end. The purpose of the second strip is to serve as a straightedge, the piece of glass to be cut being slipped under it and the cutter then run along its outer edge as in Fig. 8. With the two strips in place, the board is ruled off in 1-in. squares with a knife, starting at the inner edge of the bottom strip and the outer edge of the side strip. Finer divisions of the board may be made if desired.

The cutter should be run over the glass only once. It is not necessary that a deep cut be made. A fine, clean but continuous line is sufficient. If it should skip a few places you may carefully run it over these places again, being careful not to retrace over any part already marked. After the cut has been made the glass should be slid forward and tapped on the underside immediately under the cut, Fig. 9. While tapping the glass you will note that a deep crack forms directly under the cut. When the crack extends the full length of the cut it should be lined up with the edge of the board and broken with a sharp

④ CUTTING A GLASS DISK  ⑤ CUTTING SQUARE OPENINGS  ⑥ CUTTING CIRCULAR OPENINGS  ⑦ CUTTING OUT A SECTION

# CUTTING GLASS

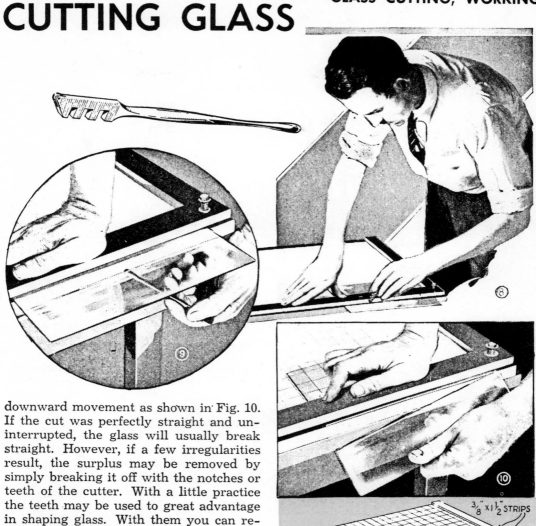

downward movement as shown in Fig. 10. If the cut was perfectly straight and uninterrupted, the glass will usually break straight. However, if a few irregularities result, the surplus may be removed by simply breaking it off with the notches or teeth of the cutter. With a little practice the teeth may be used to great advantage in shaping glass. With them you can remove very small pieces without cracking the piece.

After some experience in straight glass cutting you will get the feel of the cutter and become used to the characteristics of glass. You will then be able to tackle successfully the cutting of round and irregularly shaped pieces. Round pieces of glass are cut with a circle cutter shown in Fig. 1. This cutter is mounted on a rotating arm which pivots in the center of a heavy base. When a cutter of this type is not available, a makeshift arrangement which will do the job can be improvised from a regular cutter, a short square stick, a steel ball and a small piece of rubber or tape as in Fig. 2. The cutter is held to the end of the stick by means of a tack, one of the notches being slipped under the tack head. Mark the desired radius of the

cut on the stick, measuring from the cutter wheel to a point where the stick is placed on the ball. With a hammer sink the ball some distance into the wood and then lay the stick and ball on the piece of rubber, which will prevent the ball from slipping out of position. After the glass is cut it is turned over and tapped under the cut until a crack forms all the way around. Next, straight cuts are made in the glass as in Fig. 4, and the corners are

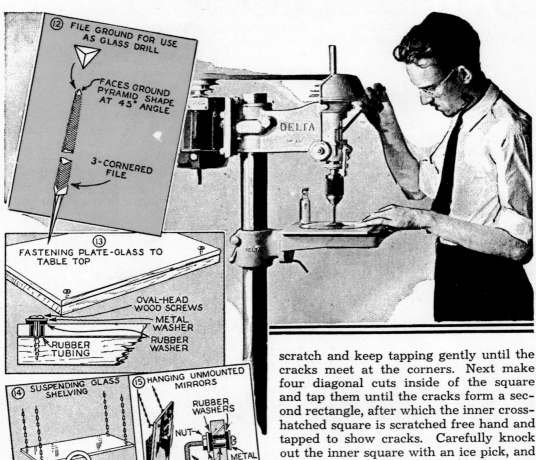

⑫ FILE GROUND FOR USE AS GLASS DRILL

FACES GROUND PYRAMID SHAPE AT 45° ANGLE

3-CORNERED FILE

⑬ FASTENING PLATE-GLASS TO TABLE TOP

OVAL-HEAD WOOD SCREWS
METAL WASHER
RUBBER TUBING
RUBBER WASHER

⑭ SUSPENDING GLASS SHELVING

⑮ HANGING UNMOUNTED MIRRORS

RUBBER WASHERS

NUT

METAL WASHERS

MACHINE SCREW
RUBBER TUBING

SCREW-EYE
RUBBER WASHERS
METAL WASHERS

broken away exactly as in straight cutting, leaving the disk as in Fig. 3. Ovals and irregular shapes are cut out by scratching around a pattern made from ¼-in. plywood. In making irregular cuts, as much surplus glass as possible should be removed by straight cutting after the design has been scratched into the glass and a complete crack produced by tapping.

The cutting of rectangular and circular openings in glass is more difficult and requires more patience than straight cutting. It is important that only very small pieces of glass be removed at a time. Cutting rectangular openings, Fig. 5, is done as follows: First scratch the edges of the opening to be made, not marking all the way to the corners. Then tap the glass to start a crack at the center of each

scratch and keep tapping gently until the cracks meet at the corners. Next make four diagonal cuts inside of the square and tap them until the cracks form a second rectangle, after which the inner cross-hatched square is scratched free hand and tapped to show cracks. Carefully knock out the inner square with an ice pick, and then remove the second rectangle, after which the remaining pieces of glass are broken away to complete the rectangular opening desired. The edges of the opening may be made smooth by light stroking with a coarse file, after which an emery stone is used for finishing. The procedure for cutting circular openings, Fig. 6, is practically the same except that a circular cut is made first. Cutting out a section of glass as in Fig. 7 is done by first scratching the arc and the straight lines, after which the inside part of the section is scratched diagonally. Cracks are then produced by tapping and the small pieces are broken out one by one.

Holes may be drilled in glass with a drill made by grinding the blunt end of a triangular file to a pyramid shape as shown in Fig. 12. The location of the hole to be drilled should be surrounded with a dam of putty. The dam is filled with turpentine to lubricate the drill, which may be rotated either in a drillpress or with an ordinary bit brace, using only a slight pressure. When the drill starts to break through, the glass should be turned over and the hole completed from the other side, very carefully, of course, to prevent breakage. If a piece of clean white paper is placed under the glass while drilling, it will be spotted by the turpentine as soon as the tip of the drill breaks through, thus warning you of the necessity of turning over the glass. Like other operations with glass, a perfectly smooth wood surface should be used as a support.

Figs. 13, 14 and 15 show methods of mounting glass. If resilient rubber mountings are not used, expansion and contraction of the glass with changes in temperature will cause breakage. These methods of mounting also make the glass less likely to break under shock and vibration.

Glass may be ground smooth on a grindstone or fine emery wheel if the work is done slowly so as to avoid chipping and heating. In all operations on glass, it is important that the glass be kept from getting hot as it will break when unevenly heated. Coarse files may be used for smoothing up rough edges, if light pressure is used in quick sweeping strokes. This treatment is the most rapid method of producing a smooth edge; however, a wet grindstone is the best tool for producing a fine finish. Ground glass may be produced by rubbing the surface of glass with water and coarse emery powder on a rag or piece of leather.

## Electrically Heated Wire Will Cut Glass Tubing

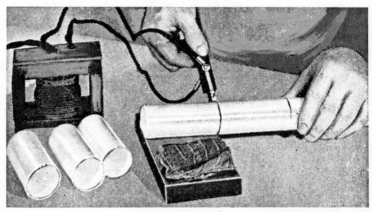

With a cutter like the one diagrammed at the right, which consists of a loop of electrically heated Nichrome wire fitted to a plierlike holder of hardwood or plastic, you can cut a number of lengths of glass tubing quickly. The resistance wire is taken from an electric iron, coil heater or a similar appliance. Power is supplied by a 6-volt storage battery or a toy transformer of 10-ampere capacity. In use, the loop is slipped over the tubing and pressed firmly against the glass at the point at which it is desired to make the cut, then current is applied for 4 or 5 seconds, after which the tube is touched to a wet cloth, causing it to break because of the sudden change in temperature. When using this device always remember, however, prolonged contact with the hot wire will cause the glass to melt, rendering it useless.

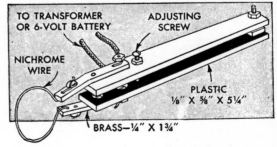

TO TRANSFORMER OR 6-VOLT BATTERY

ADJUSTING SCREW

NICHROME WIRE

PLASTIC ⅛" X ⅝" X 5¼"

BRASS—¼" X 1¾"

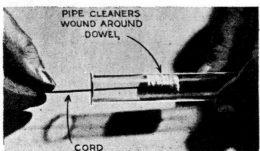

PIPE CLEANERS WOUND AROUND DOWEL

CORD

## Easy Method of Cleaning Tubes

Cleaning the inside of a long glass tube is not difficult if the following method is adopted: Select a short piece of dowel that will fit inside the tubing loosely, and drill it lengthwise so that a long cord can be attached. Wind the dowel with one or two pipe cleaners, and then pull it through the tube by means of the cord.

# MOLDED CONTOURS
## STREAMLINE YOUR PROJECTS

**In boat, trailer and sidewalk-car construction contour work pleases the eye and adds strength to the structure. Here's a simple method of contouring with glass fiber, resin and metal lath**

### By Harold Humphrey

USING GLASS-FIBER CLOTH, ordinary metal lath and resin plastics you can build up almost any desired contour and combine it with flat structural materials such as plywood, hardboard and sheet metals. Usually the finished job owes its professional appearance to the three-dimensional corners, the trailer body illustrated being a typical example. In any type of body construction you'll need to plan in advance the location of the contour work and make the necessary allowances in framing the project. It's regular practice to frame the job, apply the covering of plywood, hardboard or sheet metal and leave the corners open for later application of the contouring.

In this step the procedure is quite simple and you have a choice of several methods of application. The first, used where the nature of the assembly and type of materials will permit, is to apply metal lath to

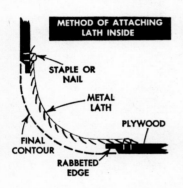

METHOD OF ATTACHING LATH INSIDE

STAPLE OR NAIL
METAL LATH
PLYWOOD
FINAL CONTOUR
RABBETED EDGE

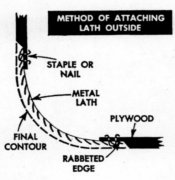

METHOD OF ATTACHING LATH OUTSIDE

STAPLE OR NAIL
METAL LATH
PLYWOOD
FINAL CONTOUR
RABBETED EDGE

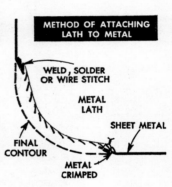

METHOD OF ATTACHING LATH TO METAL

WELD, SOLDER OR WIRE STITCH
METAL LATH
SHEET METAL
FINAL CONTOUR
METAL CRIMPED

After forming metal lath to desired contour and nailing or stapling in place, next step is to apply brush coat of resin plastic over lath to uniform thickness

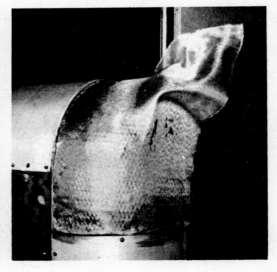

Before plastic brush coat hardens, apply glass-fiber fabric and smooth out in all directions to remove any wrinkles. Trim away any excess with scissors

the inside of the curve as in the left-hand detail below. Note that the metal lath is stapled or nailed to the inside face of the flat material. Also that the edges of the covering material are rabbeted to take the plastic. The method forms a tight, waterproof joint that won't shake loose. The center detail shows the metal lath nailed or stapled in a wide rabbet on the outside of

the covering material. This method permits applying the metal lath and plastic from the outside of the body. The third method shows how metal lath is attached to a sheet-metal covering. Here a plastic of the metal-bonding type must be used.

The photos below, left to right, show the step-by-step procedure in building up a typical contoured corner. The metal lath,

Apply a final brush coat over glass-fiber fabric taking special care to brush on plastic mix to a uniform thickness. Work plastic right up to edges all around

Final step in building up contour is applying trowel coat of resin plastic. This is mixed to consistency of light grease so that it is easily worked with trowel

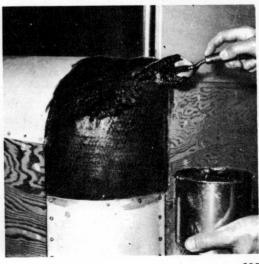

Spread glass-fiber fabric on a flat surface, the garage floor will do, mark size and cut with scissors

available from any building materials dealer, can be cut easily with tinsnips and can be shaped to three dimensional curves by hand. When attaching and shaping the lath keep in mind that it will be covered with at least 1/8 in. of plastic when the job is finished to the final contour. Check the contours carefully before finally nailing or stapling the formed lath in place.

Polyester resins of the type that will bond readily to wood or hardboard, also glass-fiber fabrics are readily available in kit form for covering boat hulls. Or, the resin can be bought by the quart or gallon and the fabric by the yard. The resin comes as a syrup-like liquid and requires the addition of a liquid hardener. For application to the metal lath the mixture must be thickened to a grease-like consistency by the addition of a small amount of powdered asbestos. When mixing resin plastic and hardener follow the instructions.

As the next step brush the mixed material onto the metal lath and before it dries apply the glass fabric and stretch to remove all wrinkles. Trim off the excess at the edges of the opening with scissors. Now coat the fabric with the same plastic mix-

ture, brushing from the center outward to the edges. Allow to harden.

Finally, finish with the trowel coat, which is mixed to a somewhat heavier consistency and laid on with a trowel or wide putty knife. Apply as uniformly as possible, building the material slightly higher than the final contour, then while wet add a second layer of glass fabric. Work out wrinkles and pull the coarse-meshed fabric into the soft trowel coat until it is below the surface. Now smooth the job by hand, taking care to work the surface to a true curvature. Wipe excess material off your hands occasionally with a cloth moistened with acetone. Don't permit the resin to dry on the hands. When applying metal-bonding plastic wear rubber gloves. Trim away any excess glass cloth with scissors and allow the job to dry about 24 hr.

After drying, the trowel coat is worked down to final contour and the curves feathered, or faired, neatly into the flat surface of the covering. This is done with a rasp and sandpaper, working with an eye to true contours and a smooth surface. Any imperfections will show up under the paint or enamel. ★ ★ ★

## GLUING

## Hardboard Gluing Tip

You will get a better bond when joining other parts to the hard, smooth face of hardboard if it is roughened before applying the glue. This can be done easily with a special serrated surfacer made from a wooden block and a few corrugated fasteners. The fasteners are inserted in a shallow saw kerf cut in one edge of the block. To insure a tight fit, the fasteners are bent slightly so as to apply tension against the sides of the kerf.—Bill Toman

In this doweled joint, end grain is joined to flat grain. End grain should have two coats of glue before joining. Dowel locators assure perfect alignment

A bar clamp is used to draw the joint tight after application of the glue. Care should be taken to assure a perfect fit between all meeting surfaces

A tub filled with water makes a good "clamp" for flat work such as veneering a small surface. Place a piece of plywood under the tub to distribute pressure

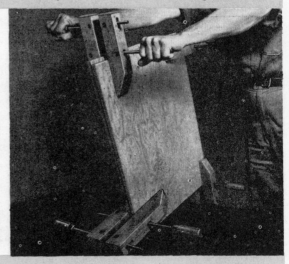

Laminating and veneering can be carried out with hand screws, using four or eight screws, depending on size of work. Adjust hand screws for uniform pressure

GLUE KNOW-HOW has been simplified by the ready-to-mix and ready-to-apply cold adhesives which eliminate heating and the temperature problem at the time of application. Liquid hide glues have supplanted the older hide glues that were supplied in the flake form and required heating for a period of time to reduce them to a usable consistency. Although the older glues were highly effective in durability and holding power, they are not so suitable for use in small manufacturing plants and home shops due to the special equipment required for preparation and application. Both the liquid hide glues and the newer resin glues, the latter having the appearance and consistency of thick cream, are especially useful in home-shop joinery. Both these glues, also the

# All About
# GLUE
# and
# GLUING

Laminating hardboard to wood is easy with the setup pictured. C-clamps should be equally spaced to distribute pressure uniformly. Wipe away excess glue

Edge clamps are large C-clamps with a sliding fixture that permits applying pressure in two directions. They are especially useful for gluing strips to edges

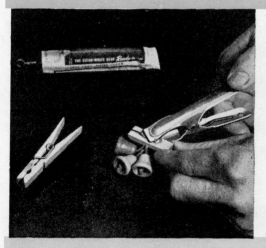

Spring clamps and clothespins of the spring type are used for joining small parts, border inlay and assembly of models. Spring clamps come in several sizes

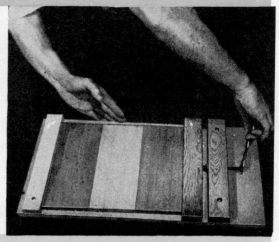

Improvised clamps for edge-gluing can substitute for bar clamps. The simple unit pictured is very effective. Bolt forces the movable jaw against the edge of work

ready-to-mix type supplied in the powder form, require only the simplest clamping equipment. All are water-resistant in the sense that holding power is affected little, if any, by ordinary dampness. When a completely waterproof glue is required, the craftsman uses a resorcinol glue supplied in a two-part container, one part of which contains a dry powder, the other a catalyst in liquid form. When the powder and liquid are mixed in accordance with instructions they form a waterproof glue of great holding power. When gluing woods which contain natural oils such as rosewood, teak, lemon and yew wood, the craftsman uses a casein glue, which comes as a powder and is mixed with water to form a fairly heavy liquid.

Edge-gluing and joint-gluing of frames and cabinet parts require not only the use of the correct glue, but a careful trial fitting of the parts to insure full contact over the whole area of the meeting surfaces. When edge-gluing a number of strips to form a wide panel, the edges of the strips must be jointed true, either by machine or by hand-planing. Craftsmen make a trial assembly of cabinet frames before applying glue to the joints. This will assure a perfect fit of the parts when they are glued and clamped. When gluing cabinet-frame members where end grain is joined to flat grain, it is important to apply two coats of glue to the end grain. Allow the first coat to become tacky, then apply a second coat and join. When joining flat grain, as in edge-to-edge work, the important thing is to apply the glue in a uniform coating. This can be done

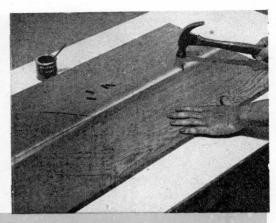

Bar clamps, or carpenter's clamps, are best for edge-gluing a number of strips to form a wide panel or top. Note spacing and alternate position of center clamp

On work where exposed metal is not objectionable, corrugated fasteners are suitable "clamps" for edge-gluing. Usually they are driven into both sides of joint

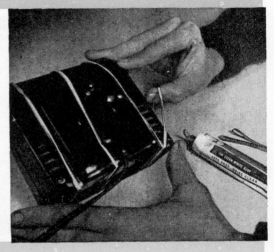

A self-adjusting miter clamp is handy in the home shop. You can make one like this in a few minutes. Note how two members are drawn tight with C-clamp

Ordinary rubber bands of various sizes are just the thing where it is necessary to apply a light, uniform pressure when gluing or cementing small parts

For certain clamping operations requiring light pressure, cellulose tape is useful. Simply spread glue on joining faces, locate parts and wrap with tape

Craftsmen often improvise bar clamps when building or repairing chairs. This simple, two-part clamp is especially effective for this type of parts assembly

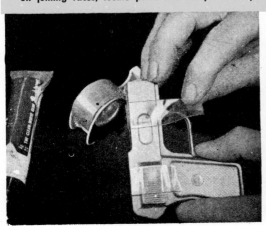

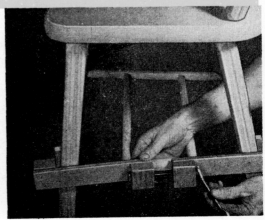

For repairing a single chair, twisted cords can be used to apply pressure until glue sets. Cord clamp is quickly improvised from a length of clothesline

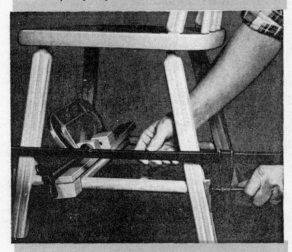

In some cases, chair assembly can be speeded up by applying pressure in two directions simultaneously. Here three bar clamps will be placed at right angles

When the amount of work to be done justifies its purchase, the band clamp is best for chair work. Here the lower assembly is clamped in one operation

with a thin wooden paddle, a brush, or best of all, a glue applicator of the roller type. This applicator operates in a manner similar to a wheel-type paint striper.

Beginning with the two right-hand photos on page 935, various methods of clamping are pictured. Correct application of the clamps and the amount of pressure applied are the two most important points about clamping. Bar clamps, C-clamps and wooden hand screws, or adjustable clamps, are the most commonly used in the small shop. Bar clamps, or carpenter's clamps, are used chiefly in edge-gluing several strips of stock, also in cabinet-frame assembly. It is important that bar clamps be located square with the work so that pressure is exerted uniformly. Also, when more than two bar clamps must be used, locate the center clamp, or clamps as the case may be, equidistant from those near the ends of the work. The upper left-hand photo on page 937 is a good example of correct bar-clamping. Note that the center clamp is placed with the bar across the opposite face of the work. This position of the third clamp helps to equalize the pressure and also prevents any tendency of the work to buckle. If the work has been cut to the finish size before clamping it will be necessary to protect the edges at the point where the metal clamp jaws engage. This is done by placing small pine blocks between the edge of the stock and the jaws, or by cementing pieces of leather to the face of the jaws. You also can improvise a good substitute for bar clamps, the clamp in the lower right-hand photo on page 936 being a good example.

C-clamps and edge clamps, upper left and upper right-hand photos on page 936, are used when it is necessary to apply pressure near the edges of the work, as in gluing on an edging strip, or in veneering. Edging clamps, upper right-hand photo, page 936, are provided with a sliding bracket, or jaw, which makes it possible to apply equal pressure in two directions. Another clamp which belongs in this classification is the simple spring clamp shown in the lower left-hand photo, page 936. This clamp works in a manner similar to pliers, the spring acting to close the pivoted jaws. Spring-type clothespins also can be used in the same manner.

Improvised miter clamps, rubber bands, cellulose tape, corrugated fasteners, "chevron type" fasteners, all these can be made to serve as clamps in certain gluing operations. In building or repairing chairs, the band clamp, lower photo at the left, is universally useful. It consists of a length of canvas or other tough fabric attached to a special fixture having a snubbing device which permits adjustment of the fabric band to any required length. ★ ★ ★

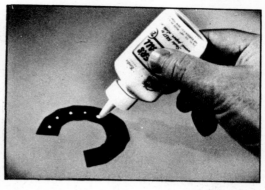

## GLUING HINTS

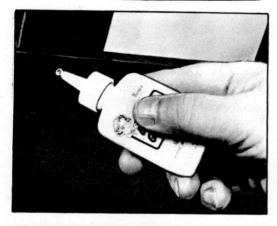

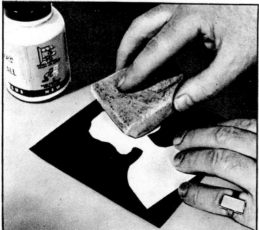

1. An easy way of attaching a letter or other insignia to a sweater is to spread white plastic glue on the back of the insignia and press it onto the garment with a warm electric iron. Either cloth or felt insignia may be attached in this manner

2. Loose crossrail of a chair can be reglued without having to pull members of the joint apart. First drill a small hole in the leg to take the tip of a plastic glue-bottle spout as shown. With the spout held firmly in the hole, squeeze the bottle to force glue into the joint, wiggling the members to get an even distribution of glue. Wipe off excess glue and fill the hole with plastic wood tinted to match

3. When gluing ungummed labels and decorations cut from thin paper, dampen them with a sponge immediately before applying the glue to assure a neat job. The moisture-expanded paper contracts as it dries, leaving a smooth, wrinkle-free appearance

4. Here is an easy way of relieving glue pressure in a dowel joint without having to cut a groove or flat surface on one side of the dowel. Wrap a length of lightweight thread around the dowel to be glued, apply glue and insert it as shown. Excess glue can flow through the spaces made by the thread which then becomes saturated and flattened. This method does not reduce contact surfaces as when a dowel is grooved or flattened, resulting in a stronger joint

Designed by John Bergen

# BUILD YOUR OWN GREENHOUSE

**F**OR THE PROPAGATION and healthy growth of plants and the production of seedlings for spring planting, there's nothing quite as effective and satisfying as a greenhouse. A separate structure, or true greenhouse, is preferable as it more nearly serves the twofold purpose of propagation and display of plants. However, a lean-to built against the house or garage, or over a basement window, offers safe growing conditions for many common seedlings, cuttings and also for the display of plants not hardened to sudden temperature changes. The one disadvantage of the lean-to type is that it is not always possible to locate it to take full advantage of light and heat from the sun.

### True Greenhouse

A separate structure like that pictured above is the choice of experienced gardeners. It offers a much better opportunity for proper management of the house during the growth period of most plants and a better utilization of available sunlight during the season. Note from the following pages that ordinary storm sashes form the glass roof and that both ends of the structure are glazed. The sashes are shown hinged at the top. If desired they also can be hinged at the lower ends. If this is done, each sash should be fitted with a storm-sash bracket so that it can be locked in the open position. The size of the structure detailed permits use of two 3'-0" x 6'-0" storm sashes on each side of the gable. When selecting these be sure there are no pronounced ripples in the glass panes. Ripples in the glass may tend to concentrate the sun's rays and damage plants.

In the sectional detail of the house, page 942, the foundations are shown without footings. In stable soils this construction is permissible. But in loose loam and in sandy or gravelly soils the foundation should be on a footing about 6 x 12 in. in sectional

Above, separate structure, or true greenhouse, is most suitable for all-around use of experienced gardener. Center, lean-to greenhouse includes a potting shed

Window greenhouse serves as starter for transplants

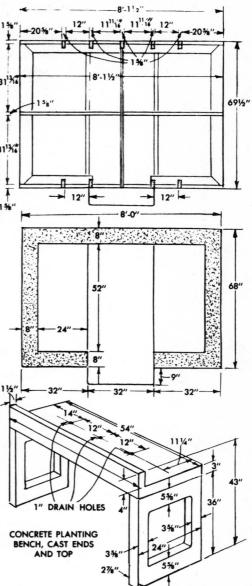

1" DRAIN HOLES

CONCRETE PLANTING BENCH, CAST ENDS AND TOP

size. The cast-concrete planting benches detailed above and on the opposite page can be omitted and planting benches constructed of cypress substituted. These can be constructed inexpensively and in considerably less time. If you do cast the benches of concrete be sure to reinforce the top either with reinforcing rods or wire mesh.

The walls can be laid up of cinder block, concrete block, or natural stone. Fill the voids in the top course of blocks with cement mortar and rubble (small stones or coarse gravel) and insert anchor bolts before the mixture hardens. The bolts provide a means of attaching the 2 x 6 plates securely to the wall. When laying the blocks be sure to bed each one in sufficient mortar

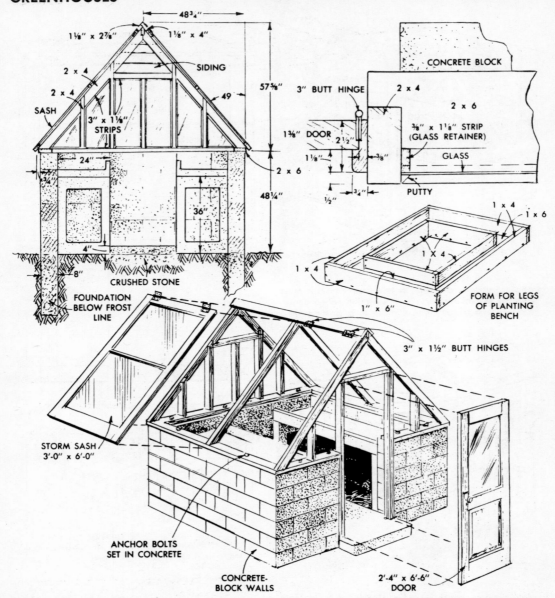

to assure watertight joints of maximum strength. Keep each course of blocks level and the corners plumb.

Cut all wooden parts of the structure to finished size, trial-fit each one, then prime with a suitable primer, making sure that the priming coat covers all surfaces, especially the end grain. Give the priming coat time to dry thoroughly, then bed the 2 x 6 plates in mortar, allow the mortar to set partially and tighten the nuts on the anchor bolts. Note that the plates are notched to take the 2 x 4 uprights that form the side jambs of the doorframe. The top jamb is end-lapped onto the upright side jambs. The sectional detail through the doorjamb shows the door hinged to swing in. This assembly can, or course, be re-versed and the door hinged to swing out, if desired. To avoid cutting triangular pieces of glass to fit over the header in the rear gable and over the top jamb above the door, these areas are covered with siding as indicated.

## Lean-to Greenhouse and Potting Shed

This unit is designed to be built against the house or garage where space is available for a southern exposure. It should not be built under a wide cornice. Sills of the structure are bolted to a concrete foundation poured to a depth well below the normal frost line. Studs, plates and rafters complete the framing ready for siding and roof boards. The concrete floor, poured over a tamped gravel fill, is an optional

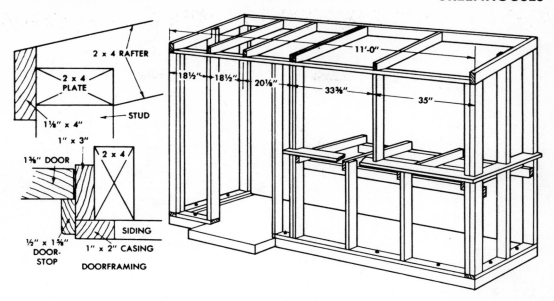

2 x 4 RAFTER

2 x 4 PLATE

STUD

1½" x 4"

1" x 3"

1⅜" DOOR

2 x 4

SIDING

½" x 1⅝" DOOR-STOP

1" x 2" CASING

DOORFRAMING

18½"    18½"    20⅛"    33⅜"    35"    11'-0"

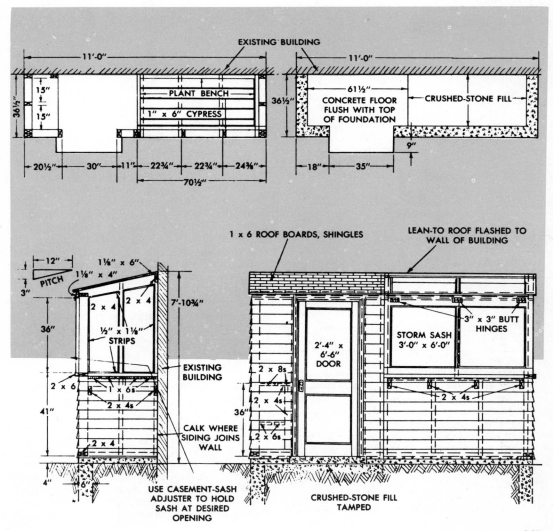

EXISTING BUILDING

11'-0"

15"

15"

36½"

PLANT BENCH

1" x 6" CYPRESS

20½"    30"    11"    22¾"    22¾"    24⅜"

70½"

11'-0"

36½"

CONCRETE FLOOR FLUSH WITH TOP OF FOUNDATION

61½"

CRUSHED-STONE FILL

18"    35"    9"

12"

PITCH

3"

1½" x 6"

1⅛" x 4"

2 x 4    2 x 4

½" x 1⅛" STRIPS

36"

2 x 6

1 x 6s

2 x 4s

41"

2 x 4

4"    6"

7'-10¾"

EXISTING BUILDING

CALK WHERE SIDING JOINS WALL

USE CASEMENT-SASH ADJUSTER TO HOLD SASH AT DESIRED OPENING

1 x 6 ROOF BOARDS, SHINGLES

LEAN-TO ROOF FLASHED TO WALL OF BUILDING

STORM SASH 3'-0" x 6'-0"

3" x 3" BUTT HINGES

2'-4" x 6'-6" DOOR

2 x 8s

2 x 4s

2 x 6s

36"

2 x 4s

CRUSHED-STONE FILL TAMPED

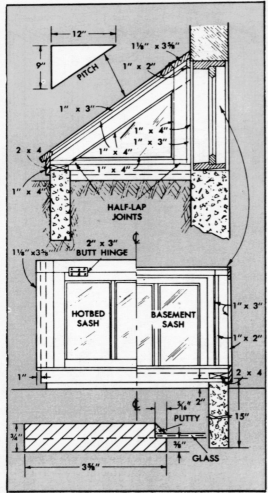

Labels in diagram:
12", 9" PITCH, 1½" x 3⅝", 1" x 2", 1" x 3", 1" x 4", 1" x 4", 1" x 3", 1" x 4", 2 x 4, 1" x 4", HALF-LAP JOINTS, 1½" x 3⅝", 2" x 3" BUTT HINGE, HOTBED SASH, BASEMENT SASH, 1" x 3", 1" x 2", 1", 2 x 4, 5/16" 2" PUTTY, 15", ¾", ⅜", GLASS, 3⅝"

feature. The greenhouse half of the structure is housed with two standard storm sashes and the end is glazed as detailed. The potting bench and plant bench can be made in any way that best suits the purpose. Cypress wood is the most durable because of its ability to resist rot.

### Window Greenhouse

For starting seedlings in flats and for advancing the growth of certain house plants which are to be reset out of doors later in the season, a window greenhouse is ideal. The details giving the construction of this unit are not fully dimensioned as certain changes may have to be made when fitting it to the basement window. Note in the construction details that the ends are shown glazed to admit the maximum amount of light. The unit should be located on the south side of the house.

### Heating

Unless used during the four seasons, the lean-to and window greenhouses will not ordinarily require heat. In an emergency a small electric heater will serve for the lean-to in the early spring and late fall months. To utilize the separate greenhouse to the fullest a reliable source of heat is necessary. In all except the more severe climates a small greenhouse usually can be adequately heated by means of lead-covered electric heating elements. ★ ★ ★

## Individual "Greenhouse" From Jug

Portable "greenhouses" for single plants can be made from 1-gal. glass jugs. To remove only the bottom yet leave the curved lower edge for extra support, use the following method: Remove the cap and place the jug in a shallow pan. Pour boiling water into the pan to a depth of ¼ in. and let the jug stand for 2 or 3 min. to heat the bottom of the jug. Remove the jug and immediately place it in another pan which contains ice water. The bottom of the jug will fracture and drop out. Because the open mouth of the jug acts as a vent, there is no problem of condensing moisture.

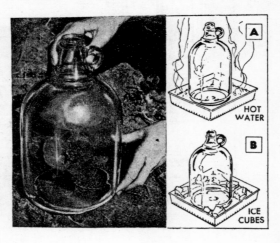

A HOT WATER
B ICE CUBES

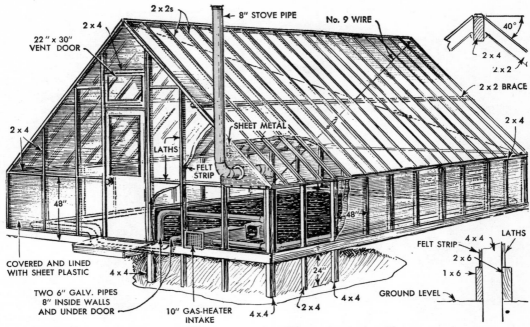

2 x 2s · 8" STOVE PIPE · No. 9 WIRE · 2 x 4 · 40° · 2 x 4 · 2 x 2
22" x 30" VENT DOOR · 2 x 2 BRACE
2 x 4 · LATHS · 2 x 4
SHEET METAL
FELT STRIP
48" · 48"
COVERED AND LINED WITH SHEET PLASTIC · 4 x 4 · 24"
TWO 6" GALV. PIPES 8" INSIDE WALLS AND UNDER DOOR · 10" GAS-HEATER INTAKE · 4 x 4 · 2 x 4 · 4 x 4 · GROUND LEVEL
FELT STRIP · 4 x 4 · LATHS · 2 x 6 · 1 x 6

# Plastic Cuts Greenhouse Costs

By H. H. Slawson

LOWER ORIGINAL construction costs plus moderate maintenance expenses, for greenhouses used by either commercial or home flower growers, are promised by innovations in a structure designed and built by horticulturists at the South Dakota Agricultural College. Polyethylene-plastic film is used in place of the glass used in conventional greenhouses. Cost of the plastic for the 18 x 40-ft. structure built at the college was 45 dollars. Material for a home-size unit would be correspondingly less costly. To construct the walls 4 x 4s were sunk in the ground every 8 ft., with 2 x 4s centered between each pair. The corner posts are 4 x 4s. Across the top of these vertical members, which project 4 ft. above the ground and extend 2 ft. into the ground, are nailed 2 x 4s. At ground level, outside the walls, are nailed 2 x 6s, while a 1 x 6 is nailed to the inside of the wall opposite each exterior member. All wood contacting the ground is treated with wood preservative. The roof of the building consists of 2 x 2 rafters fitted against a 2 x 4 ridgepole. A 2 x 2 longitudinal is positioned at right angles to the rafters on each side of the roof, and lengths of 9-ga. wire are fitted through screw eyes and tightened by turnbuckles to form an X-brace on each side of the

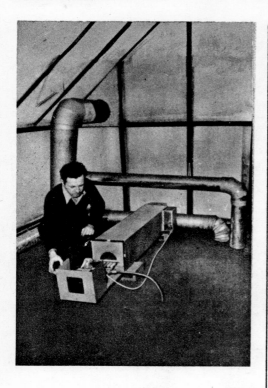

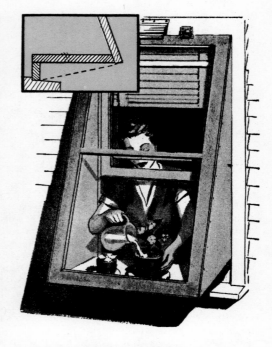

## Small Window Greenhouse Utilizes Storm Sash

A window greenhouse which utilizes the present storm sash can be built in a couple of hours and at a nominal cost. First, the storm sash should be hung on hook-and-eye hangers at the top. The bottom of the sash is extended and a platform of 1-in. stock is fitted between it and the window sill as shown. Hooks hold the platform against the sill to prevent entry from the outside. Two triangular-shaped pieces of ¾-in. exterior plywood form the sides of the greenhouse. Glue and wood screws are used throughout the assembly. Weather stripping is nailed to the window frame so it covers the opening between the top of the storm sash and the frame.

roof as indicated. Rough spots and slivers are removed or sanded before applying the sheet plastic, to minimize the chance of tearing it. The outside layer of polyethylene plastic is 3 mils (.003 in.) thick, stapled in place with laths nailed over it as added reinforcements. The inside layer of plastic is .0015 in. thick, strips of 2-in.-wide roofing felt being used rather than laths. Heat for the greenhouse is supplied by an LP gas heater, the heat being forced through metal ducts positioned 8 in. inside the walls, with the bottom duct 4 in. above the floor. The ducts run underground inside the door. A commercial version of the greenhouse has a concrete floor, with the furnace in an enclosure outside the greenhouse to conserve floor space. A home greenhouse also could have a concrete floor, with a small oil space heater to maintain temperature. The plastic deteriorates during the summer and must be replaced annually, but the college figures that, for a commercial establishment, its replacement cost is less than the cost of replacing broken glass. Also, with the continual improvement in plastics, it is quite possible that a material will be developed that will last much longer. Replacement of the plastic is made in fall, when the weather is fair. The 50-in.-wide material is lapped 3 in., for a tight, strong joint that keeps heat and humidity inside. ★ ★ ★

Birdbath is miniature greenhouse with potted plant growing inside a plastic column 12 in. in dia. Frame is aluminum

# HAND GRINDER

## *Speeds up to 25,000 r.p.m. make this tiny power tool a real shop workhorse*

WITH THE accessories available, a hand grinder can be made to do just about anything within the capacity of the motor. It can be mounted in fixtures and used as a shaper, router, vertical-spindle sander, drill press, carver, speed lathe and circular saw. Used freehand with grinding wheels of various shapes, rotary files and felt wheels, it can do any work that calls for abrading, cutting or polishing on small workpieces.

The extremely high speed of the motor and direct drive to the cutting and abrading tools results in exceptionally smooth, accurate work on both wood and metal. Free-hand sanding and rotary filing are operations that require very high speeds for acceptable accuracy and easy control of the tool. Drilling tiny holes in model parts of wood or metal calls for sustained high speeds to prevent heating and drill breakage. That's why experienced model-makers, laboratory technicians and hobbyists make wide use of hand grinders and the many accessories available. The simple **saw table detailed on the following page** converts your hand grinder into an efficient circular saw for ripping and crosscutting tiny model parts.—Edwin M. Love.

Used with rotary-file accessories of various shapes, a hand grinder in a fixture makes high-speed shaper

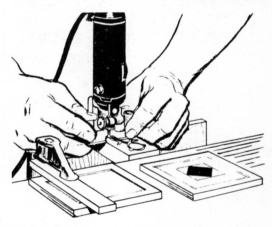

**Precision drilling is assured with this midget drill press. Handles hair-sized bits without breakage**

Above, used with veining bits, a hand grinder can't be beat as a router. Below, it's a spindle sander

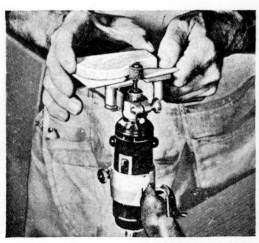

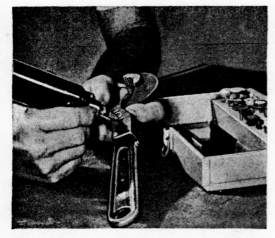

Using various sizes and types of abrasive wheels you can etch your name on tools, do light die sinking, grind small edge tools, work designs on metal or glass

Here carving is being done freehand with grinder held in a fixture. Similar work also can be done with grinder held freehand and workpiece clamped to bench

Modelmakers often have use for a midget speed lathe on which pencil-sized turnings can be made. Here's such a lathe in operation with improvised tool rest

Tiny circular saw blade is accessory for hand grinder. Make table of plywood, solid stock as in detail below, mount grinder in fixture and there you are

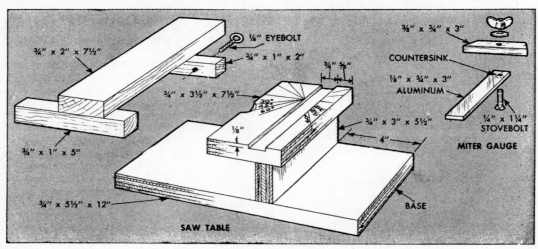

¼" EYEBOLT

¾" x 2" x 7½"

¾" x 1" x 2"

¾" x 3½" x 7½"

¾" x 1" x 5"

¾" x 5½" x 12"

⅛"

¾ ⅝"

¾" x 3" x 5½"

4"

SAW TABLE

BASE

⅜" x ¾" x 3"

COUNTERSINK

⅛" x ¾" x 3"

ALUMINUM

¼" x 1¼"
STOVEBOLT

MITER GAUGE

# GUN CLEANING

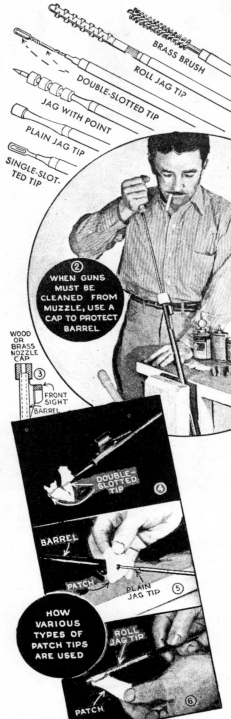

BRASS BRUSH

ROLL JAG TIP

DOUBLE-SLOTTED TIP

JAG WITH POINT

PLAIN JAG TIP

SINGLE-SLOT-TED TIP

② WHEN GUNS MUST BE CLEANED FROM MUZZLE, USE A CAP TO PROTECT BARREL

WOOD OR BRASS NOZZLE CAP

③ FRONT SIGHT BARREL

④ DOUBLE-SLOTTED TIP

BARREL

PATCH

⑤ PLAIN JAG TIP

HOW VARIOUS TYPES OF PATCH TIPS ARE USED

ROLL JAG TIP

⑥ PATCH

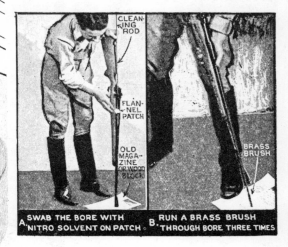

CLEANING ROD

FLANNEL PATCH

OLD MAGAZINE OR WOOD BLOCK

BRASS BRUSH

A. SWAB THE BORE WITH NITRO SOLVENT ON PATCH    B. RUN A BRASS BRUSH THROUGH BORE THREE TIMES

INCREASED accuracy, smoother shooting and longer gun life will reward the shooter who spends a little time in keeping his guns in first-class condition. Given a new gun to start with, a few minutes' cleaning time will keep it in perfect condition whereas the neglected gun becomes increasingly difficult to clean satisfactorily.

Cleaning a rifle or shotgun involves five simple operations, as shown by the photos A to E inclusive. The bore is first swabbed with a flannel patch well saturated with nitro solvent. Cleaning should be done from the breech of the barrel if possible, and the muzzle of the gun should rest on a clean magazine or a block of wood. The patch should be run up and down the bore several times to saturate the powder residue thoroughly with the solvent oil. Any brand of powder solvent available at a hardware store will do. Operation No. 2 calls for a brass brush. Running this up and down the bore will remove the sticky powder fouling partially loosened by the action of the solvent. The brush should be pushed out of the barrel on each down stroke. Reversing the direction of the brush inside the bore does nothing but ruin the brush. Next repeat the first operation. The object of the fourth operation is to dry the barrel thoroughly. Start by wiping the rod clean. You will need four to six clean patches. Run the first patch down, up, down and out at the muzzle end. Run the rest of the patches through the bore once only, discarding each at the muzzle end. The final patch should

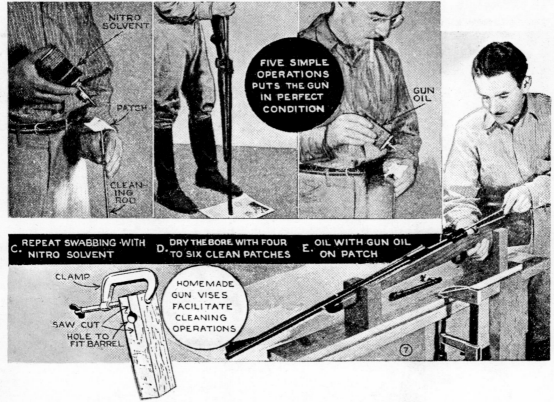

FIVE SIMPLE OPERATIONS PUTS THE GUN IN PERFECT CONDITION

NITRO SOLVENT

PATCH

CLEANING ROD

GUN OIL

C. REPEAT SWABBING WITH NITRO SOLVENT

D. DRY THE BORE WITH FOUR TO SIX CLEAN PATCHES

E. OIL WITH GUN OIL ON PATCH

HOMEMADE GUN VISES FACILITATE CLEANING OPERATIONS

CLAMP

SAW CUT

HOLE TO FIT BARREL

show perfectly clean and dry. If it shows dirt, the preceding operations must be repeated. The final operation is oiling. This is done with a clean patch. Use any good gun oil. This will protect the gun for a period of four to eight weeks. If the gun is to be stored for a longer period than this, use gun grease instead of the lighter oil.

As previously mentioned, cleaning should be done from the breech. Cleaning the gun from the muzzle permits the rod to rub at this vital point, causing wear which may influence the accuracy of the weapon. Some guns cannot be cleaned from the breech. In this case it is advisable to use a wooden or brass muzzle cap, Figs. 2 and 3, to protect the muzzle. If you use a plain jag tip for cleaning, the chamber should be fitted with a cartridge case plugged with wood. This will prevent the patch from working loose as it sometimes does when pushed into the larger diameter of the chamber.

Fig. 1 shows the five types of cleaning tips commonly used. The single slotted tip is the simplest. It has the advantage of holding onto the patch under all conditions, but has two disadvantages in that the patch sometimes jams when reversed inside the bore, and, the cleaning action is often one-sided, permitting the bare sides of the tip to rub the bore. The plain jag tip gives a uniform cleaning action, and reverses perfectly inside the barrel. The patch sticks to the tip as long as it is inside the barrel, but any chance movement beyond the muzzle or chamber will cause

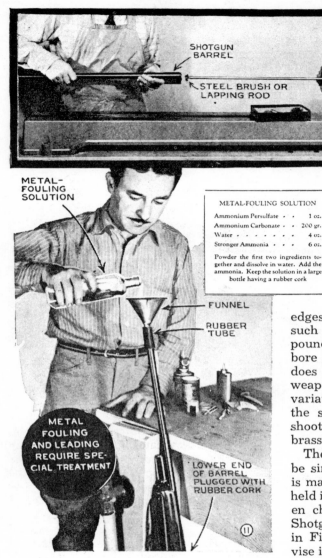

SHOTGUN BARREL

STEEL BRUSH OR LAPPING ROD

⑨

TO FIT BORE OF SHOTGUN

WOOD LAPPING ROD

WOOD ROD FOR STEEL WOOL

ADJUSTING SCREW

ABRASIVE PAPER GLUED IN PLACE

WOOD ROD FOR USE WITH ABRASIVE PAPER ⑩

METAL-FOULING SOLUTION

| METAL-FOULING SOLUTION | |
|---|---|
| Ammonium Persulfate | 1 oz. |
| Ammonium Carbonate | 200 gr. |
| Water | 4 oz. |
| Stronger Ammonia | 6 oz. |

Powder the first two ingredients together and dissolve in water. Add the ammonia. Keep the solution in a large bottle having a rubber cork

FUNNEL

RUBBER TUBE

METAL FOULING AND LEADING REQUIRE SPECIAL TREATMENT

LOWER END OF BARREL PLUGGED WITH RUBBER CORK

⑪

it to come loose. The same applies to the jag tip with point. The point is an advantage in centering the patch previous to insertion in the bore. The double-slotted tip is a first-rate cleaner, with a uniform action. The roll jag permits rolled or wrapped patches, and is preferred by many shooters on this account. The patch is wrapped around the jag as shown in Fig. 6, and can be made tight or loose as desired. Fig. 5 shows how the plain jag is used, the patch simply being centered on the tip, while Fig. 4 shows the obvious way of using either the single or double-slotted tip.

The cleaning rod itself can be brass or steel and should be of a proper diameter to fit the bore of the rifle. It must be fitted with a swivel joint so that the patch will rotate inside the bore, following the rotation of the rifling. Without this rotation, the patch will drag at right angles across the lands and will quickly destroy the sharp edges of the rifling. The patch should be of such a size as to require three or four pounds pressure to force it through the bore of the rifle. A shotgun cleaning rod does not require a swivel joint, as this weapon has a smooth bore. Other than this variation, the cleaning technique is exactly the same, with the exception that most shooters prefer a wire-gauze cleaner or a brass worm instead of a brass brush.

The cleaning operation as described can be simplified greatly if some type of vise is made to hold the gun. Rifles are easily held in a simple jig consisting of two wooden chocks nailed to a baseboard, Fig. 7. Shotguns can be clamped in the jig shown in Fig. 8. Clamping in a standard wood vise is also satisfactory, but care should be exercised in exerting too much clamping pressure.

Other than powder fouling, the shooter must sometimes give consideration to metal fouling. This is a deposit of metal left by the bullet in the bore. If you shoot lead bullets, the fouling is more specifically designated as "leading." It is obvious that a perfectly smooth, polished bore will pick up very little metal fouling, whereas the roughened, neglected bore will always foul to a greater extent. Metal fouling in itself does no particular harm to the bore, but it may trap powder residue beneath it, leading to corrosion of the bore. Metal fouling can be detected by a careful examination of the bore, in which the fouling will show as long streaks, flaky deposits or even actual lumps of metal sticking to the lands and grooves. The fouling is easily removed, if attended to promptly, by using the metal-fouling solution specified in Fig. 11. The liquid is kept in a tightly corked bottle at all times except when actually using the solution, since it loses strength quickly when exposed to air. This can be applied with a cloth patch in the usual manner if the deposit is light. For a more thorough action, the solution is poured into the bore of the gun after first plugging the chamber with a rubber cork. When first poured in, the solution will be as colorless as water but will asume a deep blue color as it begins to dissolve the metallic deposit. The action is complete in about 15 min. Care should be taken in using the metal-fouling solution as it will remove bluing or the finish on the stock. After the solution has been removed from the barrel, the regular cleaning procedure should follow immediately.

Leading can be removed with the metal-fouling solution. Many shooters, however, prefer mercury. A few ounces of this are placed in the barrel. A finger over the muzzle will hold it inside, and a few tips up and down will cause the mercury to amalgamate with the lead deposit. The solution can be used many times. Mercurial ointment is a satisfactory remedy for leading as is also common vinegar or a dilute solution of glacial acetic acid.

Metal fouling in shotgun barrels or any condition of rusting or pitting can be removed usually by mechanical methods as the smoooth bore permits almost any type of polishing. The cleaning operation is most conveniently done in a lathe, mounting the polishing barrel or abrasive in the lathe and holding the gun barrel in the hands, as shown in Fig. 9. Steel brushes and polishing heads for this purpose can be purchased, or the shooter can make his own, as in Fig. 10, to be used with paste abrasive, steel wool or abrasive paper.

# GUN RACK

## This Gun Rack Hangs in a Corner Where It Takes Little Space

Different from the usual gun rack in that it can be hung in a corner above the floor to make cleaning under it easy, this rack consists of a standard carrying a shelf at the bottom for the gun stocks and a notched holder at the top to receive the barrels. The shelf is cut on a 14-in. radius and is screwed and glued to the lower end of the standard. Metal braces add further support to the shelf. The notched holder at the top is screwed to the standard, which is chamfered at the edges. A ring at the top for hanging the rack engages a hook in the wall. If desired, small holes can be drilled in the notched holder to take cleaning rods.

# Tote Case for Your Guns

HERE IS AN IDEAL CASE for transporting shotguns and rifles on hunting trips where you are going to use more than one gun. It furnishes protection against marring and breakage, and at the same time is easy to carry. Because of its flat shape, it packs easily into a car or station wagon and at home, between trips, it provides a dry and dustproof storage cabinet.

The construction is simple, as no difficult-to-make joints are used. The over-all dimensions will be determined by the sizes of the guns to be carried in it. The top and bottom pieces are ¼-in. plywood and the sides are of 1 x 4-in. stock. Drill holes for 1-in. screws ⅜ in. from the edges of the

After box is assembled, top and bottom are separated by making a saw cut all around, shown above left

Above center, the 1 x 4 crosspieces are fitted in place. Next, at the right, gun positions are marked

Lower left, cutouts are made on a jigsaw. Center, attaching screws must not be driven through cutout

Lower right, the crosspieces are lined with strips of rubber held in place with broad-headed tacks

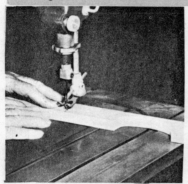

plywood pieces, 6 in. apart on the sides and 5 in. apart on the ends, with a screw at each corner. To assemble the case, a box is made first by joining the 1 x 4 sides to the plywood top and bottom. Coat the edges of the 1 x 4s with glue, put them in position and drive the screws. Next, join the corners with finishing nails driven through the long sides. Space these nails carefully so they won't interfere with the saw cut to be made later.

Now the box is cut all around to form the top and bottom of the case. The cut should be off-center, 2¾ in. from one side and 2 in. from the other. The crosspieces in the top and bottom are made by splitting 1 x 4s in the same proportion as the box was split, the smaller ones being fitted into the top and the larger ones into the bottom. These are laid in place 6 in. from each end and the guns are positioned on them. With a pencil, indicate the cutouts that will be necessary in the bottom crosspiece to take the stocks and barrels. Cut on a jigsaw, making each cut slightly larger than the marking to allow for padding to be added later. Fasten the crosspieces in place with glue and screws, then pad them with ¾-in. strips of rubber cut from an inner tube. Join the top and bottom together with two or three butt hinges or a length of piano hinge. Finally, attach a handle and two suitcase latches to the front side. ★ ★ ★

Clean gutters thoroughly after leaves have fallen, as they cause stoppages. After leaves and debris are removed, flush gutters with a hose and then check for leaks and drainage pitch

# GUTTER REPAIR AND MAINTENANCE

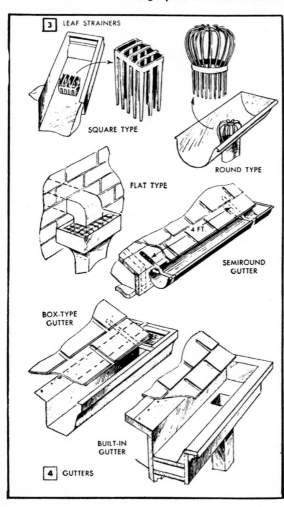

LEAF STRAINERS

SQUARE TYPE

ROUND TYPE

FLAT TYPE

4 FT.

SEMIROUND GUTTER

BOX-TYPE GUTTER

BUILT-IN GUTTER

4 GUTTERS

IT'S EASY to put off inspecting and cleaning the gutters and downspouts on your home from year to year until they finally deteriorate to a point where they are beyond repair and must be completely replaced. Yet, it is possible to lengthen the serviceable life of these important fittings from five to ten years by thoroughly cleaning them and making minor repairs on a yearly schedule that any homeowner can carry out himself. Leaky, damaged and partially clogged gutters not only give unsatisfactory service, but they also can be the indirect cause of other, more serious, troubles, such as water getting into the attic or seeping into brick walls, causing unsightly efflorescent stains, Fig. 5, and a gradual deterioration of the brickwork near the cornices. For these reasons, regular servicing of the gutters is a sure way of reducing home-upkeep costs.

**Keep gutters clean:** Immediately after the leaves come down in the fall is the time to get busy and clean out gutters and downspouts to avoid stoppage resulting from accumulations of leaves and dirt. Even if leaf guards or strainers have been installed at the downspout openings, an accumulation of wet leaves will prevent proper drainage and may cause water to overflow and seep into the walls of the house. Rotting leaves combine with cinders and soot to form an acid that hastens rusting of the sheet-metal gutters. For these reasons, it is essential to remove the leaves, and other debris, as soon as possible after they col-

Photo 5 shows efflorescent stains on brick wall subjected to water seepage from roof or gutter. Loosen tight stoppages in downspout by using sink-drain auger, then flush with a hose

lect, Fig. 1, and then flush the gutters with a hose, Fig. 2. While flushing, inspect both gutters and downspouts for leaks and repair them immediately.

**Clearing stopped downspout:** If the gutters are not fitted with leaf strainers, Fig. 3, leaves may accumulate in the leaders, Fig. 16, and completely close the passage. In cold weather, water may collect and freeze in clogged elbows and downspouts. Although these parts are corrugated for the purpose of preventing damage from freezing, a large amount of water freezing solidly behind a leaf dam may expand the metal sufficiently to force open the rolled joint. An auger of the type used for clearing obstructions in sink drains, Figs. 6 and 7, can be used to loosen tightly packed leaves in either the leader or downspout. After the mass has been loosened, insert the hose in the leader with the water turned on at full pressure. Sometimes full pressure from the hose alone will do the trick. Where the downspout connects directly to the storm sewer, masses of wet leaves and dirt may collect at the bend below grade. To clear this, remove the downspout and insert a drain auger at the joint where the lower end of the downspout enters the bell tile above grade. Then flush with a hose.

**Down pitch of gutters:** To drain properly pitch gutters down slightly toward the drop outlet at the end as in Fig. 8. Especially long runs may be fitted with a drop outlet at both ends, or one in the center as shown. Each downspout will handle about 30 to 35 ft. of gutter

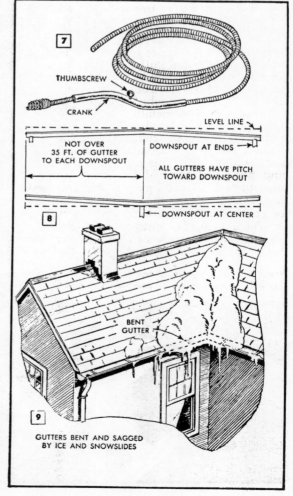

GUTTERS BENT AND SAGGED BY ICE AND SNOWSLIDES

Sheet-metal gutters of all types should be protected with asphalt-base corrosion preventives. After gutters are thoroughly cleaned, material is applied with brush

length. On some types of homes a noticeable pitch of the gutters detracts from architectural lines and in this case the gutters are installed horizontal, or level. This also is true of attached wooden gutters which usually are installed in this manner. Gutters installed level must not be permitted to sag, as otherwise some water will be left standing to evaporate after each summer shower. This accelerates rusting and provides an ideal breeding spot for mosquitoes. If metal gutters become bent or sagged in places, the cause is usually ice or snowslides from a high, steep roof, Fig. 9. As a rule, the gutter is quite easily straightened if none of the hangers has been pulled loose. In case some hangers

have been loosened, it will be necessary to renail or replace them, as the gutter will sag permanently without their support.

**Rust prevention:** Gutters and downspouts of nonrusting metals, such as copper and aluminum, have been widely used in both new and old construction, but the semi-round and box types of galvanized sheet metal are perhaps the most common. When the galvanized coating is impaired, rust attacks the bare metal and eventually eats through, causing leaks. Sometimes soldered joints pull loose, either because of stresses caused by expansion of freezing water, or because of an inadequately soldered joint. For the same reasons, slip-joint connectors sometimes open and, generally, they should be replaced. Effective rust protection for the inside surfaces of gutters and downspouts is attained by applying a heavy coating of elastic roofing cement, smokestack paint or the asphalt-base compounds used on the underside of autos as a corrosion preventive. Any of these materials will adhere tightly to clean metal and, after drying, they are sufficiently flexible to expand and contract with the metal, thus providing an unbroken protective film. This film, in most cases, also resists acids which form when wet leaves and soot are combined. Asphalt-base coatings should be used only on the inside of the gutter, as they tend to bleed through oil paints applied to the outside of the gutters. The coating is simply brushed onto the bare, clean metal, Fig. 10, after rust and loose dirt have been removed. Small breaks in the metal generally can be stopped with ordinary roofing cement, but large breaks will require a fabric retainer. First, coat the surrounding surface with cement, as in Fig. 11, and then press a piece of muslin or light canvas against the wet surface, Fig. 12. Finally, another coat of cement is applied over the fabric as in Fig. 13. To coat the inside of a downspout, alter an old paintbrush by cutting off the handle and

Small breaks in the metal can be closed by a fabric patch. First, apply compound with a brush as in Fig. 11, then press the canvas patch in place as in Fig. 12. Apply final coat over the fabric, including edges

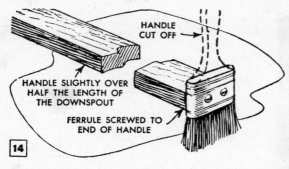

HANDLE CUT OFF

HANDLE SLIGHTLY OVER HALF THE LENGTH OF THE DOWNSPOUT

FERRULE SCREWED TO END OF HANDLE

**14**

**15**

Applying protective compounds to the inside surfaces of downspouts pays off by greatly increasing the useful life of these parts. Material is applied to the inside surfaces with an improvised brush

screwing the ferrule to one end of a long strip of wood which serves as a handle, Figs. 14 and 15.

**Replacing gutters:** Gutter and downspout units and accessories of the semiround type are detailed in Figs. 16 and 17. Box-type gutters, Fig. 4, also are used extensively and the fittings and method of attachment vary considerably. Ordinarily gutters come in 8 to 12-ft. lengths, with 10-ft. lengths being perhaps the most commonly furnished. Corner fittings and drop outlets are separate units. Leaders connect gutters to downspouts in most types of installations. When ordering the materials and parts for a major replacement job be sure to include a sufficient number of hangers, Fig. 16, to permit a 4-ft. spacing throughout the length of the gutters. Order 1-in. nails for fastening the hangers and obtain all the slip-joint connectors required. Order leaf strainers for each drop outlet, and also get the proper type of downspout hangers, or bands. If only one or two sections of the gutter require replacement, measure the old ones and renew with the same type and size. When hanging new gutters, don't forget to make sure that the pitch is the same as that of the one being replaced.

**Installing gutter hangers:** New hangers should be nailed to the roof boards and not over the shingles, as exposed nails are likely to rust away in time and cause a leak. Removing shingles to expose the roof boards

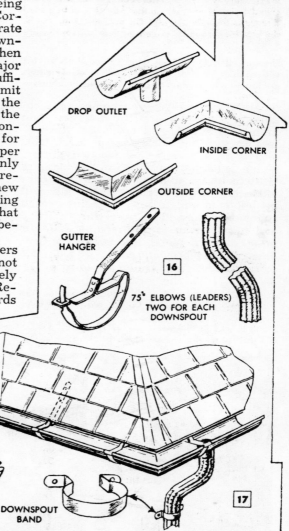

DROP OUTLET

INSIDE CORNER

OUTSIDE CORNER

GUTTER HANGER

**16**

75° ELBOWS (LEADERS) TWO FOR EACH DOWNSPOUT

END CAP

SLIP-JOINT CONNECTOR

DOWNSPOUT BAND

**17**

When applying new gutter hangers on old roofs, shingles should be lifted so that hanger can be nailed directly to the roof boards. On asphalt-shingle roofs, the individual shingles are easily removed for this job

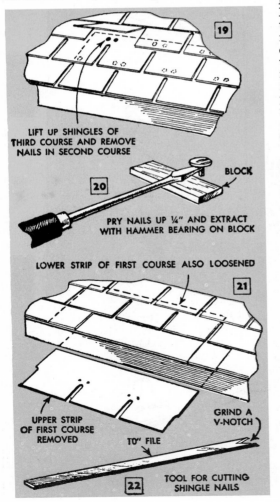

**19** LIFT UP SHINGLES OF THIRD COURSE AND REMOVE NAILS IN SECOND COURSE

**20** BLOCK — PRY NAILS UP ¼" AND EXTRACT WITH HAMMER BEARING ON BLOCK

LOWER STRIP OF FIRST COURSE ALSO LOOSENED

**21**

UPPER STRIP OF FIRST COURSE REMOVED

GRIND A V-NOTCH

TO" FILE

**22** TOOL FOR CUTTING SHINGLE NAILS

must be done with care to avoid damage. First, remove the nails from two or more individual shingles of the second row, or course. The nailheads are exposed by simply lifting up the butt ends of the third course as in Fig. 19. Pry up the nailheads with a wide-bladed screwdriver as in Fig. 20. To prevent damage to the shingle, place a strip of ⅛-in. metal or a short block of hardwood under the screwdriver blade as shown. Remember that the nails holding the second course of shingles usually go through the upper ends of shingles in the first course. Finally, removal of the nails holding the first course of shingles, which usually is of double thickness, permits you to pull the shingles out as in Fig. 21, exposing the roof boards. In some types of construction, especially on wide cornices, there will be a layer of roll roofing under the first course. It is not necessary, of course, to remove this, as the hangers can be nailed over it, provided all nail holes are sealed with roofing cement before re-laying the shingles. After prying off the old hangers and nailing on the new ones as in Fig. 18, drive the nail part way down, and then coat the area around the nail with roofing cement so that when the nail is driven down fully, the cement will form a watertight seal around the nailhead. Now, replace the double course of shingles, making sure that they are located in the same position as they were originally. Drive the new nails slightly to one side or the other of the old holes and, before driving them clear down, apply roofing cement around the heads to form a seal. Be sure all old nail holes are filled with cement. Finally, the loosened shingles of the second course are nailed down again to finish the job. The procedure is repeated at each new hanger position. In a general way the same thing applies to wooden shingles. However, these are more rigid than asphalt shingles and require a few variations in procedure. It is necessary to cut the nails holding each shingle with a special tool improvised from an old file, Fig. 22. The V-notch at one end is ground to a beveled edge and in use the tool is forced under the shingle until the V-shaped cutting edge contacts the nail. A few light taps on the outer end of the tool generally cuts the nail cleanly. When replacing a wooden shingle, the two lower nails are started at approximately the same position as the original nails. Fill the old nail holes with roofing cement. Pry up the shingles of the next course above, slip a piece of sheet metal over the nailheads and press the upper shingle down to force the nails home Don't tap the shingle with a hammer as you may break it.

When hangers must be attached to metal

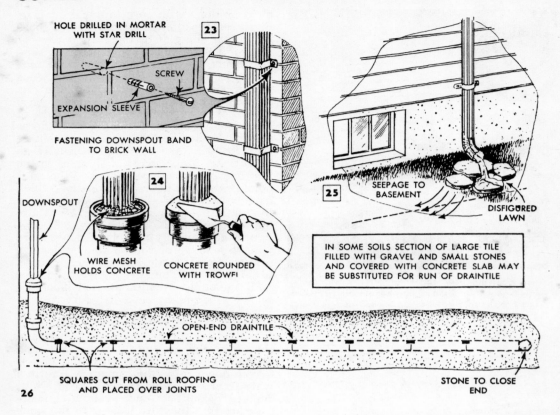

HOLE DRILLED IN MORTAR WITH STAR DRILL

23

SCREW

EXPANSION SLEEVE

FASTENING DOWNSPOUT BAND TO BRICK WALL

24

DOWNSPOUT

WIRE MESH HOLDS CONCRETE

CONCRETE ROUNDED WITH TROWEL

25

SEEPAGE TO BASEMENT

DISFIGURED LAWN

IN SOME SOILS SECTION OF LARGE TILE FILLED WITH GRAVEL AND SMALL STONES AND COVERED WITH CONCRETE SLAB MAY BE SUBSTITUTED FOR RUN OF DRAINTILE

OPEN-END DRAINTILE

SQUARES CUT FROM ROLL ROOFING AND PLACED OVER JOINTS

STONE TO CLOSE END

26

roofing, it's a common practice to solder them in place. Before soldering, the metal must be thoroughly cleaned, fluxed and preheated with a blowtorch. Downspout bands are simply nailed to wooden trim surfaces. However, when fastening the bands to brick, it is necessary to use masonry nails or screws. Screws are driven into expansion sleeves which are placed in holes drilled in the masonry with a star drill as in Fig. 23.

**Cementing downspout into draintile:** When downspouts are connected to draintile leading to the storm sewers, the opening where the downspout enters the tile should be sealed with cement mortar supported by wire mesh pressed into the bell end of the tile. Usually the bell end is only a few inches above grade and if the opening is not closed tightly, small stones, dirt and trash may clog the tile. To seal the joint, first cut and bend a disk of ½-in. wire mesh to fit into the open end of the tile. Bend up the edges of the wire disk so that it will wedge tightly in place. Then cut a round opening in the disk so that you can insert the lower end of the downspout. After the latter is in place, mix a heavy cement mortar and trowel it into the opening, building it up at the top to form a sloping surface that will shed water, Fig. 24.

**Installing splashers and draintile:** When water from the downspout is discharged at ground level, some provision must be made for spreading the flow of water, as otherwise the force of the stream of water will wash away sod and soil. Also, if drainage from the foundation is poor, water may seep into the basement. Where there is ample drainage away from the foundation, a few flat stones placed below the end of the downspout may suffice as a splasher, Fig. 25. However, unless the arrangement is only temporary, it is better to install concrete splashers of sufficient size to direct the water away from the building in a spreading flow. In some soils, a run of open-end draintile installed below grade as in Fig. 26, will serve as a dispersal unit. Sometimes, builders install a long run of tile in this manner and place a section of large draintile (24 to 36 in. in diameter) at the lower end of the run. The large draintile section is placed on end with the bell end up and filled with coarse gravel and small stones to form a dry well. The top of the tile is closed with a cast-concrete cover. Sometimes a tile elbow is cast integral with the cover and the lower end of the draintile is led into the elbow. In gravelly or sandy soils, this installation works quite satisfactorily.